A **KNOCK** ON THE **DOOR**

A
KNOCK
ON THE
DOOR

THE ESSENTIAL HISTORY OF
RESIDENTIAL SCHOOLS
FROM THE TRUTH AND RECONCILIATION
COMMISSION OF CANADA | *Edited & Abridged*

FOREWORD BY PHIL FONTAINE

UMP
University of Manitoba Press

National Centre *for*
Truth *and* Reconciliation
UNIVERSITY OF MANITOBA

University of Manitoba Press
Winnipeg, Manitoba
Canada R3T 2M5
uofmpress.ca

National Centre *for*
Truth *and* Reconciliation
UNIVERSITY OF MANITOBA

Published in collaboration with the National Centre for Truth and Reconciliation

The Introduction, Chapters 1–5, and Bibliography have been reproduced from reports of the Truth and Reconciliation Commission of Canada: *What We Have Learned: Principles of Truth and Reconciliation* (2015) and *Truth and Reconciliation Commission of Canada: Calls to Action* (2015). These texts are in the public domain and can be accessed at www.trc.ca.
Foreword © Phil Fontaine 2016
Afterword © Aimée Craft 2016

Printed in Canada
Text printed on chlorine-free, 100% post-consumer recycled paper

20 19 18 17 16   1 2 3 4 5

Cover and interior design: Jess Koroscil

Cataloguing-in-Publication information available from Library and Archives Canada

ISBN 978-0-88755-785-9 (pbk.)
ISBN 978-0-88755-540-4 (PDF)
ISBN 978-0-88755-538-1 (epub)

The University of Manitoba Press gratefully acknowledges the financial support for its publication program provided by the Government of Canada through the Canada Book Fund, the Canada Council for the Arts, the Manitoba Department of Culture, Heritage, Tourism, the Manitoba Arts Council, and the Manitoba Book Publishing Tax Credit.

A portion of all proceeds from the sale of this book will be donated to the National Centre for Truth and Reconciliation to assist with its ongoing educational and research activities.

FSC
www.fsc.org
MIX
Paper from
responsible sources
FSC® C016245

CONTENTS

FOREWORD

My name is Phil Fontaine and I am a survivor.

Survivor is a word that years ago I used in hushed tones to describe my experience at Indian Residential School. But that was then. I have now come to say the word louder and more imbued with pride with every passing year of my life. This year, "survivor" has reached a crescendo.

The Truth and Reconciliation Commission Report, and its findings, represents a historic moment for all survivors; for all Indigenous people everywhere. It is, I think, a historic moment for Canada, the significance of which rests in not only what has been, but also what is to come.

I cannot speak for every survivor—each of us has our own story—but we do have common characteristics. As survivors, we number in the thousands. But if you count our brothers and sisters who are no longer with us, we number in the hundreds of thousands, possibly many more. All of us, the living and the dead, endured the effects of a policy that sought transformation—transformation of us as a people, as parents, grandparents, a transformation of all of our descendants—forever.

And so, the story of how we came to be here today is a long and painful one. The release, the publishing, the official stamp upon the findings of the Commission represents a monumental moment, and it will help put our shared collective pain behind us.

I am pleased to write this foreword to *A Knock on the Door: The Essential History of Residential Schools from the Truth and Reconciliation Commission of Canada*. This book presents the history of the Residential School system in a way that makes it accessible to all Canadians.

It addresses one of the key objectives of the Truth and Reconciliation Commission: to educate all Canadians about the Residential School experience and how this sad chapter in our shared history has affected the relationship between Indigenous and non-Indigenous people today.

The Commission spent five years putting together a report that was given life by the thousands of stories from survivors who experienced the misguided experiment of assimilation. Their contribution is immense, and their truths now enshrined for all time. Because of this hard work, our history can no longer be denied. The incontrovertible historical record before us, before all of Canada, has put an official limit on "the range of permissible lies," to use Michael Ignatieff's term.[1]

By describing and validating our story, the Report validates Canada's story. It demonstrates the righteousness and importance of our struggle. It tells us how the fundamental systems of governance failed to protect our social, economic, and cultural rights.

Education; health care; justice; child welfare: all of these systems and benefits are enjoyed, rightfully so, without a second thought by non-Indigenous Canadians. For Indigenous Canadians, wrongfully so, access to high quality education, health care, justice, child welfare was a passing dream.

What the Commission's Report tells us is that Canada is indeed in need of transformation, but that transformation is not of us. What is needed is for Canada to transform itself to embrace our true, shared culture and history—to understand that we are all, in fact, in this together.

This year happens to be the 800th anniversary of the Magna Carta, the great charter that inspired the Royal Proclamation of

1763—our Magna Carta—which in turn inspired the Commission and its prescriptions for reconciliation.

It has taken until 2015 to get here. It took the revelation of the experiences of residential school survivors to crystallize the reality that Canada was not the nation we wished it to be. But even so, beyond my fellow survivors I know that this would not have happened without the help of our allies. There are too many to name, and so to mention but a few I thank, first, the Chief Justice of Canada, the Rt. Hon. Beverley McLachlin, for speaking the words that could not be spoken: that what Canada did to us was cultural genocide. From the Supreme Court of Canada, she changed the vocabulary and narrative around residential schools.

I thank the Hon. Frank Iacobucci for his commitment to bring about a settlement that everyone could live with. I thank the negotiators for their tenacity. I thank the Rt. Hon. Paul Martin for his support throughout. I give thanks to the Commissioners for their compassionate work, for their courage, their patience, their protection, their understanding, their vision, and their wisdom. Their work affirms the survivors' legacy.

The attempt to transform us failed. The true legacy of the survivors, then, will be the transformation of Canada.

Meegwetch,

Phil Fontaine

NUNAVU

NORTHWEST TERRITORIES

YUKON

BRITISH
COLUMBIA

ALBERTA

SASKATCHEWAN

MANITOBA

Scale

| 0 | 500 | 1000 km |

SOURCE: Truth and Reconciliation Commission of Canada.
Base map: Natural Earth. Map by Weldon Hiebert.

RESIDENTIAL
SCHOOLS IN CANADA

RESIDENTIAL SCHOOLS IN CANADA

INSTITUTION NAME	PROVINCE/TERRITORY - RELIGIOUS AFFILIATION
Ahousaht	British Columbia - United Church
Alberni	British Columbia - United Church
Anahim Lake	British Columbia - Non-denominational
Cariboo	British Columbia - Roman Catholic
Christie	British Columbia - Roman Catholic
Coqualeetza	British Columbia - United Church
Cranbrook	British Columbia - Roman Catholic
Kamloops	British Columbia - Roman Catholic
Kitimaat	British Columbia - United Church
Kuper Island	British Columbia - Roman Catholic
Lejac	British Columbia - Roman Catholic
Lower Post	British Columbia - Roman Catholic
Port Simpson	British Columbia - Anglican
Sechelt	British Columbia - Roman Catholic
St. George's	British Columbia - Anglican
St. Mary's	British Columbia - Roman Catholic
St. Michael's	British Columbia - Anglican
St. Paul's	British Columbia - Roman Catholic
Assumption	Alberta - Roman Catholic
Blue Quills	Alberta - Roman Catholic
Crowfoot	Alberta - Roman Catholic
Desmarais	Alberta - Roman Catholic
Edmonton	Alberta - United Church
Ermineskin	Alberta - Roman Catholic
Fort Vermillion	Alberta - Roman Catholic
Grouard	Alberta - Roman Catholic
Holy Angels	Alberta - Roman Catholic
Joussard	Alberta - Roman Catholic
Lac La Biche	Alberta - Roman Catholic
Lesser Slave Lake	Alberta - Anglican
Morley	Alberta - United Church
Old Sun	Alberta - Anglican
Red Deer	Alberta - United Church
Sacred Heart	Alberta - Roman Catholic
Sarcee	Alberta - Anglican

St. Albert	Alberta - Roman Catholic
St. Augustine	Alberta - Roman Catholic
St. Cyprian's	Alberta - Anglican
St. Joseph's	Alberta - Roman Catholic
St. Mary's	Alberta - Roman Catholic
St. Paul's	Alberta - Anglican
Sturgeon Lake	Alberta - Roman Catholic
Wabasca	Alberta - Anglican
Whitefish Lake	Alberta - Anglican
Battleford	Saskatchewan - Anglican
Beauval	Saskatchewan - United Church
Cote	Saskatchewan - United Church
Crowstand	Saskatchewan - Presbyterian
File Hills	Saskatchewan - Presbyterian (1889–1925) United Church (1925–1949)
Fort Pelly	Saskatchewan - Roman Catholic
Gordon's	Saskatchewan - Anglican
Lac La Ronge	Saskatchewan - Anglican
Lebret	Saskatchewan - Roman Catholic
Marieval	Saskatchewan - Roman Catholic
Muscowequan	Saskatchewan - Roman Catholic
Prince Albert	Saskatchewan - Anglican
Regina	Saskatchewan - Presbyterian
Round Lake	Saskatchewan - Presbyterian (1884–1926) United Church (1926–1950)
St. Anthony's	Saskatchewan - Roman Catholic
St. Barnabas	Saskatchewan - Anglican
St. Michael's	Saskatchewan - Roman Catholic
St. Philip's	Saskatchewan - Roman Catholic
Sturgeon Landing	Saskatchewan - Roman Catholic
Thunderchild	Saskatchewan - Roman Catholic
Assiniboia	Manitoba - Roman Catholic
Birtle	Manitoba - Presbyterian
Brandon	Manitoba - Methodist (1895–1929) United Church (1929–1970) Roman Catholic (1970–1972)
Churchill	Manitoba - Non-denominational
Cross Lake	Manitoba - Roman Catholic
Dauphin	Manitoba - Anglican

Elkhorn	Manitoba - Anglican
Fort Alexander	Manitoba - Roman Catholic
Guy	Manitoba - Roman Catholic
MacKay	Manitoba - Anglican
Norway House	Manitoba - Roman Catholic
Norway House	Manitoba - United Church
Pine Creek	Manitoba - Roman Catholic
Portage la Prairie	Manitoba - Presbyterian (1891–1926) United Church (1926–1969)
Sandy Bay	Manitoba - Roman Catholic
Bishop Horden Hall	Ontario - Anglican
Cecilia Jeffrey	Ontario - Presbyterian (1902–1925) United Church (1925–1927) Women's Missionary Society of the Presbyterian (1927–1969)
Chapleau	Ontario - Anglican
Cristal Lake	Ontario - Mennonite
Fort Frances	Ontario - Roman Catholic
Fort William	Ontario - Roman Catholic
McIntosh	Ontario - Roman Catholic
Mohawk Institute	Ontario - Anglican
Mount Elgin	Ontario - Methodist/United Church
Pelican Lake	Ontario - Anglican
Poplar Hill	Ontario - Mennonite
Shingwauk	Ontario - Anglican
Spanish Boys' School	Ontario - Roman Catholic
Spanish Girls' School	Ontario - Roman Catholic
St. Anne's	Ontario - Roman Catholic
St. Mary's	Ontario - Roman Catholic
Stirland Lake	Ontario - Mennonite
Wawanosh	Ontario - Anglican
Amos	Québec - Roman Catholic
Federal Hostel at George River	Québec - Non-denominational
Federal Hostel at Great Whale River	Québec - Non-denominational
Federal Hostel at Payne Bay	Québec - Non-denominational
Federal Hostel at Port Harrison	Québec - Non-denominational
Fort George	Québec - Anglican
Fort George	Québec - Roman Catholic
Fort George Hostels	Québec - Non-denominational

La Tuque	Québec - Anglican
Mistassini Hostels	Québec - Non-denominational
Pointe Bleue	Québec - Roman Catholic
Sept-Îles	Québec - Roman Catholic
Shubenacadie	Nova Scotia - Roman Catholic
Chesterfield Inlet	Nunavut - Roman Catholic
Coppermine	Nunavut - Anglican
Federal Hostel at Baker Lake	Nunavut - Non-denominational
Federal Hostel at Belcher Islands	Nunavut - Non-denominational
Federal Hostel at Broughton Island	Nunavut - Non-denominational
Federal Hostel at Cambridge Bay	Nunavut - Non-denominational
Federal Hostel at Cape Dorset	Nunavut - Non-denominational
Federal Hostel at Eskimo Point	Nunavut - Non-denominational
Federal Hostel at Igloolik	Nunavut - Non-denominational
Federal Hostel at Lake Harbour	Nunavut - Non-denominational
Federal Hostel at Pangnirtung	Nunavut - Non-denominational
Federal Hostel at Pond Inlet	Nunavut - Non-denominational
Frobisher Bay	Nunavut - Non-denominational
Aklavik	Northwest Territories - Anglican
Aklavik	Northwest Territories - Roman Catholic
Breynat Hall	Northwest Territories - Roman Catholic
Federal Hostel at Fort Franklin	Northwest Territories - Non-denominational
Fort McPherson	Northwest Territories - Anglican
Fort Providence	Northwest Territories - Roman Catholic
Fort Resolution	Northwest Territories - Roman Catholic
Fort Simpson	Northwest Territories - Anglican
Fort Simpson	Northwest Territories - Roman Catholic
Grandin College	Northwest Territories - Roman Catholic
Hay River	Northwest Territories - Anglican
Inuvik	Northwest Territories - Anglican
Inuvik	Northwest Territories - Roman Catholic
Yellowknife	Northwest Territories - Non-denominational
Carcross	Yukon - Anglican
Coudert Hall	Yukon - Roman Catholic
Shingle Point	Yukon - Anglican
St. Paul's Hostel	Yukon - Anglican
Whitehorse Baptist	Yukon - Baptist

CHRONOLOGY

1834   The Mohawk Institute in Brantford, Ontario, begins taking on boarders. It is the oldest residential school included in the Indian Residential Schools Settlement Agreement (IRSSA).

1851   Mount Elgin school opens in Muncey, Ontario.

1860   Beauval school (also known as Ile-à-la-Crosse) opens in what is now Saskatchewan.

1863   St. Mary's school opens in Mission, British Columbia.

1863   St. Albert school opens in what is now Alberta.

1867   *Constitution Act, 1867* assigns the federal government jurisdiction over "Indians, and Lands reserved for the Indians."

1867   Sacred Heart school opens in Fort Providence in what is now the Northwest Territories.

1868   Wikwemikong school opens on Manitoulin Island, Ontario.

1876   The *Indian Act* consolidates earlier legislation that defined and limited First Nations life in Canada. The Act becomes the basis for regulation of the residential school system.

1879   The Davin Report recommends the establishment of government-funded, church-run residential schools on the Prairies.

1883   Parliament authorizes the creation of three industrial schools in the Northwest Territories.

1883   Battleford Industrial School opens in what is now Saskatchewan.

1888   Birtle residential school, the first in Manitoba, opens.

1891   Jean L'Heureux, a translator for Indian Affairs and recruiter for Catholic residential schools in Alberta, is allowed to resign rather than face a criminal investigation into allegations of sexual abuse.

1892   A federal government order-in-council cuts funding to industrial schools.

1894   An amendment to the *Indian Act* empowers Indian agents to send children to residential schools if they deem parents "unfit or unwilling to provide for the child's education." Parents who do not return children who had run away from schools become subject to prosecution.

1899   Indian Affairs minister Clifford Sifton issues instruction that allows Métis children to be enrolled in residential schools.

1903   The first residential school for Métis children opens at Saint-Paul-des-Métis, in what is now Alberta.

1905   The boarding school at Saint-Paul-des-Métis is destroyed by a fire that kills one student.

1907   Indian Affairs Chief Medical Officer Dr. Peter Bryce reports that 24 percent of the students who had enrolled in fifteen western Canadian schools since 1886 were dead.

1910   Indian Affairs and church organizations negotiate a contract that
        increases funding and imposes standards for the schools.

1914   A father successfully sues the Mohawk Institute principal for locking his
        daughter in a cell for three days on what is described as a "water diet."

1920   The *Indian Act* is amended to make attendance at a day school or
        residential school compulsory for First Nations school-aged children.

1920   The St. Paul's hostel for Métis students opens in Dawson City, Yukon.

1927   Nineteen students and one staff member die in a fire
        that destroys the Beauval school in Saskatchewan.

1930   The *Indian Act* is amended to increase the discharge age from 15 to 16.

1930   Thirteen students and one teacher die in a fire that
        destroys the Cross Lake, Manitoba, school.

1930   Shubenacadie school opens in Nova Scotia.

1931   St. Joseph's school opens in Fort George, Québec.

1933   The *Indian Act* is amended to appoint all Royal Canadian
        Mounted Police officers as truant officers.

1937   Indian Affairs issues a policy directive ending the
        enrollment of Métis children in residential schools.

1939   The Supreme Court of Canada rules that Inuit
        are "Indians" under Canadian law.

1939   B.C. police refuse to return runaways to Kuper Island school
        after concluding the boys had likely been sexually abused at the
        school. The local Indian agent advises the suspected abusers
        to leave the province, allowing them to avoid prosecution.

1944 . Indian Affairs Superintendent of Welfare and Training
        R.A. Hoey tells a parliamentary committee that he believes
        the residential schools should be gradually closed.

1947   Dr L.B. Pett, director of the Nutrition Division of the
        Department of National Health and Welfare, reports
        that "no school was doing a good feeding job."

1948   Special Joint Committee on the *Indian Act* recommends
        that "wherever and whenever possible Indian children
        should be educated in association with other children."

1951   Amendments to the *Indian Act* authorize Indian Affairs to enter
        into agreements with school boards and provincial governments
        to have First Nations students attend public schools.

1953   The federal government institutes a nation-wide
        policy for discipline at residential schools.

1954   The federal government takes over the responsibility of
        staffing at all government-owned residential schools.

1955   The federal government approves an extensive program
        for the construction of schools and hostels in the
        Northwest Territories and northern Québec.

1958   The first three large hostels in the Northwest Territories open: Akaitcho Hall in Yellowknife, Fleming Hall in Fort McPherson, and Breynat Hall in Fort Smith.

1958   Grollier Hall, Inuvik, opens. During the next two decades, there was never a year in which the school did not employ at least one dormitory supervisor who would later be convicted for sexually abusing students at the school.

1960   Food allowances based on Canada's Official Food Rules are included in the residential school funding formula.

1969   The federal government ends its partnership with churches and takes over direct administration of residential schools.

1969   The federal government transfers responsibility for residential schools in the Northwest Territories and the Yukon to the territorial governments.

1970   Parents occupy the Blue Quills school in Alberta for seventeen days until the government agrees to transfer control to an Aboriginal education authority.

1970   The Mohawk Institute closes. Sixty-seven schools remain in operation.

1980   Twenty-two schools in operation.

1982   The *Constitution Act, 1982* recognizes and affirms the rights of "Indian, Inuit, and Métis peoples of Canada."

1986   The United Church of Canada issues an apology for its role in the colonization of Aboriginal people.

1990   Thirteen schools in operation.

1990   Phil Fontaine, Grand Chief of the Assembly of Manitoba Chiefs, speaks publicly about the abuse he suffered at Fort Alexander Residential School.

1991   The Cariboo Tribal Council organizes a national conference on residential schools.

1991   The Missionary Oblates of Mary Immaculate apologize to Aboriginal people for their role in the residential school system.

1993   The Anglican Church of Canada apologizes to Aboriginal people for its role in the residential school system.

1994   The Assembly of First Nations publishes *Breaking the Silence: An Interpretive Study of Residential School Impact and Healing as Illustrated by the Stories of First Nations Individuals.*

1994   The RCMP launches the Native Indian Residential School Task Force to investigate complaints of historic physical and sexual abuse at residential schools in B.C.

1995   The Presbyterian Church in Canada apologizes to Aboriginal people for its role in the residential school system.

1996   The Nuu-chah-nulth Tribal Council publishes *Indian Residential Schools: The Nuu-chah-nulth Experience.*

1996   The *Report of the Royal Commission on Aboriginal Peoples* calls for a public inquiry into the effects of residential schools on generations of Aboriginal peoples.

1998   Former Mohawk Institute students file a class-action claim for damages. This claim is referred to as the *Cloud* case.

1998   The Qu'Appelle school closes in Saskatchewan.

1998   The United Church of Canada apologizes to Aboriginal people for its role in the residential school system.

2000   All schools have closed.

2005   Assembly of First Nations National Chief Phil Fontaine announces a class-action lawsuit against the Government of Canada over the legacy of the residential schools.

2005   The Indian Residential Schools Settlement Agreement is negotiated as an out-of-court settlement of the student class-action suits.

2007   The Indian Residential Schools Settlement Agreement comes into effect. It provides benefits to former students of 140 schools. Certain classes of Aboriginal students and types of schools are, however, not included in the agreement.

2008   Prime Minister Stephen Harper apologizes to First Nations, Inuit, and Métis for the residential school system.

2008   The Indian Residential Schools Truth and Reconciliation Commission of Canada (TRC) is established.

2015   The National Centre for Truth and Reconciliation opens in Winnipeg, Manitoba.

2015   Prime Minister Justin Trudeau instructs the Minister of Indigenous and Northern Affairs to implement the TRC's Calls to Action.

2015   The TRC releases its final report.

A **KNOCK** ON THE **DOOR**

The Introduction, Chapters 1–5, and Bibliography have been reproduced from reports of the Truth and Reconciliation Commission of Canada: *What We Have Learned: Principles of Truth and Reconciliation* (2015) and *Truth and Reconciliation Commission of Canada: Calls to Action* (2015).

INTRODUCTION

For over a century, the central goals of Canada's Aboriginal policy were to eliminate Aboriginal governments; ignore Aboriginal rights; terminate the Treaties; and, through a process of assimilation, cause Aboriginal peoples to cease to exist as distinct legal, social, cultural, religious, and racial entities in Canada. The establishment and operation of residential schools were a central element of this policy, which can best be described as "cultural genocide."

Physical genocide is the mass killing of the members of a targeted group, and *biological genocide* is the destruction of the group's reproductive capacity. *Cultural genocide* is the destruction of those structures and practices that allow the group to continue as a group. States that engage in cultural genocide set out to destroy the political and social institutions of the targeted group. Land is seized, and populations are forcibly transferred and their movement is restricted. Languages are banned. Spiritual leaders are persecuted, spiritual practices are forbidden, and objects of spiritual value are confiscated and destroyed. And, most significantly to the issue at hand, families are disrupted to prevent the transmission of cultural values and identity from one generation to the next.

In its dealing with Aboriginal people, Canada did all these things.

Canada asserted control over Aboriginal land. In some locations, Canada negotiated Treaties with First Nations; in others, the land was simply occupied or seized. The negotiation of Treaties, while seemingly honourable and legal, was often marked by fraud and coercion, and Canada was, and remains, slow to implement their provisions and intent.[1]

On occasion, Canada forced First Nations to relocate their reserves from agriculturally valuable or resource-rich land onto remote and economically marginal reserves.[2]

Without legal authority or foundation, in the 1880s, Canada instituted a "pass system" that was intended to confine First Nations people to their reserves.[3]

Canada replaced existing forms of Aboriginal government with relatively powerless band councils whose decisions it could override and whose leaders it could depose.[4] In the process, it disempowered Aboriginal women, who had held significant influence and powerful roles in many First Nations, including the Mohawks, the Carrier, and Tlingit.[5]

Canada denied the right to participate fully in Canadian political, economic, and social life to those Aboriginal people who refused to abandon their Aboriginal identity.[6]

Canada outlawed Aboriginal spiritual practices, jailed Aboriginal spiritual leaders, and confiscated sacred objects.[7]

And, Canada separated children from their parents, sending them to residential schools. This was done not to educate them, but primarily to break their link to their culture and identity. In justifying the government's residential school policy, Canada's first prime minister, Sir John A. Macdonald, told the House of Commons in 1883:

When the school is on the reserve the child lives with its parents, who are savages; he is surrounded by savages, and though he may learn to read and write his habits, and training and mode of thought are Indian. He is simply a savage who can read and write. It has been strongly pressed on myself, as the head of the Department, that Indian children should be withdrawn as much as possible from the parental influence, and the only way to do that would

be to put them in central training industrial schools where they
will acquire the habits and modes of thought of white men.[8]

These measures were part of a coherent policy to eliminate
Aboriginal people as distinct peoples and to assimilate them into
the Canadian mainstream against their will. Deputy Minister of
Indian Affairs Duncan Campbell Scott outlined the goals of that
policy in 1920, when he told a parliamentary committee that "our
object is to continue until there is not a single Indian in Canada
that has not been absorbed into the body politic."[9] These goals
were reiterated in 1969 in the federal government's *Statement of
the Government of Canada on Indian Policy* (more often referred
to as the "White Paper"), which sought to end Indian status and
terminate the Treaties that the federal government had negotiated
with First Nations.[10]

The Canadian government pursued this policy of cultural
genocide because it wished to divest itself of its legal and financial
obligations to Aboriginal people and gain control over their land
and resources. If every Aboriginal person were "absorbed into
the body politic," there would be no reserves, no Treaties, and no
Aboriginal rights.

Residential schooling quickly became a central element in the
federal government's Aboriginal policy. When Canada was created
as a country in 1867, Canadian churches were already operating
a small number of boarding schools for Aboriginal people. As
settlement moved westward in the 1870s, Roman Catholic and
Protestant missionaries established missions and small boarding
schools across the Prairies, in the North, and in British Columbia.
Most of these schools received small, per-student grants from the
federal government. In 1883, the federal government moved to establish three, large, residential schools for First Nation children in
western Canada. In the following years, the system grew dramatically. According to the Indian Affairs annual report for 1930, there
were eighty residential schools in operation across the country at
the time.[11] The Indian Residential Schools Settlement Agreement

provided compensation to students who attended 139 residential schools and residences.[12] The federal government has estimated that at least 150,000 First Nation, Métis, and Inuit students passed through the system.[13]

Roman Catholic, Anglican, United, Methodist, and Presbyterian churches were the major denominations involved in the administration of the residential school system. The government's partnership with the churches remained in place until 1969, and, although most of the schools had closed by the 1980s, the last federally supported residential schools remained in operation until the late 1990s.

For children, life in these schools was lonely and alien. Buildings were poorly located, poorly built, and poorly maintained. The staff was limited in numbers, often poorly trained, and not adequately supervised. Many schools were poorly heated and poorly ventilated, and the diet was meagre and of poor quality. Discipline was harsh, and daily life was highly regimented. Aboriginal languages and cultures were demeaned and suppressed. The educational goals of the schools were limited and confused, and usually reflected a low regard for the intellectual capabilities of Aboriginal people. For the students, education and technical training too often gave way to the drudgery of doing the chores necessary to make the schools self-sustaining. Child neglect was institutionalized, and the lack of supervision created situations where students were prey to sexual and physical abusers.

In establishing residential schools, the Canadian government essentially declared Aboriginal people to be unfit parents. Aboriginal parents were labelled as being indifferent to the future of their children—a judgment contradicted by the fact that parents often kept their children out of schools because they saw those schools, quite accurately, as dangerous and harsh institutions that sought to raise their children in alien ways. Once in the schools, brothers and sisters were kept apart, and the government and churches even arranged marriages for students after they finished their education.

The residential school system was based on an assumption that European civilization and Christian religions were superior to Aboriginal culture, which was seen as being savage and brutal. Government officials also were insistent that children be discouraged—and often prohibited—from speaking their own languages. The missionaries who ran the schools played prominent roles in the church-led campaigns to ban Aboriginal spiritual practices such as the Potlatch and the Sun Dance (more properly called the "Thirst Dance"), and to end traditional Aboriginal marriage practices. Although, in most of their official pronouncements, government and church officials took the position that Aboriginal people could be "civilized," it is clear that many believed that Aboriginal culture was inherently inferior.

This hostility to Aboriginal cultural and spiritual practice continued well into the twentieth century. In 1942, John House, the principal of the Anglican school in Gleichen, Alberta, became involved in a campaign to have two Blackfoot chiefs deposed, in part because of their support for traditional dance ceremonies.[14] In 1947, Roman Catholic official J.O. Plourde told a federal parliamentary committee that since Canada was a Christian nation that was committed to having "all its citizens belonging to one or other of the Christian churches," he could see no reason why the residential schools "should foster aboriginal beliefs."[15] United Church official George Dorey told the same committee that he questioned whether there was such a thing as "native religion."[16]

Into the 1950s and 1960s, the prime mission of residential schools was the cultural transformation of Aboriginal children. In 1953, J.E. Andrews, the principal of the Presbyterian school in Kenora, Ontario, wrote that "we must face realistically the fact that the only hope for the Canadian Indian is eventual assimilation into the white race."[17] In 1957, the principal of the Gordon's Reserve school in Saskatchewan, Albert Southard, wrote that he believed that the goal of residential schooling was to "change the philosophy of the Indian child. In other words since they must work and live with 'whites' then they must begin to think

as 'whites.'" Southard said that the Gordon's school could never
have a student council, since "in so far as the Indian understands
the department's policy, he is against it."[18] In a 1958 article on
residential schools, senior Oblate André Renaud echoed the words
of John A. Macdonald, arguing that when students at day schools
went back to their "homes at the end of the school day and for the
weekend, the pupils are re-exposed to their native culture, however diluted, from which the school is trying to separate them." A
residential school, on the other hand, could "surround its pupils
almost twenty-four hours a day with non-Indian Canadian culture
through radio, television, public address system, movies, books,
newspapers, group activities, etc."[19]

Despite the coercive measures that the government adopted,
it failed to achieve its policy goals. Although Aboriginal peoples
and cultures have been badly damaged, they continue to exist. Aboriginal people have refused to surrender their identity. It was the
former students, the Survivors of Canada's residential schools, who
placed the residential school issue on the public agenda. Their efforts led to the negotiation of the Indian Residential Schools Settlement Agreement that mandated the establishment of a residential
school Truth and Reconciliation Commission of Canada (TRC).

The Survivors acted with courage and determination. We
should do no less. It is time to commit to a process of reconciliation. By establishing a new and respectful relationship, we restore
what must be restored, repair what must be repaired, and return
what must be returned.

CHAPTER ONE

THE HISTORY

It can start with a knock on the door one morning. It is the local Indian agent, or the parish priest, or, perhaps, a Mounted Police officer. The bus for residential school leaves that morning. It is a day the parents have long been dreading. Even if the children have been warned in advance, the morning's events are still a shock. The officials have arrived and the children must go.

For tens of thousands of Aboriginal children for over a century, this was the beginning of their residential schooling. They were torn from their parents, who often surrendered them only under threat of prosecution. Then, they were hurled into a strange and frightening place, one in which their parents and culture would be demeaned and oppressed.

For Frederick Ernest Koe, it started when the Anglican minister and the Mounted Police arrived with a message that he had to leave his parents' home in Aklavik in the Northwest Territories that morning. "And I didn't get to say goodbye to my dad or my brother Allan, didn't get to pet my dogs or nothing."[1]

The day she left for the Lestock, Saskatchewan, school, Marlene Kayseas's parents drove her into the town of Wadena. "There was a big truck there. It had a back door and that truck was full of kids and there was no windows on that truck."[2] Larry Beardy travelled by train from Churchill, Manitoba, to the Anglican residential school in Dauphin, Manitoba—a journey of 1,200 kilometres. As soon as they realized that they were leaving their parents behind, the younger children

FIG 1.1   The goal of residential schooling was to separate children from their
families, culture, and identity. A group of students and parents from the Saddle
Lake Reserve, en route to the Methodist-operated school in Red Deer, Alberta.
Library and Archives Canada, PA-040715.

started crying. At every stop, the train took on more children and
they would start to cry as well. "That train I want to call that train of
tears."[3] Florence Horassi was taken to the Fort Providence, Northwest
Territories, school in a small airplane. On its way to the school, the
plane stopped at a number of small communities to pick up students.
"When the plane took off, there's about six or five older ones, didn't
cry, but I saw tears come right out of their eyes. Everybody else was
crying. There's a whole plane crying. I wanted to cry, too, 'cause my
brother was crying, but I held my tears back and held him."[4]

The arrival at school was often even more traumatizing than
the departure from home or the journey. Lily Bruce's parents were

in tears when they left her and her brother at the Alert Bay, British Columbia, school.[5] At Fort Chipewyan in northern Alberta, Vitaline Elsie Jenner fought to stay with her mother. "I was screaming and hollering. And in my language I said, 'Mama, Mama, *kâya nakasin*' and in English it was, 'Mom, Mom, don't leave me.' 'Cause that's all I knew was to speak Cree. And so the nun took us."[6]

Nellie Ningewance was raised in Hudson, Ontario, and went to the Sioux Lookout, Ontario, school in the 1950s and 1960s. "When we arrived we had to register that we had arrived, then they took us to cut our hair."[7] Bernice Jacks became very frightened when her hair was cut on her arrival at a school in the Northwest Territories. "I could see my hair falling. And I couldn't do nothing. And I was so afraid my mom ... I wasn't thinking about myself. I was thinking about Mom. I say, 'Mom's gonna be really mad. And June is gonna be angry. And it's gonna be my fault.'"[8]

Marthe Basile-Coocoo recalled feeling a chill on first seeing the Pointe Bleue, Québec, school:

> It was something like a grey day, it was a day without sunshine. It was, it was the impression that I had, that I was only six years old, then, well, the nuns separated us, my brothers, and then my uncles, then I no longer understood. Then that, that was a period there, of · suffering, nights of crying, we all gathered in a corner, meaning that we came together, and there we cried. Our nights were like that.[9]

Pauline St-Onge was traumatized by just the sight of the Sept-Îles school in Québec. She fought back when her father tried to take her into the school. "I thought in my child's head I said: 'you would ... you would make me go there, but I will learn nothing, nothing, nothing.'"[10]

Campbell Papequash was taken, against his will, to residential school in 1946. "And after I was taken there they took off my clothes and then they deloused me. I didn't know what was happening but I learned about it later, that they were delousing me; 'the dirty, no-good-for-nothing savages, lousy.'"[11]

Roy Denny was perplexed and frightened by the clothing that the priests and sisters wore at the Shubenacadie, Nova Scotia, school. "We were greeted by this man dressed in black with a long gown. That was the priest, come to find later. And the nuns with their black, black outfits with the white collar and a white, white collar and, like a breastplate of white."[12] Calvin Myerion recalled being overwhelmed by the size of the Brandon, Manitoba, school. "The only building that I knew up to that time, that moment in my life was the one-storey house that we had. And when I got to the residential school, I seen this big monster of a building, and I've never seen any buildings that, that large, that high."[13] Archie Hyacinthe compared the experience to that of being captured and taken into captivity. "That's when the trauma started for me, being separated from my sister, from my parents, and from our, our home. We were no longer free. It was like being, you know, taken to a strange land, even though it was our, our, our land, as I understood later on."[14] When she first went to the Amos, Québec, school, Margo Wylde could not speak any French. "I said to myself, 'How am I going to express myself? How will I make people understand what I'm saying?' And I wanted to find my sisters to ask them to come and get me. You know it's sad to say, but I felt I was a captive."[15]

On their arrival at residential school, students often were required to exchange the clothes they were wearing for school-supplied clothing. This could mean the loss of homemade clothing that was of particular value and meaning to them. Murray Crowe said his clothes from home were taken and burned at the school that he attended in northwestern Ontario.[16] When Wilbur Abrahams's mother sent him to the Alert Bay school in British Columbia, she outfitted him in brand-new clothes. When he arrived at the school, he was told to hand in this outfit in exchange for school clothing. "That was the last time I saw my new clothes. Dare not ask questions."[17] Martin Nicholas of Nelson House, Manitoba, went to the Pine Creek, Manitoba, school in the 1950s. "My mom had prepared me in Native clothing. She had made me a buckskin jacket, beaded with fringes.... And my mom did beautiful work, and I was really proud of my clothes. And when I got to residential school, that first day I remember, they stripped us of our clothes."[18] On her arrival at the Presbyterian school in Kenora, Ontario, Lorna Morgan was wearing "these nice little beaded moccasins that my grandma had made me to wear for school, and I was very proud of them." She said they were taken from her and thrown in the garbage.[19]

Gilles Petiquay, who attended the Pointe Bleue school, was shocked by the fact that each student was assigned a number. "I remember that the first number that I had at the residential school was 95. I had that number—95—for a year. The second number was number 4. I had it for a longer period of time. The third number was 56. I also kept it for a long time. We walked with the numbers on us."[20]

Older brothers were separated from younger brothers, older sisters were separated from younger sisters, and brothers and sisters were separated from each other. Wilbur Abrahams climbed up the steps to the Alert Bay school behind his sisters and started following them to the girls' side of the school. Then, he felt a staff member pulling him by the ear, telling him to turn the other way. "I have always believed that, I think at that particular moment, my spirit left."[21]

When Peter Ross was enrolled at the Immaculate Conception school in Aklavik, Northwest Territories, it was the first time he had ever been parted from his sisters. He said that in all the time he was at the school, he was able to speak with them only at Christmas and on Catholic feast days.[22] Daniel Nanooch recalled that he talked with his sister only four times a year at the Wabasca, Alberta, school. "They had a fence in the playground. Nobody was allowed near the fence. The boys played on this side, the girls played on the other side. Nobody was allowed to go to that fence there and talk to the girls through the fence or whatever, you can't."[23]

The only reason Bernice Jacks had wanted to go to residential school was to be with her older sister. But once she was there, she discovered they were to sleep in separate dormitories. On the occasions when she slipped into the older girls' dormitory and crawled into her sister's bed, her sister scolded her and sent her away: "My sister never talked to me like that before."[24] Helen Kakekayash's older sister tried to comfort her when she first arrived at the McIntosh, Ontario, school. She recalled that "she would try to talk to me, and she would get spanked."[25] Bernard Catcheway said that even though he and his sister were both attending the Pine Creek school, they could not communicate with each other. "I couldn't talk to her, I couldn't wave at her. If you did you'd get, you know a push in the head by a nun."[26] On her second day at the Kamloops school in British Columbia, Julianna Alexander went to speak to her brother. "Did I ever get a good pounding and licking, get over there, you can't go over there, you can't talk to him, you know. I said, 'Yeah, but he's my brother.'"[27]

Taken from their homes, stripped of their belongings, and separated from their siblings, residential school children lived in a world dominated by fear, loneliness, and lack of affection.

William Herney, who attended the Shubenacadie school in Nova Scotia, recalled the first few days in the school as being frightening and bewildering. "Within those few days, you had to learn, because otherwise you're gonna get your head knocked off. Anyway, you learned everything. You learned to obey. And one of the rules that you didn't break, you obey, and you were scared, you were very scared."[28] Raymond Cutknife recalled that when he attended the Hobbema school in Alberta, he "lived with fear."[29] Of his years in two different Manitoba schools, Timothy Henderson said, "Every day was, you were in constant fear that, your hope was that it wasn't you today that we're going to, that was going to be the target, the victim. You know, you weren't going to have to suffer any form of humiliation."[30] Shirley Waskewitch said that in Kindergarten at the Catholic school in Onion Lake, Saskatchewan, "I learned the fear, how to be so fearful at six years old. It was instilled in me."[31]

At the Fort Alexander, Manitoba, school, Patrick Bruyere used to cry himself to sleep. "There was, you know, a few nights I remember that I just, you know, cried myself to sleep, I guess, because of, you know, wanting to see my mom and dad."[32] Ernest Barkman, who attended the Pine Creek school, recalled, "I was really lonely and I cried a lot, my brother who was with me said I cried a lot."[33] Paul Dixon, who attended schools in Québec and Ontario, said that at night, children tried to weep silently. "If one child was caught crying, eh, oh, everybody was in trouble."[34] Betsy Annahatak grew up in Kangirsuk, in northern Québec, which was then known as Payne Bay. When her parents were on the land, she lived in a small hostel in the community. "When one person would start crying, all the, all the little girls would start crying; all of us. We were different ages. And we would cry like little puppies or dogs, right into the night, until we go to sleep; longing for our families."[35]

Students' hearts were hardened. Rick Gilbert remembered the Williams Lake, British Columbia, school as a loveless place. "That was one thing about this school was that when you got hurt or got beat up or something, and you started crying, nobody comforted you. You just sat in the corner and cried and cried till you got tired of crying then you got up and carried on with life."[36] Nick Sibbeston, who was placed in the Fort Providence school in the Northwest Territories at the age of five, recalled it as a place where children hid their emotions. "In residential school you quickly learn that you should not cry. If you cry you're teased, you're shamed out, you're even punished."[37] One former student said that during her time at the Sturgeon Landing school in Saskatchewan, she could not recall a staff member ever smiling at a child.[38] Jack Anawak recalled of his time at Chesterfield Inlet, in what is now Nunavut, in the 1950s that "there was no love, there was no feelings, it was just supervisory."[39] Lydia Ross, who attended the Cross Lake school in Manitoba, said, "If you cried, if you got hurt and cried, there was no, nobody to, nobody to comfort, comfort you, nobody to put their arms."[40] Stephen Kakfwi, who attended Grollier Hall in Inuvik and Grandin College in Fort Smith, Northwest Territories, said this lack of compassion affected the way students treated one another. "No hugs, nothing, no comfort. Everything that, I think, happened in the residential schools, we picked it up: we didn't get any hugs; you ain't going to get one out of me I'll tell you that."[41] Victoria McIntosh said that life at the Fort Alexander, Manitoba, school taught her not to trust anyone. "You learn not to cry anymore. You just get harder. And yeah, you learn to shut down."[42]

These accounts all come from statements made by former residential school students to the Truth and Reconciliation Commission of Canada. These events all took place in Canada within the realm of living memory. Like previous generations of residential school children, these children were sent to what were, in most cases, badly constructed, poorly maintained, overcrowded, unsanitary fire traps. Many children were fed a substandard diet and given a substandard education, and worked too hard. For far too long, they died in tragically high numbers. Discipline was harsh and unregulated; abuse was rife and unreported. It was, at best, institutionalized child neglect.

The people who built, funded, and operated the schools offered varying justifications for this destructive intrusion into the lives of Aboriginal families. Through it, they wished to turn the children into farmers and farmers' wives. They wanted the children to abandon their Aboriginal identity and come to know the Christian god. They feared that if the children were not educated, they would be a menace to the social order of the country. Canadian politicians wished to find a cheap way out of their long-term commitments to Aboriginal people. Christian churches sought government support for their missionary efforts. The schools were part of the colonization and conversion of Aboriginal people, and were intended to bring civilization and salvation to their children. These were the rationales that were used to justify making the lives of so many children so unhappy.

THE IMPERIAL CONTEXT

The whole part of the residential school was a part of a bigger scheme of colonization. There was intent; the schools were there with the intent to

change people, to make them like others and to make them not fit.
And today, you know, we have to learn to decolonize.
— Shirley Flowers, Statement to the TRC[43]

The mandate of the Truth and Reconciliation Commission of
Canada requires it to report on "the history, purpose, operation
and supervision" of Canada's residential schools. These schools
were part of a process that brought European states and Christian churches together in a complex and powerful manner. The
history of the schools can be best understood in the context of
this relationship between the growth of global, European-based
empires and the Christian churches. Starting in the sixteenth century, European states gained control of Indigenous peoples' lands
throughout the world. It was an era of mass migration. Millions of
Europeans arrived as colonial settlers in nearly every part of the
world. Millions of Africans were transported in the European-
led slave trade, in which coastal Africans collaborated. Traders
from India and China spread throughout the Red Sea and Indian
Ocean, bringing with them indentured servants whose lives were
little different from those of slaves.[44] The activities of explorers,
farmers, prospectors, trading companies, or missionaries often set
the stage for expansionary wars, the negotiation and the breaking
of Treaties, attempts at cultural assimilation, and the exploitation
and marginalization of the original inhabitants of the colonized
lands.[45] Over time, Indigenous children in places as distant from
one another as East Africa, Australia, and Siberia would be separated from their parents and sent to residential schools.[46]

The spread of European-based empires was set in motion in
the fifteenth century when the voyages of maritime explorers revealed potential sources of new wealth to the monarchs of Europe.
The Spanish conquest of the Aztecs and the Incas gave Spain, and
ultimately all of Europe, access to the resources of North and South
America. This not only enriched the Old World, but it also unleashed
an unceasing wave of migration, trade, conquest, and colonization.[47]
It marked the beginning of the creation of a European-dominated

global economy. Although it was led initially by Spain and Portugal, this era of imperial expansion came to be directed by Holland, France, and, in the end, most stunningly by Britain.[48]

Empires were established militarily. They engaged in extensive and violent wars with one another, maintained a military presence on their frontiers, and conducted innumerable military campaigns to put down nationalist uprisings.[49] Colonies were established to be exploited economically. The benefits of empire could come directly as taxes, as precious metals, or as raw materials for industries in the homeland. Colonies often were required to purchase their imports solely from the homeland, making them a captive market.[50]

The mere presence of Indigenous people in these newly colonized lands blocked settler access to the land.[51] To gain control of the land of Indigenous people, colonists negotiated Treaties, waged wars of extinction, eliminated traditional landholding practices, disrupted families, and imposed a political and spiritual order that came complete with new values and cultural practices.[52] Treaty promises often went unfulfilled. United States General William Tecumseh Sherman is quoted as having said, "We have made more than one thousand treaties with the various Indian tribes, and have not kept one of them." In commenting on Sherman's statement in 1886, C.C. Painter, a critic of American Indian policy, observed that the United States had

> never intended to keep them. They were not made to be kept,
> but to serve a present purpose, to settle a present difficulty in
> the easiest manner possible, to acquire a desired good with
> the least possible compensation, and then to be disregarded as
> soon as this purpose was tainted and we were strong enough
> to enforce a new and more profitable arrangement.[53]

The outcome was usually disastrous for Indigenous people, while the chief beneficiaries of empire were the colonists and their descendants. Many of the colonies they settled grew to be among the most prosperous societies in the late nineteenth- and early twentieth-century world.[54] Settler colonies often went on to gain political independence. In the case of Canada and the United States of America, these newly created nations spread across North America. As they expanded, they continued to incorporate Indigenous peoples and their lands into empires. Colonialism remains an ongoing process, shaping both the structure and the quality of the relationship between the settlers and Indigenous peoples.

At their height, the European empires laid claim to most of the earth's surface and controlled the seas.[55] Numerous arguments were advanced to justify such extravagant interventions into the lands and lives of other peoples. These were largely elaborations on two basic concepts: 1) the Christian god had given the Christian nations the right to colonize the lands they "discovered" as long as they converted the Indigenous populations; and 2) the Europeans were bringing the benefits of civilization (a concept that was intertwined with Christianity) to the "heathen." In short, it was contended that people were being colonized for their own benefit, either in this world or the next.

In the fifteenth century, the Roman Catholic Church, building on the traditions of the Roman Empire, conceived of itself as the guardian of a universal world order.[56] The adoption of Christianity within the Roman Empire (which defined itself as "civilized") reinforced the view that to be civilized was to be Christian. The Catholic papacy was already playing a role in directing and legitimizing colonialism prior to Christopher Columbus's voyages to the Americas in the 1490s, largely by granting Catholic kingdoms the right to colonize lands they "discovered."[57] In 1493, Pope Alexander VI issued the first of four orders, referred to as "papal bulls" (a term that takes its name from the Latin word for the mould used to seal the document), that granted most of North and South America to Spain, the kingdom that had sponsored Columbus's voyage of the preceding year. These orders helped shape the political and legal arguments that have come to be referred to as the "Doctrine of Discovery," which was used to justify the colonization of the Americas in the sixteenth century. In return, the Spanish were expected to convert the Indigenous peoples of the Americas to Christianity.[58]

Other European rulers rejected the Pope's ability to give away sovereignty over half the world.[59] But they did not necessarily reject the Doctrine of Discovery—they simply modified it. The English argued that a claim to "discovered lands" was valid if the "discoverer" was able to take possession of them.[60] Harman Verelst, who promoted the colonization in the eighteenth century of what is now the southern coast of the United States, wrote that "this Right arising from the first discovery is the first and fundamental Right of all European Nations, as to their Claim of Lands in America."[61] This Doctrine of Discovery was linked to a second idea: the lands being claimed were *terra nullius*—no man's land—and therefore open to claim. On the basis of this concept, the British government claimed ownership of the entire Australian continent. (There, the doctrine of *terra nullius* remained the law until it was successfully challenged in court in 1992.)[62] Under this doctrine, imperialists could argue that the presence of Indigenous people did not void a claim of *terra nullius*, since the Indigenous people simply occupied, rather than owned, the land. True ownership, they claimed, could come only with European-style agriculture.[63]

Underlying these arguments was the belief that the colonizers were bringing civilization to savage people who could never civilize themselves. The "civilizing mission" rested on a belief of racial and cultural superiority. European writers and politicians often arranged racial groups in a hierarchy, each with their own set of mental and physical capabilities. The "special gifts" of the Europeans meant it was inevitable that they would conquer the lesser peoples. Beneath the Europeans, in descending order, were Asians, Africans, and the Indigenous peoples of the Americas and Australia. Some people held that Europeans had reached the pinnacle of civilization through a long and arduous process. In this view, the other peoples of the world had been held back by such factors as climate, geography, and migration. Through a civilizing process, Europeans could, however, raise the people of the world up to their level. This view was replaced in the nineteenth century by a racism that chose to cloak itself in the language of science, and held that the peoples of the world had differing abilities. Some argued that, for genetic reasons, there were limits on the ability of the less-developed peoples to improve. In some cases, it was thought, contact with superior races could lead to only one outcome: the extinction of the inferior peoples.[64]

These ideas shaped global policies towards Indigenous peoples. In 1883, Britain's Lord Rosebery, a future British prime minister, told an Australian audience, "It is on the British race, whether in Great Britain, or the United States, or the Colonies, or wherever it may be, that rest the highest hopes of those who try to penetrate the dark future, or who seek to raise and better the patient masses of mankind."[65] Residential schools were established in the shadow of these ideas. In the year that Rosebery gave this speech, the Canadian government opened its first industrial residential school for Aboriginal people at Battleford on the Canadian Prairies.[66]

The Christian churches not only provided the moral justification for the colonization of other peoples' lands, but they also dispatched missionaries to the colonized nations in order to convert "the heathen." From the fifteenth century on, the Indigenous peoples of the world were the objects of a strategy of spiritual and cultural conquest that had its origins in Europe. While they often worked in isolation and under difficult conditions, missionaries were representatives of worldwide organizations that enjoyed the backing of influential individuals in some of the most powerful nations of the world, and which came to amass considerable experience in transforming different cultures.[67] Residential schools figured prominently in missionary work, not only in Canada, but also around the world.

Christian missionaries played a complex but central role in the European colonial project. Their presence helped justify the extension of empires, since they were visibly spreading the word of God to the heathen. If their efforts were unsuccessful, the missionaries might conclude that those who refused to accept the Christian message could not expect the protection of the church or the law, thus clearing the way for their destruction.[68] Although missionaries often attempted to soften the impact of imperialism, they were also committed to making the greatest changes in the culture and psychology of the colonized. They might, for example, seek to have traders give fair prices and to have government officials provide relief in times of need, but they also worked to undermine relationships to the land, language, religion, family relations, educational practices, morality, and social custom.[69]

Missionary zeal was also fuelled by the often violent division that had separated the Christian world into Catholic and Protestant churches. Both Catholics and Protestants invested heavily in the creation of missionary organizations that were intended to engage overseas missionary work. The most well-known Catholic orders were the Franciscans, the Jesuits, and the Oblates. The Oblates originally focused their attention on the poor and working classes of France, but from the 1830s onwards, they engaged in overseas missionary work. They established themselves in eastern Canada, the Pacific Northwest, Ceylon, Texas, and Africa.[70] The Oblates administered a majority of the Roman Catholic residential schools in Canada. They could not have done this work without the support of a number of female religious orders, most particularly the Sisters of Charity (the Grey Nuns), the Sisters of Providence, the Sisters of St. Anne, and the Missionary Oblate Sisters of the Sacred Heart and of Mary Immaculate.

The British-based Church Missionary Society was also a global enterprise. By the middle of the nineteenth century, this Anglican society had missions across the globe in such places as India, New Zealand, West and East Africa, China, and the Middle East. The society's Highbury College in London provided missionaries with several years of training in arithmetic, grammar, history, geography, religion, education, and the administration of schools.[71] By 1901, the Church Missionary Society had an annual income of over 300,000 pounds. It used this money to support 510 male missionaries, 326 unmarried females, and 365 ordained pastors around the world.[72]

The Catholics and Anglicans were not the only European-based missionary societies to take up work in Canada. Presbyterians and Methodists, originally drawing support from the United Kingdom, undertook missionary work among Aboriginal people in the early nineteenth century. On the coast of Labrador, members of the Moravian Brotherhood, an order that had its origins in what is now the Czech Republic, carried out missionary work from the early eighteenth century onwards.[73] Protestant missionary work also depended on the often underpaid and voluntary labour of missionary wives and single women who had been recruited by missionary societies.

Missionaries viewed Aboriginal culture as a barrier to both spiritual salvation and the ongoing existence of Aboriginal people. They were determined to replace traditional economic pursuits with European-style peasant agriculture. They believed that cultural transformation required the imposition of social control and separation from both traditional communities and European settlements. In the light of these beliefs, it is not surprising that they were proponents of an educational world that separated children from the influences of their families and cultures, imposed a new set of values and beliefs, provided a basic elementary education, and created institutions whose daily life reflected Europe's emerging work discipline. In short, they sought to impose the foreign and transforming world of the residential school.

Colonization was undertaken to meet the perceived needs of the imperial powers. The justification offered for colonialism—the need to bring Christianity and civilization to the Indigenous peoples of the world—may have been a sincerely and firmly held belief, but as a justification for intervening in the lives of other peoples, it does not stand up to legal, moral, or even logical scrutiny. The papacy had no authority to give away lands that belonged to Indigenous people. The Doctrine of Discovery cannot serve as the basis for a legitimate claim to the lands that were colonized, if for no other reason than that the so-called discovered lands were already well known to the Indigenous peoples who had inhabited them for thousands of years. The wars of conquest that took place to strip Indigenous peoples of their lands around the globe were not morally just wars; Indigenous peoples were not, as colonists often claimed, subhuman, and neither were they living in violation of any universally agreed-upon set of values. There was no moral imperative to impose Christianity on the Indigenous peoples of the world. They did not need to be "civilized"; indeed, there is no hierarchy of societies. Indigenous peoples had systems that were complete unto themselves and met their needs. Those systems were dynamic; they changed over time and were capable of continued change.[74] Taken as a whole, the colonial process relied for its justification on the sheer presumption of taking a specific set of European beliefs and values and proclaiming them to be universal values that could be imposed upon the peoples of the world. This universalizing of European values—so central to the colonial project—that was extended to North America served as the prime justification and rationale for the imposition of a residential school system on the Indigenous peoples of Canada.

RESIDENTIAL SCHOOLS IN PRE-CONFEDERATION CANADA

In Canada, residential schooling was closely linked to colonization and missionary crusades. The first boarding school for Aboriginal people in what is now Canada was established in the early seventeenth century near the French trading post at the future site of Québec City. At this Roman Catholic school, missionaries hoped to both "civilize" and "Christianize" young Aboriginal boys.[75] The school was a failure: parents were reluctant to send their children, and the students were quick to run away and return home.[76] Later efforts in New France met with no greater success.[77] After the British conquest of New France in 1763, the idea of residential schooling lay dormant until the early nineteenth century. In the first decade of that century, the New England Company, a British-based missionary society, funded a boarding school operation in Sussex Vale, New Brunswick. The goals were to teach young Mi'kmaq and Maliseet children trades and to convert them to Protestantism.[78] In the 1820s, John West, an Anglican missionary from England, opened a boarding school for Aboriginal students at Red River.[79] Although these efforts also failed to take root, in 1834, the Mohawk Institute, a mission school on the Grand River in what is now Ontario, began taking in boarders.[80] This school would remain in operation until 1970.[81]

In 1847, Egerton Ryerson, the superintendent of schools for Upper Canada, recommended the establishment of residential schools in which Aboriginal students would be given instruction in "English language, arithmetic, elementary geometry, or knowledge of forms, geography and the elements of general history, natural history and agricultural chemistry, writing, drawing and vocal music, book-keeping (especially in reference to farmers' accounts), religion, and morals."[82] This he thought of as "a plain English education adapted to the working farmer and mechanic. In this their object is identical with that of every good common school." Pupils should be "taught agriculture, kitchen gardening, and mechanics, so far as mechanics is connected with making and repairing the most useful agricultural implements."[83]

After the release of Ryerson's report, Methodist missionaries operated a number of boarding schools in southern Ontario in the 1850s.[84] One of them, the Mount Elgin school at Munceytown (later, Muncey), did not close until 1946.[85] The first of what would be a string of Roman Catholic residential schools in what is now British Columbia opened in the early 1860s.[86] A school in Fort Providence in what is now the Northwest Territories began taking in students in 1867.[87]

THE COLONIZATION OF THE NORTHWEST

After the Canadian state was established in 1867, the federal government began making small per-student grants to many of the church-run boarding schools. Federal government involvement in residential schooling did not begin in earnest until the 1880s. The catalyst for this expansion was the 1870 transfer of much of contemporary Alberta, Saskatchewan, Manitoba, northern Québec, northern Ontario, the Northwest Territories, and Nunavut from the Hudson's Bay Company to the Canadian government. The following year, British Columbia was brought into Confederation by the promise of a continental rail link.

Canadian politicians intended to populate the newly acquired lands with settlers from Europe and Ontario. These settlers were expected to buy goods produced in central Canada and ship their harvests by rail to western and eastern ports and then on to international markets. Settling the "Northwest"—as this territory came to be known—in this manner meant colonizing the over 40,000 Indigenous people who lived there.[88]

The Rupert's Land Order of 1870, which transferred much of the Northwest to Canadian control, required that "the claims of the Indian tribes to compensation for lands required for purposes of settlement will be considered and settled in conformity with the equitable principles which have uniformly governed the British Crown in its dealings with the aborigines."[89] These principles had been set down in the Royal Proclamation of 1763, which placed limits on the conditions under which Aboriginal land could be transferred. "If at any Time any of the Said Indians should be inclined to dispose of the said Lands," they could do so, but land could be sold only to the Crown, and the sale had to be at a meeting of Indians that had been held specifically for that purpose.[90] The Royal Proclamation, in effect, ruled that any future transfer of "Indian" land would take the form of a Treaty between sovereigns.[91] In this, it stands as one of the clearest and earliest expressions of what has been identified as a long-standing element of Canadian Aboriginal policy.[92]

To enable the colonization of the Northwest, in 1871, the federal government began negotiating the first in a series of what came to be termed as "Numbered Treaties" with the First Nations of western and northern Canada. The only alternative to negotiating Treaties would have been to ignore the legal obligations of the Rupert's Land Order and attempt to subdue the First Nations militarily, but that would have been a very costly proposition. In 1870, when the entire Canadian government budget was $19 million, the United States was spending more than that—$20 million a year—on its Indian Wars alone. Despite all these pressures, the government took a slow and piecemeal approach to Treaty making.[93]

Through the Treaties, Aboriginal peoples were seeking agricultural supplies and training as well as relief during periods of epidemic or famine in a time of social and economic transition.[94] They saw the Treaty process as establishing a reciprocal relationship that would be lasting.[95] The goal was to gain the skills that would allow them to continue to control their own destinies and retain their culture and identity as Aboriginal people. As Ahtahkakoop (Star Blanket) said, "We Indians can learn the ways of living that made the white man strong."[96] The provisions varied from Treaty to Treaty, but they generally included funds for hunting and fishing supplies, agricultural assistance, yearly payments for band members (annuities), and an amount of reserve lands based on the population of the band.[97] First Nations never asked for residential schools as part of the Treaty process, and neither did the government suggest that such schools would be established. The education provisions also varied in different Treaties, but promised to pay for schools on reserves or teachers. The federal government was slow to live up to its Treaty obligations. For example, many First Nations were settled on reserves that were much smaller than they were entitled to, while others were not provided with any reserve.[98] Some obligations remain unfulfilled to this day. The commitment to establish on-reserve schools was also ignored in many cases. As a result, parents who wished to see their children educated were forced to send them to residential schools.[99]

THE ASSIMILATION POLICY

From the Canadian government's perspective, the most significant elements in the Treaties were the written provisions by which the First Nations agreed to "cede, release, surrender, and yield" their land to the Crown.[100] In the Treaty negotiations, however, federal officials left the impression that the government intended the Treaties to establish a permanent relationship with First Nations. Treaty Commissioner Alexander Morris told the Cree in 1876, "What I trust and hope we will do is not for to-day and tomorrow only; what I will promise, and what I believe and hope you will take, is to last as long as the sun shines and yonder river flows."[101] In reality, the federal government policy was very different from what Morris said. The intent of the government's policy, which was firmly established in legislation at the time that the Treaties had been negotiated, was to assimilate Aboriginal people into broader Canadian society. At the end of this process, Aboriginal people were expected to have ceased to exist as a distinct people with their own governments, cultures, and identities.

The federal *Indian Act*, first adopted in 1876, like earlier pre-Confederation legislation, defined who was and who was not an "Indian" under Canadian law.[102] The Act also defined a process through which a person could lose status as an Indian. Women, for example, could lose status simply by marrying a man who did not have status. Men could lose status in a number of ways, including graduating from a university. Upon giving up their status, individuals also were granted a portion of the band's reserve land.[103]

First Nations people were unwilling to surrender their Aboriginal identity in this manner. Until 1920, other than women who involuntarily lost their Indian status upon marriage to a non-status individual, only 250 "Indians" voluntarily gave up their status.[104] In 1920, the federal government amended the *Indian Act* to give it the power to strip individuals of their status against their will. In explaining the purpose of the amendment to a parliamentary committee, Indian Affairs Deputy Minister Duncan Campbell Scott said that "our object is to continue until there is not a single

Indian in Canada that has not been absorbed into the body politic, and there is no Indian question, and no Indian Department that is the whole object of this Bill."[105] The other major element in the bill that Scott was referring to empowered the government to compel parents to send their children to residential schools. Residential schooling was always more than simply an educational program: it was an integral part of a conscious policy of cultural genocide.

Further evidence of this assault on Aboriginal identity can be found in amendments to the *Indian Act* banning a variety of Aboriginal cultural and spiritual practices. The two most prominent of these were the west-coast Potlatch and the Prairie Thirst Dance (often referred to as the "Sun Dance").[106] Residential school principals had been in the forefront of the campaign to ban these ceremonies, and also urged the government to enforce the bans once they were put in place.[107]

The Aboriginal right to self-government was also undermined. The *Indian Act* gave the federal government the authority to veto decisions made by band councils and to depose chiefs and councillors. The Act placed restrictions on First Nations farmers' ability to sell their crops and take out loans. Over the years, the government also assumed greater authority as to how reserve land could be disposed of: in some cases, entire reserves were relocated against the will of the residents. The *Indian Act* was a piece of colonial legislation by which, in the name of "protection," one group of people ruled and controlled another.

THE INDUSTRIAL
SCHOOL INITIATIVE

It was in keeping with this intent to assimilate Aboriginal peoples and, in the process, to eliminate its government-to-government relationship with First Nations that the federal government dramatically increased its involvement in residential schooling in the 1880s. In December 1878, J.S. Dennis, the deputy minister of the Department of the Interior, prepared a memorandum for Prime

Minister Sir John A. Macdonald on the country's Aboriginal policy. Dennis advised Macdonald that the long-term goal should be to instruct "our Indian and half-breed populations" in farming, raising cattle, and the mechanical trades, rendering them self-sufficient. This would pave the way "for their emancipation from tribal government, and for their final absorption into the general community." Dennis argued that residential schools were key to fulfilling these goals. It was his opinion that in a short time, schools might become "self-sustaining institutions."[108]

In the following year, Nicholas Davin, a failed Conservative candidate, carried out a brief study of the boarding schools that the United States government had established for Native Americans. He recommended that Canada establish a series of such schools on the Prairies. Davin acknowledged that a central element of the education provided at these schools would be directed towards the destruction of Aboriginal spirituality. Since all civilizations were based on religion, it would be inexcusable, he thought, to do away with Aboriginal faith "without supplying a better [one]." For this reason, he recommended that while the government should fund the schools, the churches should operate them.[109]

The decision to continue to rely on the churches to administer the schools on a day-to-day basis had serious consequences. The government constantly struggled, and failed, to assert control over the churches' drive to increase the number of schools they operated. At various times, each denomination involved in school operation established boarding schools without government support or approval, and then lobbied later for per capita funding. When the churches concluded, quite legitimately, that the per capita grant they received was too low, they sought other types of increases in school funding. Building on their network of missions in the Northwest, the Catholics quickly came to dominate the field, usually operating twice as many schools as did the Protestant denominations. Among the Protestant churches, the Anglicans were predominant, establishing and maintaining more residential schools than the Methodists or the Presbyterians. The

United Church, created by a union of Methodist and Presbyterian congregations, took over most of the Methodist and Presbyterian schools in the mid-1920s. Presbyterian congregations that did not participate in the union established the Presbyterian Church in Canada and retained responsibility for two residential schools. In addition to these national denominations, a local Baptist mission ran a residence for Aboriginal students in Whitehorse in the 1940s and 1950s, and a Mennonite ministry operated three schools in northwestern Ontario in the 1970s and 1980s. Each faith, in its turn, claimed government discrimination against it. Competition for converts meant that churches sought to establish schools in the same locations as their rivals, leading to internal divisions within communities and expensive duplication of services.

The model for these residential schools for Aboriginal children, both in Canada and the United States, did not come from the private boarding schools to which members of the economic elites in Britain and Canada sent their children. Instead, the model came from the reformatories and industrial schools that were being constructed in Europe and North America for the children of the urban poor. The British parliament adopted the *Reformatory Schools Act* in 1854 and the *Industrial Schools Act* in 1857.[110] By 1882, over 17,000 children were in Britain's industrial schools.[111] Under Ontario's 1880 *Act for the Protection and Reformation of Neglected Children*, a judge could send children under the age of fourteen to an industrial school, where they might be required to stay until they turned eighteen.[112] Such schools could be dangerous and violent places. At the Halifax Boys Industrial School, first offenders were strapped, and repeat offenders were placed in cells on a bread-and-water ration. From there, they might be sent to the penitentiary.[113] The Canadian government also drew inspiration from the United States. There, the first in a series of large-scale, government-operated, boarding schools for Native Americans opened in 1879 in a former army barracks in Carlisle, Pennsylvania.[114]

On the basis of Davin's report and developments in the United States, the federal government decided to open three industrial

schools. The first one opened in Battleford in what is now Saskatchewan in 1883. It was placed under the administration of an Anglican
minister. The following year, two more industrial schools opened:
one at Qu'Appelle in what is now Saskatchewan, and one at High
River in what is now Alberta. Both these schools were administered
by principals nominated by the Roman Catholic Oblate order. The
federal government not only built these schools, but it also assumed
all the costs of operating them. Recruiting students for these schools
was difficult. According to the Indian Affairs annual report, in
1884, there were only twenty-seven students at the three schools.[115]

Unlike the church-run boarding schools, which provided
a limited education with a heavy emphasis on religious instruction, the industrial schools were intended to prepare First Nations
people for integration into Canadian society by teaching them basic trades, particularly farming. Generally, industrial schools were
larger than boarding schools, were located in urban areas, and,
although church-managed, usually required federal approval prior
to construction. The boarding schools were smaller institutions,
were located on or near reserves, and provided a more limited
education. The differences between the industrial schools and the
boarding schools eroded over time. By the 1920s, the federal government ceased to make any distinction between them, referring
to them simply as "residential schools."

In justifying the investment in industrial schools to Parliament in 1883, Public Works Minister Hector Langevin argued that

if you wish to educate these children you must separate them
from their parents during the time that they are being educated.
If you leave them in the family they may know how to read and
write, but they still remain savages, whereas by separating them
in the way proposed, they acquire the habits and tastes—it is
to be hoped only the good tastes—of civilized people.[116]

The federal government entered into residential schooling at a
time when it was colonizing Aboriginal lands in western Canada.
It recognized that, through the Treaties, it had made commitments

to provide Aboriginal people with relief in periods of economic distress. It also feared that as traditional Aboriginal economic pursuits were marginalized or eliminated by settlers, the government might be called upon to provide increased relief. In this context, the federal government chose to invest in residential schooling for a number of reasons. First, it would provide Aboriginal people with skills that would allow them to participate in the coming market-based economy. Second, it would further their political assimilation. It was hoped that students who were educated in residential schools would give up their status and not return to their reserve communities and families. Third, the schools were seen as engines of cultural and spiritual change: "savages" were to emerge as Christian "white men." There was also a national security element to the schools. Indian Affairs official Andsell Macrae observed that "it is unlikely that any Tribe or Tribes would give trouble of a serious nature to the Government whose members had children completely under Government control."[117] Duncan Campbell Scott succinctly summarized Indian Affairs' goals for the schools in 1909: "It includes not only a scholastic education, but instruction in the means of gaining a livelihood from the soil or as a member of an industrial or mercantile community, and the substitution of Christian ideals of conduct and morals for aboriginal concepts of both."[118] The achievement of such invasive and ambitious goals would require a substantial level of funding. This was never forthcoming.

FUNDING: THE DREAM OF SELF-SUPPORTING SCHOOLS

In announcing the construction of the three initial industrial schools, Indian Commissioner Edgar Dewdney said that although the starting costs would be high, he could see no reason why the schools would not be largely self-supporting in a few years, due to the skills in farming, raising stock, and trades that were being taught to the students.[119] In supporting an Anglican proposal for two industrial schools in Manitoba, Indian Affairs Deputy

Minister Lawrence Vankoughnet wrote to Prime Minister Macdonald that it would be "well to give a Grant of money annually to each school established by any Denomination for the industrial training of Indian children." He said that system worked well in Ontario, and it "costs the Government less than the whole maintenance of the School would cost and it enlists the sympathies and assistance of the religious denominations in the education and industrial training of the Indian children."[120]

The government believed that between the forced labour of students and the poorly paid labour of missionaries, it could operate a residential school system on a nearly cost-free basis. The missionaries and the students were indeed a source of cheap labour—but the government was never happy with the quality of the teaching and, no matter how hard students worked, their labour never made the schools self-supporting. Soon after the government established the industrial schools, it began to cut salaries.[121] Initially, the federal government covered all the costs of operating the industrial schools. In 1891, this policy was abandoned in favour of one by which schools received a fixed amount per student (referred to as a "per capita grant").[122] The system both intensified the level of competition among churches for students and encouraged principals to accept students who should have been barred from admission because they were too young or too sick.[123]

The government never adequately responded to the belated discovery that the type of residential school system that officials had envisioned would cost far more than politicians were prepared to fund. In the early twentieth century, chronic underfunding led to a health crisis in the schools and a financial crisis for the missionary societies. Indian Affairs, with the support of leading figures in the Protestant churches, sought to dramatically reduce the number of residential schools, replacing them with day schools. The government abandoned the plan when it failed to receive the full support of all the churches involved in the operation of the schools.[124] Instead, in 1911, the federal government finally implemented a significant increase to the per capita grant received by boarding schools and attempted to impose basic health standards for the schools. This resulted in a short-term improvement. However, inflation eroded the value of the grant increase, and the grant was actually reduced repeatedly during the Great Depression and at the start of the Second World War.[125]

Funding for residential schools was always lower than funding for comparable institutions in Canada and the United States that served the general population. In 1937, Indian Affairs was paying, on average, $180 a year per student. This was less than a third of the per capita costs at that time for the Manitoba School for the Deaf ($642.40) and the Manitoba School for Boys ($550). In the United States, the annual per capita cost at the Chilocco Indian Residential School in Oklahoma in 1937 was $350. According to the American Child Welfare League, the per capita costs for well-run institutions in that country ranged between $313 and $541.[126] It would not be until the 1950s that changes were made in the funding system in Canada that were intended to ensure that the schools could recruit qualified teachers and improve the student diets.[127] Even these improvements did not end the inequity in residential school funding. In 1966, residential schools in Saskatchewan were spending between $694 and $1,193 a year per student.[128] Comparable child-welfare institutions in Canada were spending between $3,300 and $9,855 a year. In the United States, the annual cost of residential care per child was between $4,500 and $14,059.[129]

COMPELLING ATTENDANCE

It was not until 1894 that the federal government put in place regulations relating to residential school attendance. Under the regulations adopted in that year, residential school attendance was voluntary. However, if an Indian agent or justice of the peace thought that any "Indian child between six and sixteen years of age is not being properly cared for or educated, and that the parent, guardian or other person having charge or control of such child, is unfit or unwilling to provide for the child's education," he could issue an order to place the child "in an industrial or boarding school, in which there may be a vacancy for such child."

If a child placed in the school under these regulations left a residential school without permission, or did not return at a promised time, school officials could get a warrant from an Indian agent or a justice of the peace authorizing them (or a police officer, truant officer, or employee of the school or Indian Affairs) to "search for and take such child back to the school in which it had been previously placed." With a warrant, one could enter—by force if need be—any house, building, or place named in the warrant and remove the child. Even without a warrant, Indian Affairs employees and constables had the authority to arrest a student in the act of escaping from a residential school and return the child to the school.[130]

It was departmental policy that no child could be discharged without departmental approval—even if the parents had enrolled the child voluntarily. The government had no legislative basis for this policy. Instead, it relied on the admission form that parents were supposed to sign. (In some cases, school staff members signed these forms.)[131] By 1892, the department required that all parents sign an admission form when they enrolled their children in a residential school. In signing the form, parents gave their consent that "the Principal or head teacher of the Institution for the time being shall be the guardian" of the child. In that year, the Department of Justice provided Indian Affairs with a legal opinion to the effect that "the fact of a parent having signed such an application is not sufficient to warrant the forcible arrest against the parents' will of a truant child who has been admitted to an Industrial School pursuant to the application." It was held that, without legislative authority, no form could provide school administrators with the power of arrest.[132] Despite this warning, well into the twentieth century, Indian Affairs would continue to enforce policies regarding attendance for which it had no legal authority.[133] This is not the only example of the government's use of unauthorized measures. In the

1920s, students were to be discharged from residential school when they turned sixteen. Despite this, William Graham, the Indian commissioner, refused to authorize discharge until the students turned eighteen. He estimated that, on this basis, he rejected approximately 100 applications for discharge a year.[134]

In 1920, the *Indian Act* was amended to allow the government to compel any First Nations child to attend residential school. However, residential school was never compulsory for all First Nations children. In most years, there were more First Nations children attending Indian Affairs day schools than residential schools. During the early 1940s, this pattern was reversed. In the 1944–45 school year, there were 8,865 students in residential schools, and 7,573 students in Indian Affairs day schools. In that year, there were reportedly 28,429 school-aged Aboriginal children. This meant that 31.1 percent of the school-aged Aboriginal children were in residential school.[135]

REGULATION

The residential school system operated with few regulations; those that did exist were in large measure weakly enforced. The Canadian government never developed anything approaching the education acts and regulations by which provincial governments administered public schools. The key piece of legislation used in regulating the residential school system was the *Indian Act*. This was a multipurpose piece of legislation that defined and limited First Nations life in Canada. The Act contained no education-related provisions until 1884. There were no residential school-specific regulations until 1894. These dealt almost solely with attendance and truancy.

It was recognized by those who worked within the system that the level of regulation was inadequate. In 1897, Indian Affairs education official Martin Benson wrote, "No regulations have been adopted or issued by the Department applicable to all its schools, as had been done by the Provincial Governments."[136] The situation did not improve over time. The education section of the 1951 *Indian Act* and the residential school regulations adopted in 1953

were each only four pages in length.[137] By comparison, the Manitoba *Public Schools Act* of 1954 was ninety-one pages in length.[138]
In addition to the Act, the Manitoba government had adopted
nineteen education-related regulations.[139]

It is also apparent that many key people within the system had
little knowledge of the existing rules and regulations. In 1922, an
Indian agent in Hagersville, Ontario, inquired of departmental
headquarters if there had been any changes in the regulations
regarding education since the adoption of a set of education regulations in 1908. His question suggests he was completely unaware
of major changes to the *Indian Act* regarding education that had
supplanted previous regulations in 1920.[140] In 1926, J.K. Irwin,
the newly appointed principal of the Gordon's school in Saskatchewan, discovered upon taking office that he could not find any
"laid down regulations as to the duties and powers of a Principal of
an Indian Boarding School." He wrote to Indian Affairs, asking for
a copy of such regulations, since he wanted to know "exactly what
I am to do and what powers I have."[141] Departmental secretary
J.D. McLean informed him that "there are no printed regulations
concerning the duties and powers of the principal of an Indian
residential school."[142]

The system was so unregulated that in 1968, after Canada
had been funding residential schools for 101 years, Indian Affairs
Deputy Minister J.A. MacDonald announced, "For the first time
we have set down in a precise and detailed manner the criteria
which is to be used in future in determining whether or not an
Indian child is eligible for these institutions."[143]

EXPANSION AND DECLINE

From the 1880s onwards, residential school enrolment climbed
annually. According to federal government annual reports, the
peak enrolment of 11,539 was reached in the 1956–57 school
year.[144] (For trends, see Graph 1.) Most of the residential schools
were located in the northern and western regions of the country.

With the exception of Mount Elgin and the Mohawk Institute, the Ontario schools were all in northern or northwestern Ontario. The only school in the Maritimes did not open until 1930.[145] Roman Catholic and Anglican missionaries opened the first two schools in Québec in the early 1930s.[146] It was not until later in that decade that the federal government began funding these schools.[147]

The number of schools began to decline in the 1940s. Between 1940 and 1950, for example, ten school buildings were destroyed by fire.[148] As Graph 2 illustrates, this decrease was reversed in the mid-1950s, when the federal department of Northern Affairs and National Resources dramatically expanded the school system in the Northwest Territories and northern Québec. Prior to that time, residential schooling in the North was largely restricted to the Yukon and the Mackenzie Valley in the Northwest Territories. Large residences were built in communities such as Inuvik, Yellowknife, Whitehorse, Churchill, and eventually Iqaluit (formerly Frobisher Bay). This expansion was undertaken despite reports that recommended against the establishment of residential schools, since they would not provide children with the skills necessary to live in the North, skills they otherwise would have acquired in their home communities.[149] The creation of the large hostels was accompanied by the opening of what were termed "small hostels" in the smaller and more remote communities of the eastern Arctic and the western Northwest Territories.

POLICY TOWARDS MÉTIS AND INUIT STUDENTS

Many of the early advocates of residential schooling in Canada expected that the schools would take in both Aboriginal children who had status under the *Indian Act* (in other words, they were Indians as defined by the Act) as well as Aboriginal children who, for a variety of reasons, did not have status. The federal government classed these individuals alternately as "non-status Indians," "half-breeds," or "Métis."[150]

GRAPH 1
Residential school enrolment, 1869–70 to 1965–66

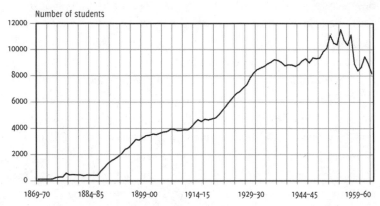

Source: Indian Affairs and Northern Affairs annual reports. After the 1965–66 school year, Indian Affairs stopped reporting on annual residential school enrolment.

GRAPH 2
Number of residential schools and residences, 1867–1998

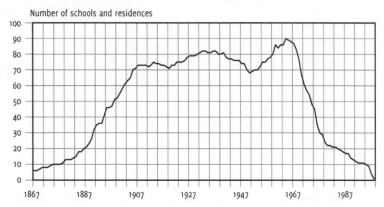

Source: Indian and Northern Affairs Canada, Indian Residential Schools of the Indian Residential Schools Settlement Agreement 2011.

The early church-run boarding schools made no distinction between status and non-status or Métis children.[151] The federal government position on the matter was constantly shifting. It viewed the Métis as members of the "dangerous classes" whom the residential schools were intended to civilize and assimilate.[152] This view led to the adoption of policies that allowed for the admission of Métis children to the schools at various times.[153] However, from a jurisdictional perspective, the federal government believed that the responsibility for educating and assimilating Métis people lay with provincial and territorial governments. There was a strong concern that if the federal government began providing funding for the education of some of the children the provinces and territories were responsible for, it would find itself subject to having to take responsibility for the rest.[154] When this view dominated, Indian agents would be instructed to remove Métis students from residential schools.[155]

Despite their perceived constitutional responsibility, provincial and territorial governments were reluctant to provide services to Métis people. They did not ensure that there were schools in Métis communities, or work to see that Métis children were admitted and welcomed into the general public school system.[156] Many Métis parents who wished to see their children educated in schools had no option but to try to have them accepted into a residential school. In some cases, these would be federally funded schools, but, in other cases, Métis students attended church-run schools or residences that did not receive federal funding.[157]

Provincial governments slowly began to provide increased educational services to Métis students after the Second World War. As a result, Métis children lived in residences and residential schools that were either run or funded by provincial governments. The Métis experience is an important reminder that the impacts of residential schooling extend beyond the formal residential school program that Indian Affairs operated.[158]

Prior to the 1950s, most of the students who attended schools in the Northwest Territories were either First Nations or Métis.

As late as 1949, only 111 Inuit students were receiving full-time schooling in the North.[159] The hostel system that Northern Affairs established in the Northwest Territories in the mid-1950s did not restrict admission to First Nations students. It was only at this point that large numbers of Inuit children began attending residential schools. The impact of the schools on the Inuit was complex. Some children were sent to schools thousands of kilometres from their homes, and went years without seeing their parents. In other cases, parents who had previously been supporting themselves by following a seasonal cycle of land- and marine-based resource harvesting began settling in communities with hostels so as not to be separated from their children.

Because of the majority of the Aboriginal population in two of the three northern territories, the per capita impact of the schools in the North is higher than anywhere else in the country. And, because the history of these schools is so recent, not only are there many living Survivors today, but there are also many living parents of Survivors. For these reasons, both the intergenerational impacts and the legacy of the schools, the good and the bad, are particularly strongly felt in the North.

THE INTEGRATION POLICY

By 1945, the Indian Affairs residential school system, starved for funding for fifteen years, was on the verge of collapse.[160] Not only was the existing Indian Affairs education system lacking money and resources, but also there were no school facilities of any sort for 42 percent of the school-aged First Nations children.[161] Having concluded that it was far too expensive to provide residential schooling to these students, Indian Affairs began to look for alternatives. One was to expand the number of Indian Affairs day schools. From 1945–46 to 1954–55, the number of First Nations students in Indian Affairs day schools increased from 9,532 to 17,947.[162] In 1949, the Special Joint Committee of the Senate and House of Commons Appointed to Examine and Consider *The Indian Act* recommended "that wherever and whenever possible Indian children should be educated in association with other children."[163] In 1951, the *Indian Act* was amended to allow the federal government to enter into agreements with provincial governments and school boards to have First Nations students educated in public schools.[164] By 1960, the number of students attending "non-Indian" schools (9,479) had surpassed the number living in residential schools (9,471).[165] The transfer of First Nations students into the public school system was described as "integration." By then, the overall policy goal was to restrict the education being given in Indian Affairs schools to the lower grades. Therefore, it was expected that during the course of their schooling, at least half of the students then in Indian Affairs schools would transfer to a "non-Indian" school.[166]

The integration policy was opposed by some of the church organizations. Roman Catholic church officials argued that residential schooling was preferable for three reasons: 1) teachers in public schools were not prepared to deal with Aboriginal students; 2) students in public schools often expressed racist attitudes towards Aboriginal students; and 3) Aboriginal students felt acute embarrassment over their impoverished conditions, particularly in terms of the quality of the clothing they wore and the food they ate.[167] These were all issues that students and parents raised, as well.[168]

CHILD-WELFARE FACILITIES

From the 1940s onwards, residential schools increasingly served as orphanages and child-welfare facilities. By 1960, the federal government estimated that 50 percent of the children in residential schools were there for child-welfare reasons. What has come to be referred to as the "Sixties Scoop"—the dramatic increase in the apprehension of Aboriginal children from the 1960s onwards—was in some measure simply a transferring of children from one form of institution, the residential school, to another, the child-welfare agency.[169] The schools were not funded or staffed to function as child-welfare institutions. They failed to provide their students with the appropriate level of personal and emotional care children need during their childhood and adolescence. This failure applied to all students, but was of particular significance in the case of the growing number of social-welfare placements in the schools.[170] Some children had to stay in the schools year-round because it was thought there was no safe home to which they could return. The residential school environment was not a safer or more loving haven. These children spent their entire childhoods in an institution.

The closure of residential schools, which commenced in earnest in 1970, was accompanied by a significant increase in the number of children being taken into care by child-welfare agencies.[171] By the end of the 1970s, the transfer of children from residential schools was nearly complete in southern Canada, and the impact of the Sixties Scoop was in evidence across the country. In 1977, Aboriginal children accounted for 44 percent of the children in care in Alberta, 51 percent of the children in care in Saskatchewan, and 60 percent of the children in care in Manitoba.[172] In those residences that remained in operation, the percentage of social-welfare cases remained high.[173]

THE ROAD TO CLOSURE, 1969

In 1968, the federal government drastically restructured the residential school system by dividing the schools into residences and day schools, each with a principal or administrator.[174] In June of the following year, the federal government took direct control over all the schools in southern Canada.[175] Because churches were allowed to continue to appoint the residence administrators, their presence continued in many schools in the coming years. They were, however, no longer directly responsible for the facilities.[176] In 1969, the federal government also began to transfer the hostels and day schools in the Yukon and Northwest Territories to their respective territorial governments. Most of the small hostels in the eastern Arctic and Nunavik (Arctic Québec) were closed by the end of 1971. (Four small hostels were also operated in the western and central Arctic. The last of these, located at Cambridge Bay, did not close until the late 1990s.)[177]

Having assumed control over the southern Canadian schools in 1969, the federal government commenced what would prove to be a protracted process of closing the system down. According to the Indian Affairs annual report for 1968–69, the department was responsible for sixty residences. Two years later, the number was down to forty-five.[178] The government takeover of the residential schools also coincided with the release of the federal government's White Paper on "Indian Policy." This document proposed a massive transfer of responsibility for First Nations people from the federal to provincial governments.[179] It called for the repeal of the *Indian Act*, the winding up of the Department of Indian Affairs, and the eventual extinguishment of the Treaties.[180] The recently formed National Indian Brotherhood (NIB) described the White Paper as a document intended to bring about "the destruction of a Nation of People by legislation and cultural genocide."[181] In its response, the NIB proposed "Indian Control of Indian Education."[182] In 1971, Indian Affairs Minister Jean Chrétien announced that, in the face of First Nations resistance, the federal government was abandoning the policy directions outlined in the White Paper.[183]

By then, First Nations communities had already taken over one residential school. In the summer of 1970, parents of children at the Blue Quills, Alberta, school occupied the school, demanding that its operation be turned over to a First Nations education authority. They took this measure in response to reports that the school was to be turned into a residence and their children were to be educated at a nearby public school. The Blue Quills conflict was the result of both long-standing local dissatisfaction with the administration of the school and First Nations opposition to the policy of integration.[184] It was estimated that over 1,000 people participated in the sit-in, with rarely fewer than 200 people being at the school on any given day.[185] Seventeen days after the sit-in commenced, Minister Jean Chrétien announced that the school would be transferred to the Blue Quills Native Education Council.[186] In coming years, the Qu'Appelle, Prince Albert, Duck Lake, Lestock, and Grayson facilities in Saskatchewan were also taken over by First Nations authorities. The Christie residence in Tofino, British Columbia, was also operated briefly by an Aboriginal authority.[187]

The federal government, however, remained committed to the closing of the facilities. Because of the government's lengthy history of underfunding residential schools, many of the schools were in poor repair. Between 1995 and 1998, the last seven residences in southern Canada were closed.[188]

Starting in the 1970s, territorial governments, in which former residential school students were serving as cabinet ministers, also began expanding the number of day schools as part of a campaign to close residential schools in the North. The last large hostel in the Yukon closed in 1985.[189] By 1986, there were only three large hostels operating in the Northwest Territories.[190] Grollier Hall, the last large hostel in the North, closed in 1997.[191] If one dates the residential school system back to the early 1830s, when the Mohawk Institute first took in boarders, the system had been in operation for over 160 years. The closing of the schools did not mark the end of the history of residential schooling in Canada. By the 1990s, former students had begun to make Canadians aware of the tremendous harm that the residential school experience had caused to Aboriginal people and Aboriginal communities.

CHAPTER TWO

THE SCHOOL EXPERIENCE

EDUCATION: "THE CHILDREN'S WORK WAS MERELY MEMORY WORK"

As educational institutions, the residential schools were failures, and regularly judged as such. In 1923, former Regina industrial school principal R.B. Heron delivered a paper to a meeting of the Regina Presbytery of the Presbyterian Church that was highly critical of the residential school system. He said that parents generally were anxious to have their children educated, but they complained that their children "are not kept regularly in the class-room; that they are kept out at work that produces revenue for the School; that when they return to the Reserves they have not enough education to enable them to transact ordinary business—scarcely enough to enable them to write a legible letter."[1] The schools' success rate did not improve. From 1940–41 to 1959–60, 41.3 percent of each year's residential school Grade One enrolment was not promoted to Grade Two.[2] Just over half of those who were in Grade Two would get to Grade Six.[3]

Many principals and teachers had low expectations of their students. Wikwemikong, Ontario, principal R. Baudin wrote in 1883, "What we may reasonably expect from the generality of children, is certainly not to make great scholars of them. Good and moral as they may be, they lack great mental capacity." He did not think it wise to expect them to "be equal in every respect to their white brethren."[4] In preparing a 1928 report on

FIG 2.1   The classroom in the Moose Factory, Ontario, school. General Synod
Archives, Anglican Church of Canada, P7538-970.

the Anglican school at Onion Lake, a Saskatchewan government
school inspector expressed his belief that "in arithmetic abstract
ideas develop slowly in the Indian child."[5] Some thought it was
a risky matter to give the students too much education. Mount
Elgin principal S.R. McVitty wrote in 1928 that "classroom work
is an important part of our training, but not by any means the
most important." He added, "In the case of the Indian 'a little
learning is a dangerous thing.'"[6]

Much of what went on in the classroom was simply repetitious
drill. A 1915 report on the Roman Catholic school on the Blood
Reserve in Alberta noted, "The children's work was merely memory work and did not appear to be developing any deductive power,

altogether too parrot like and lacking expression."[7] A 1932 inspector's report from the Grayson, Saskatchewan, school suggests there had been little change. "The teaching as I saw it today was merely a question of memorizing and repeating a mass of, to the children, 'meaningless' facts."[8]

The classrooms were often severely overcrowded. At the Qu'Appelle school in 1911, Sister McGurk had seventy-five girls in her junior classroom. The inspector of Roman Catholic schools reported to Ottawa that this was an "almost impossible" situation.[9] In 1915, two teachers were responsible for 120 students at the Coqualeetza Institute in Chilliwack, British Columbia.[10] In 1928, there were sixty students in the junior classroom at the Alberni, British Columbia, school.[11]

The Indian Affairs schools branch maintained that the principals and the staff were "appointed by the church authorities, subject to the approval of the Department as to qualifications."[12] In reality, the churches hired staff and the government then automatically approved their selections.[13] The churches placed a greater priority on religious commitment than on teaching ability.[14] Because the pay was so low, many of the teachers lacked any qualification to teach.[15] In 1908, Indian Affairs inspector F.H. Paget reported that at the Battleford school, "frequent changes in the staff at this school has not been to its advantage." The problem lay not with the principal, but with the fact that "more profitable employment is available in the District and, furthermore, the salaries paid are not as high as are paid in other public institutions."[16] When a British Columbia Indian agent recommended that schools be required to hire only qualified staff, he was told by his superior, British Columbia Indian Superintendent A.W. Vowell, that such a requirement would result in the churches applying for "larger grants." And, as Vowell understood it, Indian Affairs "is not at present disposed to entertain requests for increased grants to Indian boarding and industrial schools."[17] In 1955, 55 (23 percent) of the 241 teachers in residential schools directly employed by Indian Affairs had no teacher's certificate.[18] In 1969, Indian Affairs reported it was still paying its teachers less than they could make in provincial schools. "As a result, there are about the same number of unqualified teachers, some 140, in federal schools [residential and non-residential] now, as ten years ago."[19]

In the minds of some principals, religious training was the most valuable training the schools provided. In 1903, Brandon, Manitoba, principal T. Ferrier wrote that "while it is very important that the Indian child should be educated, it is of more importance that he should build up a good clean character." Such a heavy emphasis was required, in Ferrier's opinion, to "counteract the evil tendencies of the Indian nature."[20] Louise Moine recalled that religious instruction and observation were a constant part of life at the Qu'Appelle school in the early twentieth century: "From the time we got out of bed at the sound of the bell, we went down on our knees to pray. After we had washed and dressed, we headed for the chapel to attend Low mass which was always held at 7 a.m."[21] The staff handbook for the Presbyterian school in Kenora in the 1940s stated it was expected that, upon leaving the school, most students would "return to the Indian Reserves from which they had come." Given this future, staff members were told that "the best preparation we can give them is to teach them the Christian way of life."[22]

Not surprisingly, many of those who succeeded academically followed careers in the church. Coqualeetza graduate Peter Kelly became a Methodist Church minister. Emmanuel College graduate Edward Ahenakew became an Anglican minister. Others worked for government or taught school. Qu'Appelle graduate Daniel Kennedy became an interpreter and general assistant for the Assiniboine Indian Agency. Joseph Dion, a graduate of the Onion Lake school, taught school for many years in Saskatchewan. Still others pursued business and professional careers. After attending the Mohawk Institute, Beverly Johnson went to Hellmuth College in London, Ontario, where he excelled at sports and drama. He then went to work for the New York Life Insurance Company in Pennsylvania. A graduate of the Mohawk Institute, N.E. Lickers, was called to the bar in 1938 and was described by the *Brantford Expositor* as the "First Ontario Indian Lawyer."[23]

Despite these successes, little encouragement generally was offered to students who wished to pursue further education. Oliver Martin, who was raised on the Six Nations Reserve in Ontario and went on to become an Ontario magistrate, recalled being told by Indian Affairs Deputy Minister Duncan Campbell Scott: "It's no use sending you Indians to school you just go back to the reserve anyway."[24]

For many students, classroom life was foreign and traumatic. David Charleson said he found the regimentation at the Christie, British Columbia, school so disturbing that he "never wanted to learn, so I jumped into my shell. I took Kindergarten twice because of what happened to me. I didn't want to learn."[25] At the Birtle school in Manitoba, Isabelle Whitford said, she had a hard time adjusting to the new language and the classroom discipline. "Every time I couldn't get an answer, like, you know, she would pull my ears and shake my head."[26] Betsy Olson described class work at the Prince Albert, Saskatchewan, school as a torment, in which her "spelling was always 30, 40, it was way down. And when we did spelling, sometimes I freeze, I couldn't move, I just scribbled because I couldn't move my hand."[27] Leona Agawa never felt comfortable in the classroom at the Spanish, Ontario, school. For much of her time in school, she was frightened or intimidated. "I'd hear my name, but I never got to answer. I stood up, never got to answer what they were saying when they sat me down. And I'd get a good slap after, after you, you leave there for not being nice in school."[28]

Since the 1920s, Indian Affairs had required residential schools to adopt provincial curricula.[29] The department had also asked provincial governments to have their school inspectors inspect Indian Affairs schools.[30] The wisdom of this practice had been questioned during the hearings of the Special Joint Committee of the Senate and House of Commons inquiry into the *Indian Act* in the 1940s. Andrew Moore, a secondary school inspector for the Province of Manitoba, told the committee members that Indian Affairs took full responsibility for all aspects of First Nations

education, including curriculum.[31] Provincial education departments, including the one he worked for, were "not organized or not
interested in Indian schools."[32]

In 1963, D.W. Hepburn, the former principal of the federal
school in Inuvik, published an article with the ominous headline
"Northern Education: Façade for Failure." He argued that the
education being provided in the new federal schools was "hope-
lessly inadequate. The reasons for this failure are clear: the aims of
education set forth by the Department are thoroughly confused,
the curriculum is inappropriate, and many current practices
of the system are not only ill-conceived but actually harmful."[33]
Although 60 percent of the students at the Inuvik school were in
the first three grades, few teachers had any background in primary
education, and "almost none has any special training in native
education, and will receive none from the Department."[34] The
schools were producing individuals who "lack not only the skills
required for most permanent wage employment but also those
necessary for the traditional economy."[35]

The decision to leave curriculum to provincial education
departments meant that Aboriginal students were subjected to
an education that demeaned their history, ignored their current
situation, and did not even recognize them or their families as
citizens. This was one of the reasons for the growing Aboriginal
hostility to the Indian Affairs integration policy. An examination
of the treatment of Aboriginal people in provincially approved
textbooks reveals a serious and deep-rooted problem. In response
to a 1956 recommendation that textbooks be developed that were
relevant to Aboriginal students, Indian Affairs official R.F. Davey
commented, "The preparation of school texts is an extremely difficult matter." It was his opinion that "there are other needs which
can be met more easily and should be undertaken first."[36] In the
following years, assessments of public-school textbooks showed
that they continued to perpetuate racist stereotypes of Aboriginal
people.[37] A 1968 survey pointed out that in some books, the word

squaw was being used to describe Aboriginal women, and the word *redskins* used to describe Aboriginal people.[38]

Students also noted that the curriculum belittled their ancestry. Mary Courchene said, "Their only mandate was to Christianize and civilize; and it's written in black and white. And every single day we were reminded."[39] Lorna Cochrane could never forget an illustration in a social studies text. "There was a picture of two Jesuits laying in the snow, they were murdered by these two 'savages.' And they had this what we call 'a blood-curdling look' on their faces is how I remember that picture."[40] When the curriculum was not racist, it was bewildering and alienating. Many students could not identify with the content of the classroom materials. For instance, Lillian Elias remembers that "when I looked at Dick and Jane I thought Dick and Jane were in heaven when I saw all the green grass. That's how much I knew about Dick and Jane."[41]

Some students said that the limits of the education they had received in residential school became apparent when they were integrated into the public school system.[42] Many said there was no expectation that they would succeed. Walter Jones never forgot the answer that a fellow student at the Alberni, British Columbia, school was given when he asked if he would be able to go to Grade Twelve. "That supervisor said, 'You don't need to go that far,' he says. He says, 'Your people are never going to get education to be a professional worker, and it doesn't matter what lawyer, or doctor, or electrician, or anything, that a person has to go to school for.'"[43]

Some northern schools developed reputations for academic success. Grandin College in Fort Smith was established originally to recruit young people for the Catholic ministry. A new principal, Jean Pochat, decided to focus on providing young men and women with leadership training.[44] The school became known as a "leadership factory," producing numerous future government leaders for the North.[45] Students who attended the Churchill Vocational Centre spoke about how they were taught by open-minded teachers who were willing to expose them to the social and political changes taking place across the world in the 1960s.[46] John Amagoalik wrote that at the Churchill Vocational Centre, "we had excellent teachers. To this day we still talk about them.... They treated us as ordinary people. We had never experienced this sort of attitude before and it was, in a way, liberating to be with new teachers that treated you as their equal."[47] David Simailak spoke of how his time at residential school gave him a series of new opportunities. He fondly remembers excelling at math and spelling competitions, and travelling to Montreal for Expo '67.[48]

Specific teachers were remembered with gratitude. When Roddy Soosay lived in residence, he attended a local public school. He credited his high school principal at the Ponoka, Alberta, public school for pushing him to succeed.[49] Martha Loon said that at the Poplar Hill, Ontario, school in the 1980s, there were staff members who befriended and helped her and her siblings. There was one staff member to whom she could tell all her problems. "I could say anything to her, and we'd go for walks sometimes. So, I could tell her anything and she wouldn't, she wouldn't say anything to other staff members about it. So, in a way, that's, you know, gave me a chance to express my frustrations, and the things that I didn't like."[50]

Other students were able to concentrate on their studies. Frederick Ernest Koe said that at Stringer Hall in Inuvik, he devoted all his energies to his school work. "You kind of develop a protective mechanism on the shell that you didn't rat on anybody, you kind of behave, you followed orders and things would go smooth."[51] Madeleine Dion Stout succeeded academically at the Blue Quills school, but she did not credit the school for her success. "It's not residential school that made me a good student. My, the fundamental values and good example I had before I went to residential school by my grandfather and my parents, and all the old people on the reserve where I grew up are the ones who made me a good student."[52]

WORK: "NO IDLENESS HERE"

Student education was further undermined by the amount of work the students had to do to support the schools. Because

Indian Affairs officials had anticipated that the residential schools would be self-sufficient, students were expected to raise or grow and prepare most of the food they ate, to make and repair much of their clothing, and to maintain the schools. As a result, most of the residential schools operated on what was referred to as the "half-day system." Under this system—which amounted to institutionalized child labour—students were in class for half the day and in what was supposed to be vocational training for the other half. Often, as many students, teachers, and inspectors observed, the time allocated for vocational training was actually spent in highly repetitive labour that provided little in the way of training. Rather, it served to maintain the school operations.

FIG 2.2 Carpenter's shop in the Battleford school, 1894. Saskatchewan Archives Board, R-B7.

The half-day system was not a formally mandated system. Some schools did not use it, and those that did use it implemented it on their own terms. When, in 1922, Indian Affairs education official Russell Ferrier recommended that the Chapleau, Ontario, school implement the half-day system, he had to rely on his memory of visits to other schools in order to describe how the system operated. Indian Affairs had no official written description of the system.[53] This is telling evidence of the haphazard way in which residential schools were managed.

While the half-day system was supposed to apply only to the older students, the reality was that every student worked. Above and beyond the half-day that students spent in vocational training, it was not uncommon for them to perform daily chores both before and after school. As a result, students often spent more than half a day working for the school. At High River, Alberta, in the 1880s, students who were not learning a trade were expected to put in two hours a day of chores in the winter and four hours in the summer. According to Principal E. Claude, "To these youngest ones pertained the weeding of the garden and the house work on their side of the school, and I must say, that this summer none denied our watchword, 'No idleness here,' as all work was exclusively done by the pupils."[54]

From the time the schools were opened, parents and inspectors raised concerns about just how much work students were being required to do. Inspector T.P. Wadsworth claimed in 1884 that the boys at the Battleford school generally enjoyed their chores, but added that he would protest "against forcing these little fellows to haul water every day and all day from the river in winter, as was the case last year."[55] In 1886, Qu'Appelle school principal Joseph Hugonnard wrote, "During the summer they have more manual labor and recreation. The parents cannot understand that the pupils are here to learn how to work as well as to read and write, we therefore cannot at present devote too much time to the former."[56] Inspector Wadsworth returned to the issue of overwork in 1893, when he said that much of the farm work at the Middlechurch, Manitoba, school was too much for the boys. The girls were also set to work in the laundry at a "tender age."[57] Gilbert Wuttunee, who attended the Battleford school in the first decade of the twentieth century, recalled, "They didn't do any farm work or any kind of work until you got to, at that time, standard three, whether you were nine years old or fifteen years old." After he turned nine, he "never saw another full day of school until I left." By then, the school had drastically reduced the number of trades it taught: "There was just blacksmithing, carpentering and farming."[58] According to Lillian Elias, each fall, a barge would arrive in Aklavik, loaded with logs for the school furnace. The students would form a long chain leading from the barge to the furnace room and, with the assistance of the school staff, unload the barge.[59]

The work was inadequately supervised and often dangerous. There are accounts of students getting hands caught in power equipment in the school laundries, the kitchens, workshops, and fields.[60] Principals tended to place the blame on student carelessness and neglected to report such injuries to the government. Several injuries were recorded only after the student's parents complained or the government received a bill for the hospital treatment of a student.[61] In December 1935, a mangle (a type of clothes wringer) at the Qu'Appelle school crushed several fingers on Florence McLeod's right hand, which were amputated. The school principal, G. Leonard, stressed that "this mangle has been in use at this school for several years and all the girls are familiar with its operation." Indian Affairs secretary A.F. MacKenzie concluded that "all the necessary precautions were taken, and, while the accident to Florence McLeod is regretted, it was through no fault of the school management."[62] The school's failure to protect its students can be seen in the fact that McLeod's father, Henry, had been injured in a similar fashion when he was a student at the same school.[63] In 1941, a twelve-year-old boy lost all the fingers on one hand in an accident in the Brandon, Manitoba, school barn.[64]

FIG 2.3 Mount Elgin, Ontario, laundry room. Clothes wringers, such as the one
shown here, were a source of injury at a number of residential schools. The United
Church of Canada Archives, 90.162P1173.

Eight years later, fifteen-year-old Rodney Beardy died in a tractor
accident at the same school.[65] A student at the Edmonton school
lost a foot in 1944 after an accident during the operation of a
machine used in the preparation of fodder.[66] Two boys from the
Birtle, Manitoba, school were injured in a truck accident in 1942.
From Indian Affairs correspondence, it appears that the accident
involved a truck carrying seventy boys who were being taken from
the school to the fields to do farm work. Indian Affairs official
R.A. Hoey criticized the principal for allowing the practice to
take place, noting that "it is almost unbelievable that the principal
should permit 70 pupils to be conveyed in a truck."[67]

Even though the half-day system was supposedly eliminated in the early 1950s, students continued to be overworked.[68] After Sam Ross ran away from the Birtle school in 1959, he told Indian Affairs official J.R. Bell that he wanted to continue his education, but had been forced to work "too hard" at the school. He said that from September to Christmas of the previous year, he had worked in the school barn every day between "6:00 A.M. and 7:00 A.M. and from 8:00 A.M. to 9:00 A.M. again at recess, from 4:00 P.M. to 6:00 P.M. and had had to stoke up the furnace with coal at 10:00 o'clock before retiring." Ross said that "he liked school but not working like a hired hand." Bell recommended that the amount of student labour being done at the Birtle school be investigated.[69]

LANGUAGE AND CULTURE: "THE INDIAN LANGUAGE IS INDEED SELDOM HEARD IN THE INSTITUTION"

The government's hostile approach to Aboriginal languages was reiterated in numerous policy directives. In 1883, Indian Commissioner Edgar Dewdney instructed Battleford school principal Thomas Clarke that great attention was to be given "towards imparting a knowledge of the art of reading, writing and speaking the English language rather than that of Cree."[70] In 1889, Deputy Minister of Indian Affairs Lawrence Vankoughnet informed Bishop Paul Durieu that in the new Cranbrook, British Columbia, school, mealtime conversations were to be "conducted exclusively in the English language." The principal was also to set a fixed time during which Aboriginal languages could be spoken.[71] In 1890, Indian Commissioner Hayter Reed proposed, "At the most the native language is only to be used as a vehicle of teaching and should be discontinued as such as soon as practicable." English was to be the primary language of instruction, "even where French is taught."[72] The Indian Affairs "Programme of Studies for Indian Schools" of 1893 advised, "Every effort must be made to induce pupils to speak

English, and to teach them to understand it; unless they do the whole work of the teacher is likely to be wasted."[73]

Principals regularly reported on their success in suppressing Aboriginal languages. In 1887, Principal E. Claude boasted that his thirty students at the High River school "all understand English passably well and few are unable to express themselves in English. They talk English in recreation. I scarcely need any coercive means to oblige them to do so."[74] In 1898, the Kamloops principal reported that "English is the only language used at all times by the pupils."[75] That same year, the Mission, British Columbia, principal wrote, "English is the common language of the school, the Indian language is indeed seldom heard in the institution, except with the newly arrived pupils."[76] The 1898 report from the principal of the Anglican school at Onion Lake indicated that the school was one of the few exceptions. There, the children were taught to "read and write both Cree and English."[77] Inspectors viewed the continued use of Aboriginal languages by the students as a sign of failure. The principal of the Red Deer school was taken to task in 1903 by an inspector who felt that a "serious drawback to school work, as well as an evidence of bad discipline, was the use of the Cree language, which was quite prevalent."[78]

This policy of language suppression continued well into the twentieth century. After a 1935 tour of Canada, Oblate Superior General Théodore Labouré expressed concern over the strict enforcement of prohibitions against speaking Aboriginal languages. In his opinion, "The forbidding of children to speak Indian, even during recreation, was so strict in some of our schools that any lapse would be severely punished—to the point that children were led to consider it a serious offense."[79]

Students had strong memories of being punished for "speaking Indian." Mary Angus, who attended the Battleford school in the late nineteenth century, said that students caught speaking their own language were given a close haircut: "All the hair cut to be as a man, that what they do, for us not to talk. We were afraid of that, to have our hair cut."[80] At the Fraser Lake school in British

Columbia, Mary John said she could speak her own language only in whispers.[81] Melvina McNabb was seven years old when she was enrolled in the File Hills school, and "I couldn't talk a word of English. I talked Cree and I was abused for that, hit, and made to try to talk English."[82] Raymond Hill, who was a student at the Mohawk Institute in Brantford in the early years of the twentieth century, said, "I lost my language. They threatened us with a strapping if we spoke it, and within a year I lost all of it. They said they thought we were talking about them."[83]

Language use often continued in secret. Mary Englund recalled that while Aboriginal languages were banned at the Mission school in the early twentieth century, children would still speak it to one another.[84] Clyde Peters said he stopped speaking his Aboriginal language at the Mount Elgin school after he found out the school punished students for doing so. "I never got the strap for it but I was warned enough that I didn't do it." Even after that, he and his friends would speak to each other when they thought no one else could hear them. "When we'd go up in the dormitories in the evening I had a friend from Sarnia who I could talk with."[85]

Many of the students came to the school fluent in an Aboriginal language, with little or no understanding of French or English. This trend continued well into the post-war period. For these children, the first few months in the school were disorienting and frightening. Arthur McKay arrived at the Sandy Bay, Manitoba, school in the early 1940s with no knowledge of English. "They told me not to speak my language and everything, so I always pretended to be asleep at my desk so they wouldn't ask me anything."[86] Peter Nakogee recalled being punished for writing in his notebook in Cree syllabics at the Fort Albany, Ontario, school.[87]

Meeka Alivaktuk came to the Pangnirtung school in what is now Nunavut with no knowledge of English. When she failed to obey an instruction because she did not understand it, she was slapped on the hands. "That's how my education began."[88] On his first day of school in Pangnirtung, the teacher overheard Sam Kautainuk speaking to a friend in Inuktitut. "He took a ruler and

FIG 2.4   Inuit students at the Joseph Bernier School, Chesterfield Inlet, 1956.
Diocese of Churchill-Hudson Bay.

grabbed my head like this and then smacked me in the mouth with
the ruler four times."[89]

At the Qu'Appelle school in the mid-1960s, Greg Rainville said,
he was punished for failing to carry out instructions given to him
in a language he did not understand. "The nuns would get frus-
trated with you when they talked to you in French or English, and
you're not knowing what they're talking about, and you're pulled
around by the ear."[90] At the Shubenacadie school, a staff member
once caught William Herney speaking Mi'kmaq with his brother.
She strapped him and then washed his mouth out with soap.[91] Alphonsine McNeely underwent the same punishment at the Roman
Catholic school at Aklavik in the 1940s.[92] Pierrette Benjamin said
she was forced to eat soap at the La Tuque school. "The principal,
she put it in my mouth, and she said, 'Eat it, eat it.'"[93]

The language policy disrupted families. When John Kistabish left the Amos, Québec, school, he could no longer speak Algonquin, and his parents could not speak French, the language that he had been taught in the school. As a result, he found it almost impossible to communicate with them about the abuse he experienced at the school. "I had tried to talk with my parents, and, no, it didn't work.... We were well anyway because I knew that they were my parents, when I left the residential school, but the communication wasn't there."[94]

Culture was attacked as well as language. In his memoirs, Stoney Chief John Snow tells of how at the Morley, Alberta, school, the "education consisted of nothing that had any relationship to our homes and culture. Indeed Stoney culture was condemned explicitly and implicitly." He recalled being taught that the only good people on earth were non-Indians and, specifically, white Christians.[95] Andrew Bull Calf recalled that at the residential school in Cardston, Alberta, students were not only punished for speaking their own languages, but they also were discouraged from participating in traditional cultural activities.[96] Evelyn Kelman recalled that the principal at the Brocket, Alberta, school warned students that if they attended a Sun Dance that was to be held during the summer, they would be strapped on their return to school.[97] Marilyn Buffalo recalled being told by Hobbema, Alberta, school staff that the Sun Dance was "devil worship."[98] One year, Sarah McLeod returned to the Kamloops school with a miniature totem pole that a family member had given her for her birthday. When she proudly showed it to one of the nuns, it was taken from her and thrown out. She was told that it was nothing but devilry.[99]

School officials did not limit their opposition to Aboriginal culture to the classroom. In 1942, Gleichen, Alberta, principal John House became involved in a campaign to have two Blackfoot chiefs deposed, in part because of their support for traditional dance ceremonies.[100] In 1943, F.E. Anfield, the principal of the Alert Bay, British Columbia, school, wrote a letter encouraging former students not to participate in local Potlatches, implying that such ceremonies were based on outdated superstition, and led to impoverishment and family neglect.[101]

Even when it did not directly disparage Aboriginal culture, the curriculum undermined Aboriginal identity. Thaddee Andre, who attended the Sept-Îles, Québec, school in the 1950s, recalled how as a student he wanted "to resemble the white man, then in the meantime, they are trying by all means to strip you of who you are as an Innu. When you are young, you are not aware of what you are losing as a human being."[102]

It was not until the 1960s that attitudes began to change about the place of Aboriginal language and culture in residential schools.[103] Alex Alikashuak said that at the Churchill school, which operated in the 1960s, there were no restrictions on the use of Aboriginal languages. He recalled, "The only time, real time we spoke English was when we were in the classroom, or we're talking to one of the administration staff, and or somebody from town that's not Inuit, but otherwise we, everybody spoke our language."[104] The Canadian Welfare Council's 1967 report on nine Saskatchewan residential schools described "an emphasis on relating course content to the Indian culture" as "imaginative" and a sign of progress in "making the educational experience meaningful for the Indian child."[105] By 1968, the Roman Catholic school in Cardston was incorporating Blackfoot into its educational program.[106] In some schools, Aboriginal teachers were brought in to teach dancing and singing.[107] However, as late as the 1969–70 school year, there were only seven Indian Affairs schools that offered courses in Aboriginal languages or used Aboriginal languages as the language of instruction.[108]

Despite the encouragement that was offered in some schools, and the students' efforts to keep their language alive, the overall impact was language loss. Of her experiences at the Baptist school in Whitehorse and the Anglican school in Carcross, Rose Dorothy Charlie said, "They took my language. They took it right out of my mouth. I never spoke it again."[109] In some cases, the residential school experience led parents to decide not to teach their children an Aboriginal language. Both of Joline Huskey's parents attended residential school in the Northwest Territories. As a result of their experience in the schools, they raised their daughter to speak English.[110] When Bruce Dumont was sent to residential school in Onion Lake, Saskatchewan, his mother warned him not to speak Cree.[111]

ARRANGING AND BLOCKING MARRIAGES

Through the residential schools, Indian Affairs and church officials sought to extend their control into the most intimate aspects of the lives of Aboriginal children. Indian Affairs officials believed that because the department had spent money educating students, it had gained the right to determine whom they married. Government officials feared that if students married someone who had not also been educated at a residential school, they would revert to traditional "uncivilized" ways.[112] The control of marriage was part of the ongoing policy of forced assimilation. In 1890, Indian Commissioner Hayter Reed criticized Qu'Appelle principal Joseph Hugonnard for allowing female students from the Qu'Appelle school to marry boys who had not gone to school, without first getting Indian Affairs' approval. Reed argued, "The contention that the parents have the sole right to decide such matters cannot for one moment be admitted."[113]

The government not only encouraged marriage between students, but it also began to make marriage part of the process of getting out of residential school. In his annual report for 1896, Deputy Minister Hayter Reed wrote, "It is considered advisable, where pupils are advanced in years and considered capable of providing for themselves, to bring about a matrimonial alliance, either at the time of being discharged from the school or as soon after as possible."[114] In other words, the principals were expected to arrange marriages for the older students.

Principals regularly reported and celebrated student marriages, and, indeed, did often arrange them.[115] Reverend P. Claessen, principal of the Kuper Island school, reported in 1909 that he had succeeded in "engaging one of our leaving girls with one of our best old boys."[116] Kamloops school principal A.M. Carion reported, "It is gratifying to note again that since my last report, two more couples of ex-pupils have been united in the bonds of holy wedlock. The ex-pupils who marry other ex-pupils are better able to retain the habits of civilized life, which they acquired at the school."[117]

Efforts were also made to block marriages deemed to be unsuitable. In 1895, Indian agent Magnus Begg told members of the Blackfoot Reserve that "no young man could marry a girl from an Industrial or board [sic] School without having prepared a house with two rooms, and owning cows, with the necessary stabling, &c."[118] In that same year, principals and Indian agents were instructed to seek departmental permission prior to allowing students to marry.[119]

Principals continued to arrange marriages into the 1930s. In 1936, the principal of the Roman Catholic school at Onion Lake prepared a list of students who had turned sixteen and who, he believed, should not be discharged. He noted that he insisted on keeping the students, since he would "always try to marry them as soon as they leave the school." He wanted to keep one eighteen-year-old student in the school until the fall threshing was complete. Then, she would be married to a former pupil. He wanted to keep another eighteen-year-old until "she gets married during the year."[120] In 1922, the head of the Presbyterian Church's Winnipeg Committee on Indian Work urged the government to make it "unlawfull [sic] for a pupil or ex-pupil of the School to marry or be married without the permission of the Indian Agent." The Presbyterians proposed that the children of such unauthorized marriages be denied Treaty annuities until they reached the age of twenty-one and be prohibited from attending school.[121] Although the measure was not adopted, it is reflective of the church's lack of respect for the autonomy of Aboriginal people.

FOOD: "ALWAYS HUNGRY"

In his memoir of his years as a student at the Mount Elgin school in southern Ontario in the early twentieth century, Enos Montour wrote that the boys "were always hungry. Grub was the beginning and end of all conversations."[122] According to Eleanor Brass, the dinners at the File Hills, Saskatchewan, school consisted "of watery soup with no flavour, and never any meat." One winter, it seemed to her that they ate fish every day.[123] In fair weather, the boys would trap gophers and squirrels, and roast them over open fires to supplement their meagre diets. Sometimes, they would share these treats with the girls at the school.[124] Mary John, who attended the Fraser Lake, British Columbia, school, recalled that the meals were dull and monotonous: a regular diet of porridge interspersed with boiled barley and beans, and bread covered with lard. Weeks might go by without any fish or meat; sugar and jam were reserved for special occasions.[125] A former student of the Hay River school in the Northwest Territories recalled that in the years following the First World War, he "didn't see jam from the time I got off the boat to the time I got back on to come back down."[126] Another student from that school recalled a constant diet of fish: "They would boil it up real good until the meat falls away, the bones and scales all floating around, then mix in flour and serve it up. I won't use flour for my dogs because there's not much good in it."[127]

The reports of government inspectors confirm these student memories. An 1895 report on an inspection of the Middlechurch school concluded, "The 'bill of fare' is plain. I believed it to be barely sufficient for the older pupils, who have now, at fifteen to eighteen years of age, larger apetites [sic] than they will have when older."[128] In 1918, Indian agent John Smith inspected the Kamloops school and reported his "suspicion that the vitality of the children is not sufficiently sustained from a lack of nutritious food, or enough of the same for vigorous growing children."[129] A local doctor concurred, writing that "for some months past the food supplied has been inadequate for the needs of the children."[130] There were some positive assessments, but Indian Affairs official Martin

Benson questioned their accuracy. "In almost every instance when meals are mentioned by Inspectors they are said to be well cooked. I doubt very much whether they ever took a full regulation school meal of bread and dripping, or boiled beef and potatoes." In Benson's opinion, "The bill of fare is decidedly monotonous and makes no allowance for peculiarities of taste or constitution."[131]

When funding was cut during the Depression of the 1930s, it was the students who paid the price—in more ways than one. At the end of the 1930s, it was discovered that the cook at the Presbyterian school at Kenora was actually selling bread to the students, at the rate of ten cents a loaf. When asked if the children got enough to eat at meals, she responded, "Yes, but they were always hungry." The Indian agent ordered an end to the practice.[132] The fact that hungry students would be reduced to buying bread to supplement their meals in 1939 highlights the government's failure to provide schools with the resources needed to feed students adequately.

Milk was in constant shortage at many schools, in part due to the poor health and small size of the school dairy herds.[133] As late as 1937, disease among the cows at the Kamloops school had cut milk production by 50 percent. To the principal's frustration, Ottawa refused to fund the construction of an additional barn, which would have allowed for an increase in milk production and the isolation of sick animals.[134] Even when the dairy herds were producing satisfactorily, the students did not always get the full benefit. Often, the milk was separated, with the skimmed milk served to the children.[135] The milk fat was turned to butter and cream, which was frequently sold to raise funds for the schools. Inspector W. Murison noted in 1925 that the cows at the Elkhorn, Manitoba, school were producing enough milk for the school, but the students were not getting "the full benefit of this milk as I found that they were making about 30 lbs. of butter a week, and a great deal of the milk given the children is separated milk, which has not much food value."[136]

In 1942, the federal government issued Canada's Official Food Rules, an early version of the Canada Food Guide.[137] Inspectors quickly discovered that residential school diets did not measure up to the Food Rules. Dr. L.B. Pett, the head of the federal government's Nutrition Division, concluded in 1947, on the basis of inspections his staff had done, that "no school was doing a good feeding job."[138] It was not until the late 1950s that the federal government adopted a residential school food allowance calculated to provide a diet deemed "fully adequate nutritionally."[139] Even with the increase in funding, schools still had difficulty providing students with adequate meals. A 1966 dietician's report on Yukon Hall in Whitehorse observed that although the Canada Food Guide requirements were being met, "because of the appetite of this age group, the staff are finding 66¢ per day per student is limiting."[140] In 1969, an official at Coudert Hall in Whitehorse wrote, "The $0.80 alloted [sic] per student for food is not sufficient. In the north we find prices sky high." To cope with the problem, the residence sometimes had to buy "less meat and served maccaroni [sic] products."[141] A November 1970 inspection of the Dauphin, Manitoba, school noted that the "menu appears to be short of the recommended two servings of fruit per day."[142]

In their home communities, many students had been raised on food that their parents had hunted, fished, or harvested. These meals were very different from the European diets served at the schools. This change in diet added to the students' sense of disorientation. Daisy Diamond found the food at residential school to be unfamiliar and unpalatable. "When I was going to Shingwauk, the food didn't taste very good, because we didn't have our traditional food there, our moose meat, our bannock, and our berries."[143] Dora Fraser, from the eastern Arctic, found it difficult to adjust to the food served in the hostels. "We were eating canned food, beans, peas, red beans. The food was terrible."[144] Even when traditional foods were prepared, the school cooks made them in ways that were unfamiliar and unappetizing to the students. Ellen Okimaw, who attended the Fort Albany, Ontario, school, had vivid memories of poorly cooked fish served at the schools. The school cook had simply "dumped the whole thing, and boiled them like that, just like that without cleaning them."[145]

Bernard Catcheway recalled that in the 1960s at the Pine Creek, Manitoba, school, "we had to eat all our food even though we didn't like it. There was a lot of times there I seen other students that threw up and they were forced to eat their own, their own vomit."[146] Bernard Sutherland recalled students at the Fort Albany school being forced to eat food that they had vomited. "I saw in person how the children eat their vomit. When they happened to be sick. And they threw up while eating."[147] These abuses led in 1999 to the conviction of Anna Wesley, a former staff member of the Fort Albany school, on three charges of administering a noxious substance.[148]

Some schools did make allowances for traditional foods. Simon Awashish recalled being allowed to trap for food while attending the Amos, Québec, school:

> When we brought in hares, we were asked if … there was some members of our nation that came to work in the kitchen, and we asked them to cook the hare for us in the traditional Atikameg way, in order to keep some sort of contact with our traditional food that we had before, before we were separated from our community.[149]

Students who spoke of hunger also spoke of their efforts to improve their diet secretly. Woodie Elias recalled being hungry all the time at the Anglican school in Aklavik. "Once in a while we go raid the cellar and you can't call that stealing; that was our food."[150] When Dorothy Nolie helped out in the Alert Bay school kitchen, she and her co-workers would eat bread as they sliced it. "Kids would come to me and ask me for bread, and I'd sneak it to them."[151] At the Moose Factory school in Ontario, Nellie Trapper said, students "used to steal food, peanut butter, whatever's cooking in a pot. There were big pots in there. I remember taking figs from that pot."[152]

Complaints about the limited, poorly prepared, monotonous diet were intensified by the fact that at many schools, the students

FIG 2.5 Students working in the kitchen at the Cross Lake, Manitoba, school in the early 1920s. St. Boniface Historical Society Archives; Roman Catholic Archbishop of Keewatin-The Pas Fonds; N1826.

knew the staff members were being served much better fare than they had. At the school she attended in Saskatchewan, Inez Dieter said, "the staff used to eat like kings, kings and queens." Like many students, she said, she used the opportunity of working in the staff dining room to help herself to leftovers. "I'd steal that and I'd eat, and I'd feel real good."[153] Gladys Prince recalled how, at the Sandy Bay school in Manitoba, the "priests ate the apples, we ate the peelings. That is what they fed us. We never ate bread. They were stingy them, their own, their own baking."[154] When Frances Tait was given a position in the staff dining room, she said, she thought she had "died and gone to heaven 'cause even eating their leftovers were better than what we got."[155] Hazel Bitternose, who attended schools in Lestock and Qu'Appelle, said she enjoyed working in the priests' dining room. "They had some good food there and I used to sneak some food and able to feed myself good there. So that's why I liked to work there."[156]

The federal government knowingly chose not to provide schools with enough money to ensure that kitchens and dining rooms were properly equipped, that cooks were properly trained, and, most significantly, that food was purchased in sufficient quantity and quality for growing children. It was a decision that left thousands of Aboriginal children vulnerable to disease.

HEALTH: "FOR SICKNESS, CONDITIONS AT THIS SCHOOL ARE NOTHING LESS THAN CRIMINAL"

The number of students who died at Canada's residential schools is not likely ever to be known in full. The most serious gap in information arises from the incompleteness of the documentary record. Many records have simply been destroyed. According to a 1935 federal government policy, school returns could be destroyed after five years, and reports of accidents after ten years. This led to the destruction of fifteen tonnes of waste paper. Between 1936 and 1944, 200,000 Indian Affairs files were destroyed.[157] Health records were regularly destroyed. For example, in 1957, Indian and Northern Health Services was instructed to destroy "correspondence re routine arrangements re medical and dental treatments of Indians and Eskimos, such as transportation, escort services, admission to hospital, advice on treatment, requests for treatment, etc." after a period of two years. Reports by doctors, dentists, and nurses were similarly assigned a two-year retention period.[158]

Often, the existing record lacks needed detail. For example, it was not uncommon for principals, in their annual reports, to state that a specific number of students had died in the previous year, but not to name them.[159] It was not until 1935 that Indian Affairs adopted a formal policy on how deaths at the schools were to be reported and investigated.[160]

There can be no certainty that all deaths were, in fact, reported to Indian Affairs—the Truth and Reconciliation Commission of Canada has located reports of student deaths in church records that are not reported in government documents.[161] In some cases, school officials appear not to have recognized a responsibility to report student deaths to provincial vital statistics officials, meaning that these records may also be deficient.[162]

As part of its work, the Truth and Reconciliation Commission of Canada has established a National Residential School Student Death Register. The creation of this register marks the first effort in Canadian history to properly record the number of students who died in residential schools. The register is made up of three sub-registers:

1) the Register of Confirmed Deaths of Named Residential
    School Students (the "Named Register");

2) the Register of Confirmed Deaths of Unnamed Residential
    School Students (the "Unnamed Register"); and

3) the Register of Deaths that Require Further Investigation
    (to determine if they should be placed on either the Named
    or Unnamed register).

A January 2015 statistical analysis of the Named Register for the period from 1867 to 2000 identified 2,040 deaths. The same analysis of a combination of the Named and Unnamed registers identified 3,201 reported deaths. The greatest number of these deaths (1,328 on the Named Register and 2,434 on the Named and Unnamed registers) took place prior to 1940. Graph 3 shows the overall death rate per 1,000 students for the residential schools during this period (figures are based on information in the combined Named and Unnamed registers).

This graph suggests that the peak of the health crisis in the schools occurred in the late nineteenth and early twentieth centuries. It also shows that the death rate remained high until the 1950s.

The death rates for Aboriginal children in the residential schools were far higher than those experienced by members of the general Canadian population. Graph 4 compares the death rate per 1,000 of the general population of Canadian children aged five to fourteen with the death rates per 1,000 of the Named Register and the Named and Unnamed registers combined. (Given the limitations in Statistics Canada's historical data, the death rates are provided as five-year averages.) As can be seen, until the 1950s Aboriginal children in residential schools died at a far higher rate than school-aged children in the general population. It is only in the 1950s that the residential school death rates declined to a level comparable to that of the general school-aged population. As late as the 1941–45 period, the Named and Unnamed Combined residential school death rate was 4.90 times higher than the general death rate. In the 1960s, even though the residential school death rates were much lower than their historic highs, they were still double those of the general school-aged population.

In nearly 50 percent of the cases (both in the Named and Unnamed registers), there is no recorded cause of death. From those cases where the cause of death was reported, it is clear that until the 1950s, the schools were the sites of an ongoing tuberculosis crisis. Tuberculosis accounted for just less than 50 percent of the recorded deaths (46.2 percent for the Named Register, and 47 percent for the

GRAPH 3
*Residential school death rates per 1,000 students, Named and
Unnamed registers combined, 1869 to 1965*

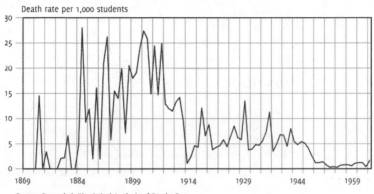

Source: Rosenthal, "Statistical Analysis of Deaths," 11.

GRAPH 4
*Comparative death rates per 1,000 population, residential schools (Named and
Unnamed registers combined) and the general Canadian population of school-aged
children, using five-year averages from 1921 to 1965*

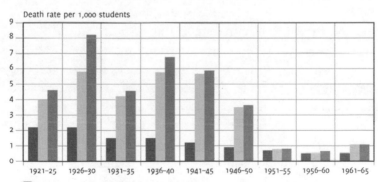

■ Death Rate, General Population, Ages 5–14
■ Named Residential School Death Rate
■ Combined Residential School Death Rate

Source: Fraser, Vital Statistics and Health, Table B35-50, http://www.statcan.gc.ca/pub/11-516-x/section-
b/4147437-eng.htm; Rosenthal, "Statistical Analysis of Deaths," 13.

GRAPH 5
Residential school tuberculosis death rates per 1,000 population, Named and
Unnamed registers combined, 1869-1965

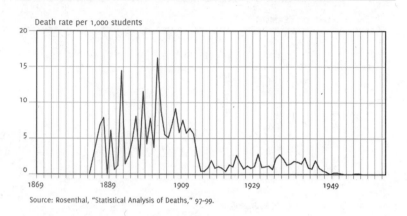

Source: Rosenthal, "Statistical Analysis of Deaths," 97–99.

Named and Unnamed registers combined). The tuberculosis death
rate remained high until the 1950s: its decline coincides with the
introduction of effective drug treatment. The next most frequently
recorded causes of death were influenza (9.2 percent on the Named
Register, and 9.1 percent of the deaths on the combined Named
and Unnamed registers), pneumonia (6.9 percent on the Named
Register, and 9.1 percent of the deaths on the combined Named
and Unnamed registers), and general lung disease (3.4 percent on
the Named Register, and 5.5 percent of the deaths on the combined
Named and Unnamed registers). Graph 5 shows the residential
school tuberculosis death rate (figures are based on information in
the combined Named and Unnamed registers).

The tuberculosis health crisis in the schools was part of a
broader Aboriginal health crisis that was set in motion by colonial
policies that separated Aboriginal people from their land, thereby
disrupting their economies and their food supplies. This crisis was
particularly intense on the Canadian Prairies. Numerous federal
government policies contributed to the undermining of Aboriginal
health. During a period of starvation, rations were withheld from

bands in an effort to force them to abandon the lands that they had initially selected for their reserves. In making the Treaties, the government had promised to provide assistance to First Nations to allow them to make a transition from hunting to farming. This aid was slow in coming and inadequate on arrival. Restrictions in the *Indian Act* made it difficult for First Nations farmers to sell their produce or borrow money to invest in technology. Reserve land was often agriculturally unproductive. Reserve housing was poor and crowded, sanitation was inadequate, and access to clean water was limited. Under these conditions, tuberculosis flourished. Those people it did not kill were often severely weakened and likely to succumb to measles, smallpox, and other infectious diseases.[163]

For Aboriginal children, the relocation to residential schools was generally no healthier than their homes had been on the reserves. In 1897, Indian Affairs official Martin Benson reported that the industrial schools in Manitoba and the Northwest Territories had been "hurriedly constructed of poor materials, badly laid out, without due provision for lighting, heating or ventilation." In addition, drainage was poor, and water and fuel supplies were inadequate.[164] Conditions were not any better in the church-built boarding schools. In 1904, Indian Commissioner David Laird echoed Benson's comments when he wrote that the sites for the boarding schools on the Prairies seemed "to have been selected without proper regard for either water-supply or drainage. I need not mention any school in particular, but I have urged improvement in several cases in regard to fire-protection."[165]

Students' health depended on clean water, good sanitation, and adequate ventilation. But little was done to improve the poor living conditions that were identified at the beginning of the twentieth century. In 1940, R.A. Hoey, who had served as the Indian Affairs superintendent of Welfare and Training since 1936, wrote a lengthy assessment of the condition of the existing residential schools. He concluded that many schools were "in a somewhat dilapidated condition" and had "become acute fire hazards." He laid responsibility for the "condition of our schools, generally," upon their "faulty construction." This construction, he said, had failed to meet "the minimum standards in the construction of public buildings, particularly institutions for the education of children."[166] By 1940, the government had concluded that future policy should concentrate on the expansion of day schools for First Nations children. As a result, many of the existing residential school buildings were allowed to continue to deteriorate. A 1967 brief from the National Association of Principals and Administrators of Indian Residences—which included principals of both Catholic and Protestant schools—concluded, "In the years that the Churches have been involved in the administration of the schools, there has been a steady deterioration in essential services. Year after year, complaints, demands and requests for improvements have, in the main, fallen upon deaf ears."[167]

When E.A. Côté, the deputy minister responsible for Indian Affairs, met with church and school representatives to discuss the brief, he told them that only emergency repairs would be undertaken at schools that Indian Affairs intended to close.[168]

The badly built and poorly maintained schools constituted serious fire hazards. Defective firefighting equipment exacerbated the risk, and schools were fitted with inadequate and dangerous fire escapes. Lack of access to safe fire escapes led to high death tolls in fires at the Beauval and Cross Lake schools.[169] The Truth and Reconciliation Commission of Canada has determined that at least fifty-three schools were destroyed by fire. There were at least 170 additional recorded fires. At least forty students died in residential school fires.[170] The harsh discipline and jail-like nature of life in the schools meant that many students sought to run away. To prevent this, many schools deliberately ignored government instructions in relation to fire drills and fire escapes. These were not problems only of the late nineteenth or early twentieth centuries. Well into the twentieth century, recommendations for improvements went unheeded, and dangerous and forbidden practices were widespread and entrenched. In the interests of cost containment, the Canadian government placed the lives of students and staff at risk for 130 years.

The buildings were not only fire traps. They were also incubators of disease. Rather than helping combat the tuberculosis crisis in the broader Aboriginal community, the poor condition of the schools served to intensify it. The 1906 annual report of Dr. Peter Bryce, the chief medical officer for Indian Affairs, observed that "the Indian population of Canada has a mortality rate of more than double that of the whole population, and in some provinces more than three times." Tuberculosis was the prevalent cause of death. He described a cycle of disease in which infants and children were infected at home and sent to residential schools, where they infected other children. The children infected in the schools were "sent home when too ill to remain at school, or because of being a danger to the other scholars, and have conveyed the disease to houses previously free."[171] The following year, Bryce published a damning report on the conditions at prairie boarding schools. In an age when fresh air was seen as being central to the successful treatment of tuberculosis, he concluded that, with only a few exceptions, the ventilation at the schools was "extremely inadequate."[172]

He found the school staff and even physicians

> inclined to question or minimize the dangers of infection
> from scrofulous or consumptive pupils [scrofula and
> consumption were alternate names for types of tuberculosis]
> and nothing less than peremptory instructions as to how
> to deal with cases of disease existing in the schools will
> eliminate this ever-present danger of infection.[173]

He gave the principals a questionnaire to complete regarding the health condition of their former students. The responses from fifteen schools revealed that "of a total of 1,537 pupils reported upon nearly 25 per cent are dead, of one school with an absolutely accurate statement, 69 per cent of ex-pupils are dead, and that everywhere the almost invariable cause of death given is tuberculosis." He drew particular attention to the fate of the thirty-one students who had been discharged from the File Hills school: nine were in good health, and twenty-two were dead.[174]

The extent of the health crisis was so severe that some people within the federal government and the Protestant churches became convinced that the only solution was to close the schools and replace them with day schools. However, the Indian Affairs minister of the day, Frank Oliver, refused to enact the plan without the support of the churches involved. The plan foundered for lack of Roman Catholic support. During the same period, Bryce recommended that the federal government take over all the schools and turn them into sanatoria under his control. This plan was rejected because it was viewed as being too costly, and it was thought that it would have met with church opposition.[175]

Instead of closing schools or turning them into sanatoria, the government's major response to the health crisis was the negotiation in 1910 of a contract between Indian Affairs and the churches. This contract increased the grants to the schools and imposed a set of standards for diet and ventilation. The contract also required that students not be admitted "until, where practicable, a physician has reported that the child is in good health."[176]

As noted earlier, although the contract led to improvements in the short term, inflation quickly eroded the benefit of the increase in grants. The situation was worsened by the cuts to the grants that were repeatedly imposed during the Great Depression of the 1930s. The underfunding created by the cuts guaranteed that students would be poorly fed, clothed, and housed. As a result, children were highly susceptible to tuberculosis. And, because the government was slow to put in place policies that would have prohibited the admission of children with tuberculosis, and ineffective in enforcing such policies once they were developed, healthy children became infected. As late as the 1950s, at some schools, pre-admission medical examinations appear to have been perfunctory, ineffective, or non-existent.[177] In the long run, the 1910 contract proved to be no solution for the tuberculosis crisis.

The schools often lacked adequate facilities for the treatment of sick children. In 1893, Indian Affairs inspector T.P. Wadsworth reported that at the Qu'Appelle school, the "want of an infirmary is still very much felt."[178] Those infirmaries that existed were often primitive. On an 1891 visit to the Battleford school, Indian Commissioner Hayter Reed concluded that the hospital ward was in such poor shape that they had been obliged to move the children in it to the staff sitting room. According to Reed, "The noise, as well as the bad smells, come from the lavatory underneath."[179] Proposals to construct a small hospital at the Red Deer school in 1901 were not implemented.[180] There were also reports of inadequate isolation facilities at the Regina school (1901), the Anglican school in Onion Lake, Saskatchewan (1921), the Mission, British Columbia, school (1924), and the Muncey, Ontario, school (1935).[181] When diphtheria broke out at Duck Lake, Saskatchewan, in 1909, the nine students who fell ill were placed in a "large isolated house."[182]

Even though the 1910 contract required all schools to have hospital accommodation to prevent the spread of infectious disease, many schools continued to be without a proper infirmary. The 1918 global influenza epidemic left four children dead at the Red Deer, Alberta, school. When the influenza epidemic subsided, Principal J.F. Woodsworth complained to Indian Affairs, "For sickness, conditions at this school are nothing less than criminal. We have no isolation ward and no hospital equipment of any kind."[183] The Roman Catholic principals petitioned the federal government for the establishment of sick rooms, under the supervision of a competent nurse, at each school in 1924. At the same time, they objected to the sanitary inspection of the schools by government appointed nurses, since they recommended changes "leading to the transformation of our schools into hospitals or sanatoriums."[184] There were also regular reports that schools could not afford to hire needed nursing staff.[185] Indian Affairs officials continued to be critical of the quality of care provided by school infirmaries at the end of the 1950s.[186] Complaints from principals make it clear that into the late 1960s, there were still severe limitations on the range of health services being provided to residential school students.[187]

General Aboriginal health care was never a priority for the Canadian government. Tuberculosis among Aboriginal people largely was ignored unless it threatened the general Canadian population.[188] In 1937, Dr. H.W. McGill, the director of Indian Affairs, sent out an instruction that Indian health-care services "must be restricted to those required for the safety of limb, life or essential function." Hospital care was to be limited, spending on drugs was cut in half, and sanatoria and hospital treatment for chronic tuberculosis were eliminated.[189]

The high death rates led many parents to refuse to send their children to residential school. In 1897, Kah-pah-pah-mah-am-wa-ko-we-ko-chin (also known as Tom) was deposed from his position as a headman of the White Bear Reserve in what is now Saskatchewan for his vocal opposition to residential schools. In making his case for a school on the reserve, he pointed to the death rate at the Qu'Appelle industrial school, adding, "Our children are not strong. Many of them are sick most of the time, many of the children sent from this Reserve to the Schools have died.[190]

Death casts a long shadow over many residential school memories. Louise Moine attended the Qu'Appelle school in the early twentieth century. She recalled one year when tuberculosis was "on the rampage in that school. There was a death every month on the girls' side and some of the boys went also."[191] Of his years at the Roman Catholic school in Onion Lake, Joseph Dion recalled, "My schoolmates and I were not long in concluding that the lung sickness was fatal, hence as soon as we saw or heard of someone spitting blood, we immediately branded him for the grave. He had consumption: he had to die."[192] Simon Baker's brother Jim died from spinal meningitis at the Lytton, British Columbia, school. "I used to hear him crying at night. I asked the principal to take him to the hospital. He didn't. After about two weeks, my brother was in so much pain, he was going out of his mind. I pleaded with the principal for days to take him to a doctor."[193]

Ray Silver said that he always blamed the Alberni school for the death of his brother Dalton. "He was a little guy, laying in the bed in the infirmary, dying, and I didn't know 'til he died. You know that's, that was the end of my education."[194] The death of a child often prompted parents to withdraw the rest of their children from a school. One former student said her father came to the school when her sister became ill at the Anglican school at Aklavik, Northwest Territories. "He came upstairs and there we were. He cried over us. He took me home. He put her in a hospital, and she died."[195]

The high deaths rates in the schools were, in part, a reflection of the high death rates among the Aboriginal community in general. Indian Affairs officials often tried to portray these rates as simply the price that Aboriginal people had to pay as part of the process of becoming civilized. In reality, these rates were the price they paid for being colonized.[196] Aboriginal livelihoods were based on access to the land; colonization disrupted that access and introduced new illnesses to North America. Colonial policies helped wipe out food sources and confined Aboriginal people to poorly located reserves, with inadequate sanitation and shelter. The schools could have served as institutions to help counter these problems. To do that, however, they would have had to have been properly constructed, maintained, staffed, and supplied. Government officials were aware of this. They were also aware that death rates among students at residential schools were disproportionately high. It would be wrong to say the government did nothing about this crisis: the 1910 contract did provide a substantial funding increase to the schools. But the federal government never made the type of sustained investment in Aboriginal health, in either the communities or the schools, that could have addressed this crisis—which continues to the present. The non-Aboriginal tuberculosis death rate declined before the introduction of life-saving drugs. It was brought down by improvements in diet, housing, sanitation, and medical attention. Had such measures been taken by the federal government earlier, they would have reduced both the Aboriginal death rates and the residential school students' death rates. By failing to take adequate measures

that had been recommended to it, the federal government blighted
the health of generations of Aboriginal people.

BURIAL POLICY

Many of the early schools were part of larger church mission centres
that might include a church, a dwelling for the missionaries, a farm,
a sawmill, and a cemetery. The mission cemetery might serve as a
place of burial for students who died at school, members of the local community, and the missionaries themselves. For example, the
cemetery at the Roman Catholic St. Mary's mission, near Mission,
British Columbia, was intended originally for priests and nuns from
the mission as well as for students from the residential school.[197]

FIG 2.6 Residential school students at the Roman Catholic cemetery in Fort
George, Québec. Deschâtelets Archives.

During the influenza pandemic of 1918–19, many of the schools and missions were overwhelmed. At the Fort St. James school and mission in British Columbia, the dead were buried in a common grave.[198] At the Red Deer school, four students who died there were buried two to a grave to save costs.[199] In some cases, student and staff graves were treated differently. At the Spanish, Ontario, school, the graves of staff members were marked with headstones that, in the case of former priests and nuns, provided name and date of birth and death. The burial spots of students were identified only by plain white crosses.[200]

The general Indian Affairs policy was to hold the schools responsible for burial expenses when a student died at school. The school generally determined the location and nature of that burial.[201] Parental requests to have children's bodies returned home for burial were generally refused as being too costly.[202] In her memoirs, Eleanor Brass recalled how the body of one boy, who hung himself at the File Hills school in the early twentieth century, was buried on the Peepeekisis Reserve, even though his parents lived on the Carlyle Reserve.[203] As late as 1958, Indian Affairs refused to return the body of a boy who had died at a hospital in Edmonton to his northern home community in the Yukon.[204]

The reluctance to pay the cost of sending the bodies of children from residential schools home for burial ceremonies continued into the 1960s. For example, Indian Affairs was initially unwilling to pay to send the body of twelve-year-old Charlie Wenjack back to his parents' home community in Ogoki, Ontario, in 1966.[205] When Charles Hunter drowned in 1974 while attending the Fort Albany school, it was decided, without consultation with his parents, to bury him in Moosonee rather than send him home to Peawanuck near Hudson Bay. It was not until 2011, after significant public efforts made on his behalf by his sister Joyce, who had never got to meet her older brother, that Charles Hunter's body was exhumed and returned to Peawanuck for a community burial. The costs were covered by funds that the *Toronto Star* raised from its readership.[206]

A school closing might mean the cemetery would be left unattended. When the Battleford school closed in 1914, Principal E. Matheson reminded Indian Affairs that there was a school cemetery that contained the bodies of seventy to eighty individuals, most of whom were former students. He worried that unless the government took steps to care for the cemetery, it would be overrun by stray cattle.[207] In short, throughout the system's history, children who died at school were buried in school or mission cemeteries, often in poorly marked graves. The closing of the schools has led, in many cases, to the abandonment of these cemeteries.

DISCIPLINE: "TOO SUGGESTIVE OF THE OLD SYSTEM OF FLOGGING CRIMINALS"

When Indian agent D.L. Clink returned a runaway student to the Red Deer industrial school in 1895, he noted that the boy's head was bruised from where a teacher had hit him with a stick. The school principal, John Nelson, told Clink that he "had been severe with him before but he would be more severe now." Worried that if he "left the boy he would be abused," Clink took the boy away from the school. He also recommended to Indian Affairs that the teacher who had struck the student be dismissed and brought up on charges, since "his actions in this and other cases would not be tolerated in a white school for a single day in any part of Canada."[208] Clink's report led Indian Affairs Deputy Minister Hayter Reed to direct his staff:

> Instructions should be given, if not already sent, to the Principals
> of the various schools, that children are not to be whipped
> by anyone save the Principal, and even when such a course is
> necessary, great discretion should be used and they should not
> be struck on the head, or punished so severely that bodily harm
> might ensue. The practice of corporal punishment is considered

unnecessary as a general measure of discipline and should only be resorted to for very grave offences and as a deterrent example.[209]

Reed's instruction underlines a number of the recurrent problems with the Indian Affairs approach to discipline in residential schools. First, Reed, who had previously been the Indian commissioner in western Canada, did not know whether there were regulations dealing with school discipline. Second, his directive is vague: while it indicates where students should *not* be struck, it does not specify where they could be struck, or place limits on what students could be struck with; and neither are there limits on the number of blows. Third, it is not clear that these instructions were ever issued to the principals. If they were, they were soon lost and forgotten. In later years, when conflicts arose over discipline at the schools, Indian Affairs officials made no reference to the policy. In 1920, Canon S. Gould, the general secretary of the Missionary Society of the Church of England in Canada, asked Deputy Minister Campbell Scott, "Is corporal punishment for disciplinary purposes recognized, or permitted in the Indian Boarding schools?" He noted that whether or not it was permitted, he imagined that it was applied in every residential school in the country.[210] The first—and only—evidence of a nation-wide discipline policy for residential schools that the Truth and Reconciliation Commission of Canada has been able to locate in the documents reviewed to date was issued in 1953.[211]

The failure to establish and enforce a national policy on discipline meant that students were subject to disciplinary measures that would not, as Clink noted in 1895, be tolerated in schools for non-Aboriginal children. Four years after Reed asked his staff to issue instructions on corporal punishment, Indian Commissioner David Laird reported that several children had been "too severely punished" at the Middlechurch school. "Strappings on the bare back," he wrote, was "too suggestive of the old system of flogging criminals."[212]

Corporal punishment was often coupled with public humiliation. In December 1896 in British Columbia, the Kuper Island school's acting principal gave two boys "several lashes in the Presence of the Pupils" for sneaking into the girls' dormitory at night.[213] When, in 1934, the principal of the Shubenacadie school could not determine who had stolen money and chocolates from a staff member, he had the suspects thrashed with a seven-thonged strap and then placed on bread-and-water diets.[214]

Some schools had a specific room set aside to serve as a "punishment room."[215] After a 1907 inspection of the Mohawk Institute in Brantford, the Ontario inspector for Indian agencies, J.G. Ramsden, reported, "I cannot say that I was favourably impressed with the sight of two prison cells in the boys [sic] play house. I was informed, however, that these were for pupils who ran away from the institution, confinement being for a week at a time when pupils returned."[216] In 1914, a father successfully sued the Mohawk Institute principal for locking his daughter in a cell for three days on what was described as a "water diet."[217]

Boys at the Anglican school in Brocket, Alberta, were chained together as punishment for running away in 1920.[218] At the Gleichen, Alberta, school, a principal was accused of shackling a boy to his bed and beating him with a quirt (a riding whip) until his back bled. The principal admitted to having beaten the boy with the whip, but denied breaking the boy's skin.[219]

Abusive punishment often prompted children to run away. The father of Duncan Sticks, a boy who died from exposure after running away from the Williams Lake school in British Columbia, told a coroner's inquest in 1902 that, in the past, his son had run away because he had been "beaten with a quirt."[220] A boy who ran away from the Anglican school in The Pas, after being severely beaten by the principal, nearly died of exposure.[221]

The violent nature of the discipline at the schools came as a shock to students. Isabelle Whitford said that prior to coming to the Sandy Bay school, she had never been physically disciplined. "All my dad have to do was raise his voice, and we knew what he meant. So, when I first got hit by the nuns, it was really devastating 'cause how can they hit me when my parents didn't hit me, you know?"[222] Rachel Chakasim said that at the Fort Albany school, "I saw violence for the first time. I would see kids getting hit. Sometimes in the classrooms, a yardstick was being used to hit."[223]

Fred Brass said that his years at the Roman Catholic school at Kamsack, Saskatchewan, were "the hellish years of my life. You know to be degraded by our so-called educators, to be beat by these people that were supposed to have been there to look after us, to teach us right from wrong. It makes me wonder now today a lot of times I ask that question, who was right and who was wrong?"[224] According to Geraldine Bob, the staff members at the Kamloops school she attended were not able to control their tempers once they began to punish a student. "They would just start beating you and lose control and hurl you against the wall, throw you on the floor, kick you, punch you."[225]

It was a common practice to shave the heads of students who ran away. William Antoine recalled that at the Spanish, Ontario, school, this was done in front of the other students. "They got all the boys to look at what is happening to this boy, what they were doing to him because he ran away. They cut all his hair off and they pulled, pulled his pants down and he was kneeling on the floor, and holding onto the chair."[226] Eva Simpson said that at the Catholic school in The Pas, her cousin's head was shaved for running away.[227]

Many students spoke of teachers punishing them by pulling their ears. At Sioux Lookout, Dorothy Ross said, "one time me and this other girl were, we were, were fooling around, we were teasing each other in our own language, we got, I got caught. She pulled my ear so hard."[228] Archie Hyacinthe could recall that in the classrooms of the Roman Catholic school in Kenora, "every time we didn't listen, they would tug us behind the ear, or behind the neck, or on the elbows."[229] Jonas Grandjambe recalled how the nun in charge of the boys' dormitory at the Roman Catholic school in Aklavik, in the Northwest Territories, would "grab our ear and twist it."[230] Delores Adolph said that the discipline she received at the Mission school impaired her hearing.[231] Joseph Wabano said that at the Fort Albany, Ontario, school, the staff would hit students with a one-inch-thick board.[232] Noel Starblanket recalled being constantly "slapped on the side of the head" at the Qu'Appelle school. One teacher struck him in the face and broke his nose.[233]

Mervin Mirasty said that at the Beauval, Saskatchewan, school, boys who were caught throwing snowballs were punished with blows to their hands from the blade of a hockey stick.[234] As a punishment, Nellie Trapper, who attended the Moose Factory, Ontario, school in the 1950s, was assigned to "scrubbing the stair, the stairwell with a toothbrush, me and this other girl. Like, I don't remember what I did wrong, but that was something that I won't forget. I remember sitting on the steps, and she, our supervisor was standing there, watching us."[235] Former students also spoke of how, in winter, they might be forced to stand or sit, inadequately clothed, in the snow as a form of punishment.

It was not uncommon for residential school students, traumatized by being placed in such a harsh and alien environment, to wet their beds. These students were subjected to humiliating punishments. Wendy Lafond said that at the Prince Albert, Saskatchewan, school, "if we wet our beds, we were made to stand in the corner in our pissy clothes, not allowed to change."[236] Don Willie recalled that students who wet their beds were publicly humiliated at the Alert Bay school. "And they used to, they used to line up the wet bed, bedwetters, and line them up in the morning, and parade them through, parade them through breakfast, the breakfast area, pretty much to shame them."[237]

Policies that were seen as being unacceptable in the early twentieth century were still in place in the 1960s. Many students compared residential schools to jails: some spoke of being locked up in dormitories, broom closets, basements, and even crawl spaces. In 1965, students who ran away from the Presbyterian school in Kenora were locked up with just a mattress on the floor and put on a bread-and-milk diet.[238] Students were still being locked up in what was referred to as the "counselling" room at the Poplar Hill, Ontario, school in the 1980s.[239] Despite the fact that Indian Affairs had given orders to abandon the practice, students were still having their hair cropped into the 1970s.[240] In the 1990s, students at the Gordon's, Saskatchewan, school were still being struck, and pushed into lockers and walls by one staff member.[241]

The failure to develop, implement, and monitor effective discipline sent an unspoken message that there were no real limits on what could be done to Aboriginal children within the walls of a residential school. The door had been opened early to an appalling level of physical and sexual abuse of students, and it remained open throughout the existence of the system.

ABUSE: "AND HE DID AWFUL THINGS TO ME"

From the nineteenth century onwards, the government and churches were well aware of the risk that staff might sexually abuse residential school students. As early as 1886, Jean L'Heureux, who worked as a translator for Indian Affairs and a recruiter for Roman Catholic schools in Alberta, was accused of sexually abusing boys in his care. The officials responsible for the schools recognized that his actions were not appropriate. Despite this, there is no record of a criminal investigation being carried out at the time.[242] When new allegations against L'Heureux emerged in 1891, he was allowed to resign. In dealing with the matter, Indian Affairs Deputy Minister Lawrence Vankoughnet hoped "it would not be necessary to state the cause which led to the same [the resignation]."[243]

When it came to taking action on the abuse of Aboriginal children, early on, Indian Affairs and the churches placed their own interests ahead of the children in their care and then covered up that victimization. It was cowardly behaviour.

This set the tone for the way the churches and government would treat the sexual abuse of children for the entire history of the residential school system. Complaints often were ignored. In some cases where allegations were made against a school principal, the only measure that Indian Affairs took was to contact the

principal.[244] In at least one case, Indian Affairs officials worked
with school officials to frustrate a police investigation into abuse
at a school. When attempting to return some runaway boys to the
Kuper Island school in 1939, British Columbia Provincial Police
officers concluded that there was good reason to believe the boys
had run away because they were being sexually abused at the
school. The police launched an investigation and refused to return
the boys to the school.[245] When Indian Affairs officials finally investigated, they concluded that the allegations had merit. However,
to protect the school's reputation, the local Indian Affairs official
advised the suspected abusers to leave the province, allowing them
to avoid prosecution.[246] Nothing was done for the students who
had been victimized or for their parents.

These patterns persisted into the late twentieth century. Officials continued to dismiss Aboriginal reports of abuse.[247] In some
cases, staff members were not fired, even after being convicted of
assaulting a student.[248] Complaints were improperly investigated.
For example, charges of sexual impropriety made against the
principal of the Gordon's school were investigated by a school staff
member in 1956.[249] Church officials failed to report cases of abuse
to Indian Affairs, and Indian Affairs failed to report cases of abuse
to families.[250] It was not until 1968 that Indian Affairs began to
compile and circulate a list of former staff members who were not
to be hired at other schools without the approval of officials in Ottawa.[251] The churches and the government remained reluctant to
take matters to the police. As a result, prosecutions were rare.

In the documents it has reviewed, the Truth and Reconciliation Commission of Canada has identified over forty successful
convictions of former residential school staff members who
sexually or physically abused students.[252] Most of these prosecutions were the result of the determination of former students to
see justice done.

The full extent of the abuse that occurred in the schools is
only now coming to light. As of January 31, 2015, the Independent

Assessment Process (IAP), established under the Indian Residential Schools Settlement Agreement (IRSSA) had received 37,951 claims for injuries resulting from physical and sexual abuse at residential schools. The IAP is a mechanism to compensate former students for sexual and physical abuse experienced at the schools and the harms that arose from the assaults. By the end of 2014, the IAP had resolved 30,939 of those claims, awarding $2,690,000,000 in compensation.[253] The Common Experience Payment (CEP) established under IRSSA provided compensation to individuals who attended a school on the IRSSA's approved list of schools. The CEP recognized the claims of 78,748 former residential school students. Although claims for compensation under the IAP could be made by non-residential school students who were abused at the schools, the vast majority of IAP claims were made by former residential school students. The number of claims for compensation for abuse is equivalent to approximately 48 percent of the number of former students who were eligible to make such claims. This number does not include those former students who died prior to May 2005.

As the numbers demonstrate, the abuse of children was rampant. From 1958, when it first opened, until 1979, there was never a year in which Grollier Hall in Inuvik did not employ at least one dormitory supervisor who would later be convicted for sexually abusing students at the school. Joseph Jean Louis Comeau, Martin Houston, George Maczynski, and Paul Leroux all worked at Grollier Hall during this period. All were convicted of abusing Grollier Hall students.[254] William Peniston Starr served as director of the Gordon's, Saskatchewan, residence from 1968 until 1984.[255] Prior to that, he worked at a series of schools in Alberta and Québec.[256] In 1993, he was convicted of ten counts of sexually assaulting Gordon's school students.[257] Arthur Plint worked as a boys' supervisor at the Alberni residential school for two five-year periods between 1948 and 1968. In 1995, he pleaded guilty to eighteen counts of indecent assault. In sentencing him to eleven years in jail, Justice D.A. Hogarth described Plint as "a sexual terrorist."[258]

Physical abuse and sexual abuse often were intertwined. Jean Pierre Bellemare, who attended the Amos, Québec, school, spoke for many students when he told the Commission that he had been subjected to "physical violence, verbal violence, touchings, everything that comes with it."[259] Andrew Yellowback was "sexually, physically, emotionally, and mentally abused" at the Cross Lake, Manitoba, school for eight years.[260] There was no single pattern of abuse: students of both sexes reported assaults from staff members of both the opposite sex and the same sex as themselves.[261]

First-year students, traumatized by separation from their parents and the harsh and alien regime of the school, were particularly vulnerable to abusive staff members who sought to win their trust through what initially appeared to be simple kindness. In some cases, this might involve little more than extra treats from the school canteen. This favouritism, however, was often the prelude to a sexual assault that left the student scared and confused.[262]

Many students spoke of having been raped at school.[263] These were moments of terror. Josephine Sutherland was cornered by one of the lay brothers in the Fort Albany school garage: "I couldn't call for help, I couldn't. And he did awful things to me."[264] Other students recalled being assaulted in the church confessional.[265] A student in the change room would suddenly have a bag pulled over his head.[266] The abuse could begin with an instruction to report to the shower room in the middle of the night or to take lunch to a staff member's room.[267] An abusive staff person might stalk a student, blocking her or his way, or grope a passing student.[268] Female students spoke of how some staff members took advantage of their innocence, rubbing against them sexually while they were sitting on their laps.[269] Abuse also took the form of voyeuristic humiliation: some staff insisted on watching the students shower.[270]

Some dormitory supervisors used their authority to institute dormitory-wide systems of abuse. Many students spoke of the fear and anxiety that spread across their dormitories in the evenings.[271] They went to bed fearful that they might be called into the supervisor's room.[272] To protect themselves, some students attempted to never be alone.[273] Older children sometimes sought to protect younger ones.[274]

Most students came to school with little knowledge or understanding of sexual activity, let alone the types of sexual abuse to which they might be subjected. Abuse left them injured, bewildered, and often friendless or subject to ridicule by other students.[275] Many students thought they were the only children being abused. This confusion made it difficult for them to describe or report their abuse.[276] Some were told they would face eternal damnation for speaking of what had been done to them.[277]

Many students fought back against their far larger and more powerful assailants, especially as they got older and stronger.[278] Some succeeded in forcing their tormentors to leave them alone.[279] Many others, such as Lawrence Waquan, concluded that there was "nothing you can do."[280] Some students ran away from school in an attempt to escape abuse.[281] Others begged their parents not to return them to school after a break.[282]

Some students never reported abuse for fear they would not be believed.[283] Other students who did report abuse were told that they were to blame.[284] In some cases, school officials took immediate action when abuse was reported to them, but the rarity of such actions is itself noteworthy.[285] Former students spoke of how betrayed they felt when nothing was done about their complaints.[286] Many simply felt too ashamed to ever speak of the abuse.[287] Family members often refused to believe their children's reports of abuse, intensifying their sense of isolation and pain.[288] This was especially so within families that had adopted Christianity, and could not believe that the people of God looking after their children would ever do such things.[289]

The impact of abuse was immediate and long-lasting. It destroyed the students' ability to function in the school, and led many to turn to self-destructive behaviours.[290]

Staff abuse of children created conditions for the student abuse of other students. Every school system has to deal with school bullies, student cliques, and inter-student conflict. It is part of the socialization process. Ideally, corrective lessons in how to treat others well are taught, as well as shown by example. Residential school staff had a responsibility not only to model such behaviour, but also to protect students from being victimized. In many cases, they failed to provide that protection. Conflicts between students are not unique to residential schools, but they take on greater significance in a residential school setting where children cannot turn to adult family members for comfort, support, and redress. The moral influences that a child's home community can exert are also absent. Instead, the children were left vulnerable and unprotected. Residential schools failed to live up to their responsibility to protect students from being victimized by other students.

Older or bigger students used force—or the threat of force—to establish their dominance over younger students. In some cases, this dominance was used to coerce younger or smaller students to participate in sexual acts. In other cases, bullies forced vulnerable students to turn over their treats, their food, or their money, or to steal on their behalf. In addition, bullies might simply seek a measure of sadistic satisfaction from beating those who were weaker. Bullies operated individually or in groups. Such groups were often formed initially as a defensive response to the level of violence within the school, but, over time, would take on their own offensive characteristics. Sometimes, such groups not only focused their anger and/or frustration on other students, but also sought to disrupt the general operation of the school. The fact that Catholic and Protestant church leaders continued to disparage one another's religions throughout this period meant that conflicts between students could also take on religious overtones, particularly in communities with more than one residential school, such as Inuvik in the Northwest Territories.

Student victimization of students was an element of the broader abusive and coercive nature of the residential school system. Underfed, poorly housed, and starved for affection, students often formed groups based on age, community of origin, or First Nation. Such groups gave students a measure of identity and status, but also provided protection to their members and dominated more vulnerable students.

William Garson recalled that at the Elkhorn, Manitoba, school, "we were always like hiding in the corners; you know away from any abusement. From other, older, from older, elder boys, students."[291] Percy Thompson said that at the Hobbema school, "one bully used to come at me and he'd pretend he was going to talk to me and all of sudden hit me in the belly. And of course I gag, gag, and he'd laugh his head off and, you know, to see me in such a predicament."[292] Alice Ruperthouse spoke of "the cruelty of the other children" at the Amos, Québec, school. "It was, you know, like in a jungle. Like in a jungle, you don't know what's going to come out but you know you had to watch out."[293] Albert Elias felt that the classroom at the Anglican school in Aklavik "was the safest place to be in 'cause that's where nobody could beat me up. I dreaded recesses and lunches and after school, I dreaded those times."[294]

Bullying might start shortly after arrival. In some schools, all new male students were put through a hazing. Denis Morrison said that each new arrival at the Fort Frances school underwent a beating. "They used to initiate you, like, they would beat the hell out of you, the other kids would. It wasn't anybody else, it was the other kids, the older ones, eh."[295] Bob Baxter recalled that there were student gangs at the Sioux Lookout school. He was beaten up and knifed on one occasion. He had a vivid memory of people tying him to his bed and throwing hot water over him.[296] Clara Quisess said that at the Fort Albany school in Ontario, older girls would threaten the younger ones with knives.[297] Louisa Birote recalled that the girls at the La Tuque, Québec, school all formed themselves into hostile groups. "We hated each other. So, this little gang didn't like the other gang. That's the way at the school, that's what we were taught, fears, and we were scared, and I went to hide in what we called the junk room, the junk closet."[298]

A lack of adequate supervision in the schools and residences meant that such domination could give rise to physical and sexual abuse. The assaults ranged from being forced to kiss someone, to being forced to simulate a sex act, to being raped. In some cases, victims were given small treats to encourage them to be silent; in other cases, they were told they would be killed if they reported the assault.[299] Agnes Moses recalled being molested by older girls at a hostel in northern Canada. "I never quite understood it, and it really wrecked my life, it wrecked my life as a mother, a wife, a woman, and sexuality was a real, it was a dirty word for us."[300] The experience of being abused at a British Columbia school by a group of boys left Don Willie distrustful of most people. "The only, only friends I kept after that were my relatives."[301]

Complaints were infrequent, as students had good reason not to report their abuse. Some feared that bullies would retaliate if they were reported. Others were ashamed of what had been done to them, and some did not fully understand what had been done to them. Many students feared they would not be believed—or would be blamed for somehow bringing the abuse upon themselves. Still others were further punished when they did tell. So, rather than report the abuse, many students chose to fight back; to seek admission into a receptive group, where violence could be fought with violence; or to endure the pain in silence. This victimization left many students feeling intensely betrayed, fearful, isolated, and bereft of home teachings and protection. The betrayal by fellow students has contributed significantly to the schools' long-term legacy of continuing division and distrust within Aboriginal communities. The residential school system's shameful inability to protect students from such victimization, even from among themselves, represents one of its most significant and least-understood failures.

SPORTS AND CULTURE: "IT WAS A RELIEF"

Many students stated that sports helped them make it through residential school. Christina Kimball attended the Roman Catholic school near The Pas, where she experienced physical, sexual, and emotional abuse. She believes that it was only through her involvement with sports that she survived. "I was very sports-oriented. I played baseball. Well, we play baseball, and even hockey. We had a hockey team. That has benefited, benefited me in a way 'cause I loved playing sports. Well, that's one way, too. I don't know how I did it but I was pretty good in sports."[302] Noel Starblanket said that at the Qu'Appelle school, "I had some good moments, in particular in the sports side, 'cause I really enjoyed sports. I was quite athletic, and basically that's what kept me alive, that's what

FIG 2.7   Boys playing hockey at the McIntosh, Ontario, school. Many students said that they would not have survived their residential school years, were it not for sports. St. Boniface Historical Society, Oblates of Mary Immaculate, Manitoba Province Fonds, SHSB 29362.

kept me going was the sports."[303] At the Lestock school, Geraldine
Shingoose took refuge in extracurricular activities:

> One of the good things that I would do to try and get out of just
> the abuse was try to, I would join track-meet, try and be, and
> I was quite athletic in boarding school. And I also joined the
> band, and I played a trombone. And, and that was something
> that took me away from the school, and just to, it was a relief.[304]

Paul Andrew spent seven years at Grollier Hall in Inuvik.
One of his strongest and most positive memories related to school
sports. "There were times when I felt dumb and stupid. But put me
in a gym, there was not too many people better than I am."[305]

Recreational activities were always underfunded and under-
supplied at the schools. A national survey of Indian Affairs schools
(both day and residential) in 1956 concluded:

> In most of the schools there appeared to be little or no physical
> education program. A number of schools had no facilities for
> such activities. Basement areas were obviously designed for
> playing areas, but they were very inadequate and were utilized
> for storage or for assembly purposes. A large number of school
> sites were not properly cleared, graded, and prepared for
> playing purposes. Many were still in the wild state; others
> were overgrown with shrubs, thistles, grasses and other weeds
> presenting a very unkempt and neglected appearance.[306]

Oblate Provincial L. Poupore wrote to Indian Affairs about
conditions at the Williams Lake, British Columbia, school in 1957.
He pointed out that a year and half earlier, he had informed Indian
Affairs about the need for a school gymnasium. At that time, he
said, "The boys' play room, a room about 35 by 60, was a scene
of bedlam during recreation periods. There were about 150 boys
trying to play; the mud they had brought in on their feet had dried
and there was so much dust in the room that you could not recognize a boy at the opposite end." Although the department had

assured him the construction of a gymnasium would be a priority, nothing had been done, and "the problem of playroom space is worse than ever."[307]

Despite the lack of financial support, hockey teams from a number of schools achieved considerable success in the 1940s and 1950s. Teams from Duck Lake and Qu'Appelle in Saskatchewan, in particular, established enviable records. The Duck Lake school team, the St. Michael's Indians, won the championship of an eight-team league in the Rosthern area in 1946.[308] In 1948, the same team, coached by Father G.-M. Latour, won the northern Saskatchewan midget hockey championship. The following year, it won the provincial championship.[309] According to the *Prince Albert Daily Herald*, "While the Duck Lake boys were outweighed in their midget series they made it up in hockey know-how, skating ability and shooting accuracy. Their drives, from any angle, had the Regina players scared and baffled at the same time."[310] Among the players on the 1949 Duck Lake provincial championship team was Fred Sasakamoose, who went on to become the first status Indian to play in the National Hockey League.[311]

While hockey dominated boys' sports in most residential schools, British Columbia residential schools gained renown for their boxers. In 1947, the Roman Catholic school at Sechelt in North Vancouver advertised for a volunteer to run a school athletics program. Navy veteran Alex Strain took on the job. At the time, the school had no recreation program and no facilities. Under Strain's direction, the students cleared out a storage building and turned it into a gymnasium. Putting in four days of volunteer work a week, Strain created what *Vancouver Sun* reporter Gerry Pratt described as "the smoothest tumbling team in the province." He then established a boxing program at the school. The limits of the first ring were marked out by four rows of chairs. The first punching bag was a navy duffle bag filled with tumbling mats. After two years, Strain purchased a used truck and took the students on a boxing tour of Vancouver Island. After four years in existence, the team had won over 100 trophies. Sister John Lawrence made

FIG 2.8 Grandin College girls' basketball team, Northwest Territories. One Grandin student wrote in the school newsletter, "At Grandin, Education comes first." Although students could participate in school sports teams, "if you are behind in your school work, you are forced to quit your sports." Deschâtelets Archives.

robes and shorts for each member of the team and also served as trainer.[312] Frederick Baker, the winner of the first national Tom Longboat award, was a member of the Sechelt boxing team. Baker had won three championships in 1948, two in 1949, one in 1950, and one in 1951.[313]

Other students sought solace in the arts. A number of former residential school students went on to prominent careers in the visual arts, including Alex Janvier, Jackson Beardy, Judith Morgan, and Norval Morrisseau. Some, such as Beardy, were encouraged in their artistic endeavours by sympathetic staff.[314] Like sports, cultural activities were underfunded. They were also often intended to encourage assimilation. In 1967, the students attending the Shingwauk, Ontario, school put on a four-act play called *Arrow to the Moon*. One act used a dialogue between an Elder and a young man to contrast what were seen as the old and new ways open to Aboriginal people. Billy Diamond played the role of the young man, who concludes at the scene's end, "The new ways show a way to work and live but the old ways have shown us how to die." The performance was filmed and shown to the James Bay Cree, who refrained from making any public comment, but were shocked to discover the degree to which their children were being manipulated.[315]

Albert Canadien recalled in his memoirs from Akaitcho Hall:

> A few of the boys had guitars and there were other instruments in the common room. Sometimes, a few of the boys would get together and play to pass the time. John, the boys' supervisor, noticed this was going on and took an interest, encouraging us to play and sing.
>
> At first we got together just for fun. But eventually ... we formed a band. There were five or six of us, and we call ourselves the Arctic Ramblers. We had guitars, fiddle, bass guitar, drums, and there was even a piano for a while.

They played at dances at the residence and in Hay River.[316] Canadien went on to play in the Chieftones, a rock-and-roll band that toured extensively across North America.[317]

On the rinks, the athletic fields, and parade grounds, or in the arts and handicraft rooms and on performance stages, many students found a way to express themselves, and, through that, gained the opportunity to explore their own talents and sometimes other parts of the country or the world. Most importantly, they gained some confidence in their ability to achieve.

RESISTANCE: "I AM THE FATHER OF THIS CHILD"

Parents and children developed a variety of strategies to resist residential schooling. Parents might refuse to enrol students, refuse to return runaways, or they might refuse to return students to school

at the end of the summer holidays. They also called on the government to increase school funding; to establish day schools in their
home communities; and to improve the quality of education, food,
and clothing. In taking such measures, they often put themselves
at risk of legal reprisals. Almost invariably, the system declined
to accept the validity of parental and student criticisms. Parental
influences were judged by school and government officials to be
negative and backward. The schools also suspected parents of
encouraging their children in acts of disobedience.[318] Once parents
came to be viewed as the "enemy," their criticisms, no matter how
valid, could be discounted.

Prior to 1920, when the *Indian Act* was amended to allow
Indian Affairs to compel children to attend residential school, the
most effective form of resistance that parents could make was to
simply refuse to enrol their children. This measure was so effective
that it contributed to the closure of a number of residential schools.
The Battleford, Saskatchewan, school, which had a capacity of 150
students, had an enrolment of thirty-five in 1915.[319] The school was
closed two years later.[320] The High River, Alberta, school could also
hold over 100 students, but by 1922, the year it closed, the school
had an enrolment of only forty.[321] The Middlechurch, Manitoba,
school was not rebuilt after it burned down in 1906, in large measure because it could not recruit enough students.[322] For similar
reasons, the St. Boniface, Manitoba, school closed in 1905; the
Calgary, Alberta, school closed in 1907; the Regina, Saskatchewan,
school closed in 1910; the Elkhorn, Manitoba, school closed in
1919; and the Red Deer, Alberta, school closed in 1919.[323]

By refusing to enrol their children in the industrial schools on
the Prairies, parents not only undermined the federal government's
assimilation policies, but also deprived the schools of per capita
grant revenue and student labour. As a result, the industrial schools
ran significant deficits, and overworked and underfed the children
they did recruit. This led other parents to withdraw their children
from the schools. This was never a risk-free choice for parents.

FIG 2.9 Boys cutting wood at the Williams Lake, British Columbia, school in
either the late nineteenth or early twentieth century. In February 1902 Duncan
Sticks froze to death after running away from the school. Museum of the Cariboo
Chilcotin.

Often, residential schools were the only available schools. Parents
who wished to see their children schooled had few, if any, options.[324]

Sometimes, government officials also took reprisals against
parents who kept their children out of school, in some cases deny-
ing them food rations and Treaty payments.[325] Parents continued
to keep their children out of school well into the twentieth century: in 1941, only forty-five students were enrolled in the Fort
Providence school, which had an authorized attendance of 100.[326]

In at least one instance, parents home-schooled their children.
In 1941, Muriel, Doreen, and Kathleen Steinhauer were kept home
from the Edmonton residential school because their parents were
not satisfied with the progress they were making at the school.
Their mother, Isabel, had been a schoolteacher prior to her marriage, and home-schooled the children.[327]

Sometimes, parents took their children out of school against the wishes of the principal. In 1904, a husband and wife attempted to remove their daughter from the Kuper Island school. When Principal G. Donckele informed them that when they signed the admission form, they had given the government the right to determine when their daughter would be discharged, the father said, "I am the father of this child and I do not care for what you and the government have to say about it." After being told that he could be prosecuted, the father left with his daughter anyway.[328]

In 1913, when a mother removed her daughter from the Fort Resolution school, the Mounted Police were called in and the mother surrendered the girl to the school.[329] In response to the death of a student in 1922, local parents withdrew their children from the Kitamaat, British Columbia, residential school. They agreed to return them only on the condition that the principal "sign her name to a paper before us that she would see that the children got all the food they wanted, that they would be well cared for, and be supplied with sufficient clothing."[330]

In March 1948, the principal of the Roman Catholic school at Cardston, Alberta, struck a father who was attempting to take his son out of the school. In discussing the issue with Indian Affairs, the Blood Indian Council insisted on having the record note that this was "not the first time that Father Charron had hit an Indian."[331]

It was not uncommon for the parents of an entire community or region to refuse to return their children to school. In the fall of 1926, for example, parents from communities in Manitoba's Interlake region announced they were not sending their children back to the Elkhorn school. According to the parents, the children were not well fed, the older boys compelled the younger boys to steal, and all children were poorly clothed.[332] In October 1927, seventy-five school-aged children from the Blood Reserve in Alberta either had not returned to school or had not been enrolled in school. It took a letter from the police, plus a follow-up visit from the Indian agent, to fill the Anglican and Catholic schools on the reserve.[333] Two weeks after the start of the 1940 school year, fifty-four students had yet to return to the Fraser Lake, British Columbia, school. The police were called in, and by October 2, twenty-five of the students had been returned.[334] This form of parental action was common throughout the 1940s.[335]

Parents were eager to have their children properly educated, and often proposed realistic and effective solutions. In 1905, parents of children attending the Roman Catholic boarding school in Squamish, British Columbia, petitioned to have the school converted into an industrial school. The request was not granted, despite the fact that Indian Affairs officials recognized that the boarding school grant allowed for only "the bare necessities in the line of food and clothing."[336]

Some First Nations leaders who had originally supported residential schools later publicly regretted their decision. Chief Napahkesit of the Pine Creek Band in Manitoba said in 1917 that he was sorry he had ever supported the construction of the Pine Creek school. According to the local Indian agent, the chief felt "the children know less when they come out than they did when they went in." What was needed, the chief said, was a day school.[337] Calls for day schools were, in fact, a common parental request.[338] A 1949 call from parents for a day school at the Cowessess Reserve eventually proved to be successful.[339]

Parents might also demand the dismissal of a principal.[340] In 1917, to back up their call for the resignation of the Shoal Lake school principal, parents refused to return their children to the school.[341] In this case, the principal did resign.[342] The parents of the Kahkewistahaw Band unsuccessfully petitioned the federal government to remove a teacher from the Round Lake, Saskatchewan, school in July 1949. They said that "the children's report cards are very unsatisfactory, worst ever received, and she abuses the children too much.[343] Parents also complained that their children were not learning the skills they needed to survive. Chief Kejick of the Shoal Lake Band told Indian Affairs officials in 1928 that the students from his reserve "did not know how to make a living when they left school and would like trades taught."[344] Eight years later, Charlie Shingoose of the Waywayseecappo Band sought to have his fifteen-year-old son discharged from the Birtle school so he could teach him to "work, trap, etc."[345]

Parents also hired lawyers to press their cases for investigations into the deaths of children who had run away, to complain about the harshness of discipline, to advocate on behalf of children who had been injured working at the schools, and to attempt to have their children discharged from school.[346]

One of the more unusual protests was mounted by First Nations people (Dene) in the Northwest Territories, who, in 1937, refused to accept their Treaty payments in protest of conditions at the Fort Resolution school. Their children, they said, were "living in hell."[347]

Residential schools also came under criticism from early First Nations organizations. At its meeting in Saddle Lake, Alberta, in 1931, the League of Indians of Canada called for the construction of more day schools to augment residential schools.[348] The following year, the league, by then known as the League of Indians of Western Canada, called for the closure of boarding schools.[349] The league also recommended that only qualified teachers be hired to work at residential schools, that medical examinations be given to students before they were sent to the schools, and that the half-day system be changed to allow for greater class time.[350]

In an effort to bring their own residential schooling to an end, some students attempted to burn their schools down. There were at least thirty-seven such attempts, two of which ended in student and staff deaths.[351] For students, the most effective form of resistance was to run away. The principal of the Shingwauk Home in Sault Ste. Marie, Ontario, school in the 1870s, E.F. Wilson, devoted a chapter of his memoirs to the topic of "Runaway Boys." It included the story of three boys who tried to make their way home by boat. They were found alive more than ten days later, stranded on an island in the North Channel of Lake Huron.[352]

After 1894, children enrolled in a residential school (or who had been placed there by government order because it was felt that they were not being properly cared for by their parents) but who were refusing to show up at school were considered to be "truant." Under the *Indian Act* and its regulations, they could be returned to the school against their will. Children who ran away from residential schools were also considered to be truants. Parents who supported their children in their truancy were often threatened with prosecution.[353]

Most runaway students headed for their home communities. Students knew they might be caught, returned, and punished. Still, they believed the effort to make it home and have a measure of freedom was worth it. In some cases, in fact, the schools failed to force runaways to return.[354] Some students eluded capture. Instead of

FIG 2.10 Aboriginal family at the Elkhorn, Manitoba, school. Indian Affairs took the position that once parents enrolled their children in a residential school, only the government could determine when they would be discharged. General Synod Archives, Anglican Church of Canada, P75-103-S8-56.

heading home, some went to work for local farmers and, as a result, were able to avoid their pursuers for considerable periods of time.[355]

Running away could be risky. At least thirty-three students died, usually due to exposure, after running away from school.[356] In a significant number of cases, parents and Indian Affairs officials concluded that the deaths could have been prevented if school officials had mounted earlier and more effective searches and notified police officials and family members.[357] In the case of Charles and Tom Ombash, two brothers who ran away from the Sioux Lookout school on October 5, 1956, school officials waited until November before informing police or Indian Affairs.[358] The boys were never found—community members continued to search for their remains decades after their disappearance.[359]

These deaths date back to the beginning of the twentieth century. However, the first system-wide policy outlining the procedures to be taken when a child ran away from school that the Truth and Reconciliation Commission of Canada has located in the documents it has reviewed dates from 1953. This was seventy-five years after the government began its residential school system. That policy simply stated, "The principal shall take prompt action to effect the return to school of any truant pupil, and shall report promptly to the Superintendent, Indian Agency, every case of truancy."[360] The nature of the prompt action was undefined. In particular, there was no requirement to contact either the child's parents or the police. It was not until 1971 that a more encompassing, nation-wide, policy was announced.[361]

In pursuing children to their parents' homes, the actions of school employees could be both invasive and disrespectful.[362] In the town of Lebret, Saskatchewan, "all the houses were checked" by the police as part of a search for two runaways from the File Hills school in 1935.[363]

Running away was not in itself a crime. However, most students were wearing school-issued clothing when they ran away, and, in some cases, principals tried, and even succeeded, in having them prosecuted for stealing the clothing they were wearing.[364]

Students who ran away numerous times also could be charged under the *Juvenile Delinquents Act*. In such cases, they could be sentenced to a reformatory until they turned twenty-one.[365]

The 1894 *Indian Act* amendments made parents who did not return truants to school subject to prosecution. The Mounted Police were often called in to force parents to send their children to school.[366] The Blue Quills, Alberta, school journal entry for May 1, 1932, reads: "The savages having received the order to bring their children to school unless they want the police to get involved, some parents did obey the order today. But there are still those who turn a deaf ear."[367] In 1937, a father who refused to return his son to the Sandy Bay, Manitoba, school was sentenced to ten days in jail. To prevent him from running away again, the boy was sent to a school in Saskatchewan.[368]

Parents were often outraged at having to return runaways. Wallace Hahawahi's father was reported as being "very indignant" at the prospect of sending his son back to the Brandon school in 1936. The boy was over sixteen and needed to help out at home. In this case, the father's argument prevailed and the boy was discharged.[369] Another runaway from the same school, Kenneth Thompson, told the police, "I am a Treaty Indian of Assiniboine Indian Reserve, I am 17 year of Age. I wish to state the reason I ran away from school was because I have to work too hard in fact I do not study at all. I am working around the school all the time. I consider if I have to work I may as well work at home for my father."[370] Despite his argument, he was returned to the school.[371]

Indian agents often referred to ongoing truancy issues at specific schools as "epidemics." The agents viewed such epidemics as a sign of underlying problems at a school. In 1928, Indian agent J. Waddy wrote that at the Anglican school in The Pas, "hardly a day goes bye [sic] that one or more do not take leave on their own account."[372] In 1935, ten pupils ran away from the Birtle, Manitoba, school.[373] In the closing years of the 1930s, the Shubenacadie school in Nova Scotia experienced continual truancy problems. It was not uncommon for some students to make numerous attempts to leave the school. On the morning of July 7, 1937, Andrew Julian decided not to join the other boys assigned to milk the school's dairy herd. Instead, he headed for Truro, where he was reported as being sighted in the rail yard. He was not located until the end of the month. By then, he had made it to Nyanza in Cape Breton, a distance of 260 miles (418.4 kilometres) from the school.[374] The following year, Steven Labobe (also given as LaBobe) managed to make it back to his home on Prince Edward Island. The principal decided not to demand the boy's return.[375] Other boys were not so lucky. One boy, who ran away five times, was eventually placed in a private reformatory.[376]

Many students said they ran away to escape the discipline of the school. Ken Lacquette attended residential schools in Brandon and Portage la Prairie, Manitoba. "They used to give us straps all the time with our pants down they'd give us straps right in the public. Then … this started happening, after awhile when I was getting old enough I started taking off from there, running away."[377] Others were seeking to escape something far more sinister than corporal punishment. After being subjected to ongoing sexual abuse, Anthony Wilson ran away from the Alberni school.[378]

In the 1940s, Arthur McKay regularly ran away from the Sandy Bay school. "I didn't even know where my home was, the first time right away. But these guys are the ones; my friends were living in nearby reserve, what they call Ebb and Flow, that's where they were going so I followed."[379] Ivan George and a group of his friends ran away from the Mission, British Columbia, school when he was eleven years old. They were strapped on their return. Despite this, he ran away two more times that school year.[380]

Muriel Morrisseau ran away from the Fort Alexander school almost every year she was at the school. The experience was often frightening. "I remember running away again trying to cross the river and it started freezing up, we all got scared, we had to come back again with a tail under our legs."[381] Isaac Daniels ran away from the Prince Albert, Saskatchewan, school with two older boys.

Their escape route involved crossing a railway bridge. Partway across, Daniels became too frightened to continue and turned back.[382] Dora Necan ran away from the Fort Frances school with a friend. They made it to the United States and stayed there for three days before returning to the school.[383] Nellie Cournoyea was sheltered by Aboriginal families along her route when she ran away from an Anglican hostel in the Northwest Territories after a confrontation with a teacher.[384] When Lawrence Waquan ran away from the Fort Chipewyan school in 1965, there were no roads and no one along the way to support him. "I walked from Fort Chipewyan in northern Alberta to Fort Smith, 130 miles. It took me about five days. I was only about sixteen. And I just ate berries and drank water to survive."[385]

When Beverley Anne Machelle and her friends ran away from the Lytton, British Columbia, school, they had to contend with the school's isolated and mountainous location:

It was halfway down this big hill, and then from there you could see town. And we got halfway down there, and we were all feeling, like, woo-hoo, you know, and we got out of there, and, and we're gonna go do something fun, and, and then we got halfway down, and then we realized, well, we have no money, and we have no place to go. There was no place to go. There was no safe place to go.[386]

The girls at the Sioux Lookout school rebelled in 1955 when they were all sent to bed early after a number of girls had been caught stealing. They barricaded themselves in their dormitory and refused to allow any staff to enter.[387] There was a similar revolt in Edmonton in the 1960s, when students blocked staff entry to the dormitory at night, to protest the abuse of students.[388]

Collectively and individually, parents and students did resist the residential school attack on Aboriginal families and communities. On occasion, they won small victories: a child might be discharged; a day school might be built. However, as long as Aboriginal people were excluded from positions of control over their children's education, the root causes of the conflict remained unresolved.

THE STAFF: "MY AIM WAS TO DO SOMETHING GOOD"

For most of their history, residential schools were staffed by individuals who were recruited by Christian missionary organizations. Generally, the churches appointed a priest or minister, as opposed to an educator, as the principal. The Roman Catholic schools could draw staff from a number of Catholic religious orders, whose members had made explicit vows of obedience, poverty, and chastity. In the spirit of those vows, they would be obliged to go where they were sent, would not expect payment, and would have no families to support. Indian Commissioner David Laird believed that since members of Roman Catholic religious orders received very little in exchange for their services, the Roman Catholic schools could "afford to have a much larger staff than where ordinary salaries are paid, and there is consequently less work for each to do, without interfering with the quality of the work done."[389] The Protestant schools recruited many of their staff members through missionary organizations.

Many of the early school staff members believed they were participating in a moral crusade. In her history of the McDougall Orphanage, the predecessor of the Morley school in Alberta, Mrs. J. McDougall described the work of the mission and orphanage as "going out after the wild and ignorant and bringing them into a Christian home and blessing the body, culturing the mind and trying to raise spiritual vision."[390]

Staff members were often motivated by a spirit of adventure as well as a religious commitment. As a young seminary student in Corsica, a French island in the Mediterranean, Nicolas Coccola wanted more than a life as a priest. In his memoir, he wrote, "The desire of foreign missions with the hope of martyrdom appeared to me as a higher calling." He ended up living out his life as a residential school principal in British Columbia.[391] As a small boy in England in the middle of the nineteenth century, Gibbon Stocken read with enthusiasm the missionary literature sent to him by an aunt. When he turned seventeen, he volunteered his services to the Anglican Church Missionary Society. He hoped to be sent to India. Instead, he was offered a position on the Blackfoot Reserve in what is now southern Alberta.[392] British-born nurse and midwife Margaret Butcher managed to get to India, where she worked for a British family. From there, she made her way to British Columbia, where she worked with a Methodist mission to Japanese immigrants.[393] In 1916, she was on her way to a job at the Methodist residential school in Kitamaat, British Columbia.[394]

This mix of motivations continued throughout the system's history. Lorraine Arbez, who worked at the Qu'Appelle school in the 1950s, said, "I chose this career to work with the children and my aim was to do something good with them and I hope I was of some use."[395] For Noreen Fischbuch, who worked at schools in Ontario and Alberta in the 1950s and 1960s, the residential schools offered much-needed experience: "As far as I was concerned, it was a teaching job, it was with the kids and I liked the kids.... The kids were getting an education; I had a job."[396] George Takashima, who taught at Sioux Lookout, explained, "I was just sort of adventuresome, you might say."[397]

Almost all the staff members were poorly paid. Government officials took the position that because many of the staff members belonged to missionary organizations, pay was a "minor consideration."[398] As a result, the schools had problems recruiting and keeping staff. Alexander Sutherland of the Methodist Church was particularly outspoken about the link between low wages and the difficulties the schools had in recruiting staff. In 1887, he wrote to the minister of Indian Affairs about the "difficulty of obtaining efficient and properly qualified teachers, on account of the meagre salaries paid."[399] The issue of low pay never went away. More than half a century later, in 1948, C.H. Birdsall, the chair of the United Church committee responsible for the Edmonton school, complained that it "is impossible for the Residential School to offer salaries in competition with" rates that Indian Affairs was paying teachers at day schools. Given the inadequate quality of accommodation, equipment, and staff at the school, he felt that it was "doubtful the present work with Indian Children could properly

be called education."[400] Many of the Catholic schools survived on
what amounted to volunteer labour. In 1948, Sechelt principal H.F.
Dunlop informed Ottawa, "If this school kept out of the red during the past year it was largely due to the fact that four Oblates,
working here full time, received in salaries from Jan 1947 to Jan
1948 the grand total of $1800."[401] As late as 1960, the nuns at the
Christie Island school were being paid $50 a month—a fact that
made Principal A. Noonan "feel like a heel."[402]

Many qualified and experienced people worked in the
schools. Miss Asson, the matron at the Kitamaat school in 1930,
was a graduate of the Ensworth Deaconess Hospital in St. Joseph,
Missouri. She had also trained as a deaconess in Toronto, and
worked in China from 1909 to 1927.[403] The matron at the Anglican Wabasca, Alberta, school in 1933 was a nurse.[404] Among the
staff at the Norway House school in the early twentieth century
were the sisters Charlotte Amelia and Lilian Yeomans. Charlotte
had trained as a nurse, and Lilian was one of the first women in
Canada to qualify as a doctor.[405] Theresa Reid had four years of
teaching experience and a teaching certificate before she applied to
work at Norway House,[406] George Takashima had a teaching certificate,[407] and Olive Saunders had a university degree and several
years of teaching experience.[408] In 1966, E.O. Drouin, the principal
of the Roman Catholic school in Cardston, boasted that out of the
twenty-one people on his staff, ten had university degrees. Drouin,
himself, had left his position as a university professor to go to work
at the school.[409]

A number of people devoted their adult lives to working in
residential schools. At least twelve principals died in office.[410]
Kuper Island principal George Donckele resigned in January 1907;
by June of that year, he was dead.[411] Sherman Shepherd served at
the Anglican schools in Shingle Point on the Arctic Ocean in the
Yukon, Aklavik (Northwest Territories), Fort George (Québec),
and Moose Factory (Ontario), resigning in 1954 after twenty-five
years of service in northern Canada.[412] Others worked into their
old age, since, due to low pay, their savings were also low and

pensions were minimal. When the seventy-three-year-old matron of the Ahousaht school in British Columbia retired in 1929, Principal W.M. Wood recommended that she be given an honorarium of a month's salary as appreciation for her years of service. Woods noted that she was "retiring with very limited means."[413]

Such long service was not the norm. Because the pay was often low and the working and living conditions were difficult, turnover was high throughout the system's history. From 1882 to 1894, there was what amounted to an annual full turnover of teachers at the Fort Simpson (now Port Simpson), British Columbia, school. At one point, all the teaching was being done by the local Methodist missionary Thomas Crosby, his wife, Emma, and the school matron.[414] Between January 1958 and March 1960, a period of just over two years, the Alert Bay school lost fifty-eight staff members. Of these, nineteen had been fired because they were deemed to be incompetent. Eight others left because they were angry with the principal.[415] In 1958, the Benedictine Sisters announced that their order would no longer be providing the Christie, British Columbia, school with staff from its monastery in Mount Angel, Oregon. According to the prioress of the Benedictine monastery, Mother Mary Gemma, meeting residential school needs had left the members of the order physically and mentally exhausted. "One of my youngest teachers had to have shock treatments this year and two others may have to." In the previous two and a half years, the order had lost fourteen teachers.[416] These examples are confirmed by the overall statistics. The average annual turnover rate for all Indian Affairs schools from 1956–57 to 1963–64 was 25 percent.[417]

The schools were heavily dependent on female labour. The Roman Catholics relied on female religious orders to staff and operate the residential schools.[418] The Protestants were equally reliant upon the underpaid work of female staff. Austin McKitrick, the principal of the Presbyterian school at Shoal Lake in northwestern Ontario, acknowledged this when he wrote in 1901, "I think if we men were to put ourselves in the places of some overworked, tired-out women, we would perhaps not stand it so patiently as they often do."[419] One missionary wrote that, knowing what he did about what was expected of female missionaries, he would discourage any daughter of his from working for the Methodist Women's Missionary Society.[420]

Although women usually worked in subordinate roles, the 1906 Indian Affairs annual report listed eleven female principals. All worked at boarding schools, as opposed to industrial schools. Seven of them were Roman Catholic, two were Anglican, one was Methodist, and one was Presbyterian.[421] One of these principals was Kate Gillespie. After teaching at day schools on reserves near Kamsack and Prince Albert, she was appointed principal of the File Hills school in 1901, a position she held until her marriage in 1908.[422]

The schools employed many more people than principals and teachers. Most schools were mini-communities. There were cooks, seamstresses, housekeepers, matrons, disciplinarians, farmers, carpenters, blacksmiths, engineers (to operate the heating and electrical generators), shoemakers, and even bandmasters.[423] Smaller schools such as the United Church Crosby Girls' Home in Port Simpson, British Columbia, made do with a staff of only three people in 1935.[424] The Roman Catholic school at Kamloops, British Columbia, had at least nineteen staff in that same year.[425] The Prince Albert, Saskatchewan, residence had over fifty employees during the 1966–67 school year.[426]

Workloads were heavy, and time off was rare. The seven-day week was the norm for many employees. An 1896 report on the Mount Elgin school noted, "No holidays are given or allowed to the staff; all days or parts of days lost time are deducted from their wages."[427] The policy at the Anglican schools into the 1920s was to allow "one full day off duty each month."[428] Indian agent F.J.C. Ball predicted that a sixty-three-year-old employee of the Lytton school was headed for a nervous breakdown in 1922. According to Ball, the man was "acting as teacher, minister, janitor and general handy man around the School. He also has charge of the boys [sic] dormitory at night."[429]

Staff meals were generally superior to those provided to the students. Staff members, particularly in the early years of the system, had greater immunity than their students to many of the diseases that plagued residential schools. Despite this, the living conditions that prevailed in many schools took a toll on staff. In 1896, E.B. Glass, the principal of the Whitefish Lake school in what is now Alberta, said the deterioration in the health of one staff member was the result of having to work in an inadequately heated and poorly insulated schoolhouse in which the "cold wind whistled up through the floor." Glass said that "the Department which charges itself with building, repairing and furnishing school houses, should also charge itself with neglect and the suffering endured by the teacher from that neglect."[430]

Disease and illness also claimed the children of married staff members. Emma Crosby, who helped found the Crosby Girls' Home in Port Simpson in the late 1870s, buried four of her children at Port Simpson. Two of them had succumbed to diphtheria.[431] Elizabeth Matheson, the wife of the Onion Lake principal, lost a daughter to whooping cough and a son to meningeal croup in the early years of the twentieth century.[432] During her fourth pregnancy, Elizabeth Matheson was so depressed that she considered suicide.[433]

Missionary staff, particularly in the early years of the system, were extremely hostile to Aboriginal culture.[434] They commonly described Aboriginal people as "lazy."[435] The long-time principal of the Shubenacadie school in Nova Scotia, J.P. Mackey, was expressing these views in the 1930s. In one letter, he described Aboriginal people as natural liars. "For myself, I never hope to catch up with the Indian and his lies, and in fact I am not going to try."[436] Others, however, spoke out on behalf of Aboriginal people. Hugh McKay, the superintendent of Presbyterian missionary work among Aboriginal people, criticized the federal government for failing to implement its Treaty promises and for failing to alleviate the hunger crisis on the Prairies.[437] Similarly, William Duncan, the Anglican missionary at Metlakatla, British Columbia, advised the Tsimshian on how to advance arguments in favour of Aboriginal title.[438]

Sometimes, staff protested the way students were treated. When two staff members of the Prince Albert, Saskatchewan, school resigned in 1952, they complained of the harsh disciplinary regime at the school.[439] In 1957, Helen Clafton, an ex-dormitory supervisor, wrote of how, at the Lytton, British Columbia, school, "the 'strap' is altogether too much in evidence."[440]

Aboriginal people also worked for the schools. The Mohawk Institute hired former student Isaac Barefoot to work as a teacher in 1869. Barefoot went on to serve as acting principal and was later ordained as an Anglican minister.[441] Another former student, Susan Hardie, obtained her teaching certificate in 1886.[442] She was the school governess as early as 1894, and was paid $200 a year.[443] She retired at the beginning of the 1936–37 school year.[444] A young Oneida woman, Miss Cornelius, taught at the Regina school in the early twentieth century.[445] She left the following year, lured away to a better paying school in the United States.[446] In the early 1930s, the Brandon school hired former student Lulu Ironstar as a teacher.[447] But these were exceptions, not the rule. As late as 1960, there were only twenty-three First Nations teachers working in residential schools across the country. Nineteen taught academic subjects and the other four taught home economics and industrial arts.[448] Stan McKay, who was educated at the Birtle and Brandon residential schools, taught in the Norway House, Manitoba, school in the 1960s. Although there was much that he enjoyed about the work, he left after two years. In his opinion, the education he was being forced to provide was not relevant to the lives of the children. There was, for example, a heavy emphasis on English, and no recognition of the role of Cree in the communities from which the children came. "They were doomed to fail under the system that existed. The majority of them would certainly and did."[449]

Verna Kirkness, who was raised on the Fisher River First Nation in Manitoba, taught at both the Birtle and Norway House schools.[450] She did not like the atmosphere at the Birtle school,

where, she felt, administrators discouraged students from spending additional time with her. In her memoir, she wrote that she
"wondered if they were afraid the children would tell me things
about their lives away from the classroom."[451]

It was in the 1960s that a number of Aboriginal people were
promoted to the position of school principal. Ahab Spence, a
former residential school student, was appointed principal of the
Sioux Lookout school in 1963.[452] Under Spence's administration,
the school had a staff of twenty-three, half of whom were Aboriginal.[453] Colin Wasacase became the principal of the Presbyterian
school in Kenora in 1966.[454] In keeping with past practice, his wife
was made school matron.[455] This trend continued into the 1970s,
when Aboriginal people were appointed to administrative positions at numerous residential schools, including those in Mission
and Kamloops, British Columbia; Blue Quills, Alberta; Prince Albert, Duck Lake, and Qu'Appelle, Saskatchewan; and Fort George,
Québec.[456] Although the total number of schools declined rapidly
from 1969 onwards, they became a significant source of Aboriginal employment, particularly in Saskatchewan, where six schools
were operated by First Nations educational authorities. Of the 360
people working in the Saskatchewan schools in 1994, 220 were of
Aboriginal ancestry—almost two-thirds of the total.[457]

Most of the Aboriginal people who were hired by the schools
worked as cooks, cleaners, and handymen. In 1954, Mrs. Clair, a
Cree woman who had attended the school at Lac La Ronge, Saskatchewan, was working at the Carcross school in the Yukon. She
was described by a superintendent as a "very fine person, willing
worker and everyone likes her. Can certainly get the most out of
the children."[458] At the Wabasca, Alberta, school, Alphonse Alook
was seen as being "a tower of strength to the Principal especially of
late. Can do fair carpentering and is loyal to the school. Principal
recommends an increase in his salary."[459] Four young Aboriginal
women, three of whom were sisters, had been hired to work at the
Fort George, Québec, school in 1953.[460] A 1956 report on three of
them said, "The Herodier girls are all doing a fine job." They were

not, however, being housed in the same way as non-Aboriginal staff. The report observed that it was fortunate that "the native girls do not mind doubling up in cramped quarters otherwise staff accommodation would be insufficient."[461]

A number of former Aboriginal staff members felt they helped make an important difference in the lives of the students. Jeanne Rioux went to the Edmonton school and later worked as a supervisor at the Hobbema school in Alberta. There, she challenged staff about the way they disciplined children.[462] Mary Chapman was a former residential school student who later worked in the kitchen of the Kuper Island school. At her prompting, the school began serving students and staff the same meals. It was her rule that "if we run out of roast, the kids run out of roast, I don't give them bologna, I take the roast from the staff and I give it to them."[463] Vitaline Elsie Jenner, who had unhappily attended the Fort Chipewyan, Alberta, residential school, worked as a girls' supervisor at Breynat Hall, the Roman Catholic residence at Fort Smith, Northwest Territories. To her surprise, she enjoyed most of the experience. She recalled being asked by one staff person what sort of games she thought the children would like to play to make them feel at home. "I said, 'You know I bet you they all want to be hugged, like I was in that residential school. 'Cause you know what? They're away from their parents.'"[464]

Former staff and the children of former staff members have expressed the view that much of the discussion of the history of residential schools has overlooked both the positive intent with which many staff members approached their work, and the positive accomplishments of the school system. Although they certainly believed the system was underfunded, they also believed that they and their parents devoted much of their lives to educating and caring for Aboriginal children.

Most of the staff members did not make a career in residential schools, spending only a year or two at a school before moving on. Others stayed for many years in conditions that were often very different from what they grew up with, working for low pay, and living in cramped and confined quarters with, at times, less than congenial colleagues. They spent their time teaching, cooking, cleaning, farming, and supervising children. On their own, these can be seen as positive, not negative, activities. For the most part, the school staff members were not responsible for the policies that separated children from their parents and lodged them in inadequate and underfunded facilities. In fact, many staff members spent much of their time and energy attempting to humanize a harsh and often destructive system. Along with the children's own resilience, such staff members share credit for any positive results of the schools.

AGREEMENT AND APOLOGIES

During the years in which the federal government was slowly closing the residential school system, Aboriginal people across the country were establishing effective regional and national organizations. In the courts and the legislatures, they argued for the recognition of Aboriginal rights, particularly the right to self-government. They forced the government to withdraw its 1969 White Paper that aimed at terminating Aboriginal rights, they placed the settling of land claims on the national agenda, ensured that Aboriginal rights were entrenched in the Constitution, and saw the creation of a new jurisdiction within Canada—the territory of Nunavut—with an Inuit majority population. These developments were part of a global movement asserting the rights of Indigenous peoples. Canadian Aboriginal leaders played a key role in this movement. For example, they were central in the creation of the World Council of Indigenous Peoples in 1975.[465] The work of the council laid the groundwork for the 2007 *United Nations Declaration on the Rights of Indigenous Peoples.*[466]

From the 1960s onwards, many people within the churches began to re-evaluate both the broader history of the relations between the churches and Aboriginal peoples, and the specific history of the residential schools. Many church organizations

provided support to Aboriginal campaigns on such issues as
land and Treaty rights. In the 1980s, the churches began to issue
apologies to Aboriginal people. One of the first of these, issued in
1986 by the United Church of Canada, focused on the destructive
impact that church missionary work had on Aboriginal culture.[467]
The Oblate order offered an apology in 1991 that referred to the
residential schools.[468] Apologies relating specifically to their roles
in operating residential schools were issued by the Anglicans in
1993, the Presbyterians in 1994, and the United Church in 1998.[469]

Aboriginal people also began both individually and collectively to push for the prosecution of individuals who had abused
students at residential schools and for compensation for former
students. In 1987, Nora Bernard, a former student of the Shubenacadie residential school, began interviewing fellow Survivors
in the kitchen of her home in Truro, Nova Scotia.[470] In 1995, she
formed the Shubenacadie Indian Residential School Survivors
Association and started registering Survivors. The work of former
students from the schools in places as distant as Fort Albany,
Ontario; Chesterfield Inlet, then in the Northwest Territories;
and Williams Lake, British Columbia, led to several police investigations, and a limited number of prosecutions and convictions.
They also led to the creation of local and national organizations
of former residential school students. Phil Fontaine, then Grand
Chief of the Assembly of Manitoba Chiefs, placed the issue on the
national agenda in October 1990 when he spoke publicly about the
abuse that he and his fellow students had experienced at the Fort
Alexander school.[471]

Former students also filed lawsuits against the federal government and the churches over the treatment that they received in
the schools. Although they were successful in a number of these
cases, courts were not willing to provide compensation for some
issues of importance to Aboriginal peoples, such as the loss of language and culture. By October 2001, more than 8,500 residential
school Survivors had filed lawsuits against the federal government,
the churches, related organizations, and, where possible, the

individual who committed the abuse.[472] By 2005, it was estimated
that the volume surpassed 18,000 lawsuits.[473] Former students also
commenced class-action lawsuits for compensation. Although
lower courts rejected their right to pursue such claims, in 2004, the
Ontario Court of Appeal ruled that one of these cases (known as
the "Cloud case") should be allowed to proceed.[474] Within months,
the federal government agreed to enter into a process intended to
negotiate a settlement to the growing number of class-action suits.
The Indian Residential Schools Settlement Agreement (IRSSA)
was reached in 2006 and approved by the courts in the following
year. The IRSSA has five main components: 1) a Common Experience Payment; 2) an Independent Assessment Process; 3) support
for the Aboriginal Health Foundation; 4) support for residential
school commemoration; and 5) the establishment of a Truth and
Reconciliation Commission of Canada. Through the Common
Experience Payment, former students would receive a payment of
$10,000 for the first year that they attended a residential school,
and an additional $3,000 for each additional year or partial year of
attendance. The Independent Assessment Process adjudicated and
compensated the claims of those students who were physically or
sexually abused at the schools. Funding was also provided to the
Aboriginal Healing Foundation to support initiatives addressing
the residential school legacy. The Settlement Agreement committed the federal government to funding initiatives to commemorate
the residential school experience. The Truth and Reconciliation
Commission of Canada was mandated to tell Canadians about the
history of residential schools and the impact those schools had on
Aboriginal peoples, and to guide a process of reconciliation.

The court approval of the IRSSA in 2007 was followed in June
2008 with Prime Minister Stephen Harper's apology on behalf of
Canada. In his statement, the prime minister recognized that the
primary purpose of the schools had been to remove children from
their homes and families in order to assimilate them better into
the dominant culture. Harper said, "These objectives were based
on the assumption Aboriginal cultures and spiritual beliefs were

inferior and unequal. Indeed, some sought, as it was infamously said, 'to kill the Indian in the child.' Today, we recognize that this policy of assimilation was wrong, has caused great harm, and has no place in our country."[475]

The prime minister was joined by the leaders of the other parties represented in the Canadian House of Commons. The Liberal leader of the opposition, the Honourable Stéphane Dion, recognized that the government's policy had "destroyed the fabric of family in First Nations, Métis and Inuit communities. Parents and children were made to feel worthless. Parents and grandparents were given no choice. Their children were stolen from them."[476] The Bloc Québecois leader, the Honourable Gilles Duceppe, asked Canadians to "picture a small village, a small community. Now picture all of its children, gone. No more children between seven and sixteen playing in the lanes or the woods, filling the hearts of their elders with their laughter and joy."[477] The New Democratic Party leader, the Honourable Jack Layton, called on Canadians to help

> reverse the horrific and shameful statistics afflicting Aboriginal populations, now: the high rates of poverty, suicide, the poor or having no education, overcrowding, crumbling housing, and unsafe drinking water. Let us make sure that all survivors of the residential schools receive the recognition and compensation that is due to them.[478]

In his response, Phil Fontaine, then National Chief of the Assembly of First Nations, said the apology marked a new dawn in the relationship between Aboriginal people and the rest of Canada. He also called attention to the "brave survivors," who, by "the telling of their painful stories, have stripped white supremacy of its authority and legitimacy. The irresistibility of speaking truth to power is real."[479] National Chief of the Congress of Aboriginal Peoples Patrick Brazeau spoke of how the resiliency, courage, and strength of residential school Survivors had inspired all Aboriginal people.[480] Mary Simon, President of the Inuit Tapiriit Kanatami, said, in tackling the hard work that remained to be done, "Let us now join forces with the common goal of working together to ensure that this apology opens the door to a new chapter in our lives as aboriginal peoples and in our place in Canada."[481] Clem Chartier, President of the Métis National Council, noted that he had attended a residential school, and pointed out that many issues regarding the relationship between Métis people and residential schools still were not resolved. He said, "I also feel deeply conflicted, because there is still misunderstanding about the situation of the Métis Nation, our history and our contemporary situation."[482] Beverley Jacobs, President of the Native Women's Association of Canada, spoke of how Aboriginal communities were recovering their traditions. "Now we have our language still, we have our ceremonies, we have our elders, and we have to revitalize those ceremonies and the respect for our people not only within Canadian society but even within our own peoples."[483]

The Settlement Agreement and the formal apology by Prime Minister Stephen Harper represent the culmination of years of political struggle, changes in societal attitudes, court decisions, and negotiation. Through it all, the Survivors kept the issue alive.

These events do not bring the residential school story to an end. The legacy of the schools remains. One can see the impact of a system that disrupted families in the high number of Aboriginal children who have been removed from their families by child-welfare agencies. An educational system that degraded Aboriginal culture and subjected students to humiliating discipline must bear a portion of responsibility for the current gap between the educational success of Aboriginal and non-Aboriginal Canadians. The health of generations of Aboriginal children was undermined by inadequate diets, poor sanitation, overcrowded conditions, and a failure to address the tuberculosis crisis that was ravaging the country's Aboriginal community. There should be little wonder that Aboriginal health status remains far below that of the general population. The over-incarceration and over-victimization of Aboriginal people also have links to a system that subjected Aboriginal children to punitive discipline and exposed them to physical and sexual abuse.

The history of residential schools presented in this report commenced by placing the schools in the broader history of the global European colonization of Indigenous peoples and their lands. Residential schooling was only a part of the colonization of Aboriginal people. The policy of colonization suppressed Aboriginal culture and languages, disrupted Aboriginal government, destroyed Aboriginal economies, and confined Aboriginal people to marginal and often unproductive land. When that policy resulted in hunger, disease, and poverty, the federal government failed to meet its obligations to Aboriginal people. That policy was dedicated to eliminating Aboriginal peoples as distinct political and cultural entities and must be described for what it was: a policy of cultural genocide.

Despite being subjected to aggressive assimilation policies for nearly 200 years, Aboriginal people have maintained their identity and their communities. They continue to assert their rights to self-governance. In this, they are not alone. Like the Settlement Agreement in Canada, the *United Nations Declaration on the Rights of Indigenous Peoples* is a milestone in a global campaign to recognize and respect the rights of Indigenous peoples. It is time to abandon the colonial policies of the past, to address the legacy of the schools, and to engage in a process of reconciliation with the Aboriginal people of Canada.

CHAPTER THREE

THE LEGACY

The closing of the schools did not bring the residential school story to an end. Their legacy continues to this day. It is reflected in the significant disparities in education, income, and health between Aboriginal people and other Canadians—disparities that condemn many Aboriginal people to shorter, poorer, and more troubled lives. The legacy is also reflected in the intense racism and the systemic discrimination Aboriginal people regularly experience in this country. More than a century of cultural genocide has left most Aboriginal languages on the verge of extinction. The disproportionate apprehension of Aboriginal children by child-welfare agencies and the disproportionate imprisonment and victimization of Aboriginal people are all part of the legacy of the way that Aboriginal children were treated in residential schools.

Many students were permanently damaged by residential schools. Separated from their parents, they grew up knowing neither respect nor affection. A school system that mocked and suppressed their families' cultures and traditions destroyed their sense of self-worth and attachment to their own families. Poorly trained teachers working with an irrelevant curriculum left them feeling branded as failures. Children who had been bullied and physically or sexually abused carried a burden of shame and anger for the rest of their lives. Overwhelmed by this legacy, many succumbed to despair and depression. Countless lives were lost to alcohol and drugs.[1] Families were destroyed, and generations of children have been lost to child welfare.

The Survivors are not the only ones whose lives have been disrupted and scarred by the residential schools. The legacy has also profoundly affected the Survivors' partners, their children, their grandchildren, their extended families, and their communities. Children who were abused in the schools sometimes went on to abuse others. Some students developed addictions as a means of coping. Students who were treated and punished as prisoners in the schools sometimes graduated to real prisons.

The Commission recognizes that these impacts cannot be attributed solely to residential schooling. But they are clearly attributable to the Aboriginal policies of the federal government over the last 150 years. Residential schooling, which sought to remake each new generation of Aboriginal children, was both central to, and emblematic of, those policies. The beliefs and attitudes that were used to justify the establishment of residential schools are not things of the past: they continue to animate official Aboriginal policy today. Reconciliation will require more than apologies for the shortcomings of those who preceded us. It obliges us to recognize the ways in which the legacy of residential schools continues to disfigure Canadian life and to abandon policies and approaches that currently serve to extend that hurtful legacy.

CHILD WELFARE

The federal government and the churches believed that Aboriginal parenting, language, and culture were harmful to Aboriginal children. Consequently, a central objective of the residential schools was to separate Aboriginal children from their parents and communities, in order to "civilize" and Christianize them. For generations, children were cut off from their families. The schools were in many ways more a child-welfare system than an educational one. A survey in 1953 suggested that of 10,112 students then in residential schools, 4,313 were either orphans or from what were described as "broken homes."[2] From the 1940s onwards, residential schools increasingly served as orphanages and child-welfare facilities. By 1960, the federal government estimated that 50 percent of the children in residential schools were there for child-welfare reasons.[3]

The schools were intended to sever the link between Aboriginal children and parents. They did this only too well. Family connections were permanently broken. Children exposed to strict and regimented discipline in the schools sometimes found it difficult to become loving parents. Genine Paul-Dimitracopoulos's mother was placed in the Shubenacadie residential school in Nova Scotia at a very early age. She told the Commission that knowing this helped her understand "how we grew up because my mom never really showed us love when we were kids coming up. She, when I was hurt or cried, she was never there to console you or to hug you. If I hurt myself she would never give me a hug and tell me it would be okay. I didn't understand why."[4] Alma Scott of Winnipeg told the Commission that as "a direct result of those residential schools, I was a dysfunctional mother.... I spent years of my life stuck in a bottle, in an addiction where I didn't want to feel any emotions, and so I numbed out with drugs and with alcohol.... That's how I raised my children, that's what my children saw, and that's what I saw."[5]

Old Crow Chief Norma Kassi spoke a powerful truth when she told the TRC's Northern National Event in Inuvik in 2011, "The doors are closed at the residential schools but the foster homes are still existing and our children are still being taken away."[6] The closing of the residential schools, starting in the 1960s, was accompanied by the commencement of what has come to be known as the "Sixties Scoop"—the wide-scale apprehension of Aboriginal children by child-welfare authorities.

Child-welfare agencies across Canada removed thousands of Aboriginal children from their families and communities and placed them in non-Aboriginal homes with little consideration of the need to preserve their culture and identity. Children were placed in homes in different parts of the country, in the United

States, and even overseas. This practice actually extended well beyond the 1960s, until at least the mid- to late 1980s.[7] By 1980, 4.6 percent of all First Nations children were in care; the comparable figure for the general population was 0.96 percent.[8] There has been little improvement since then: a 2011 Statistics Canada study found that 14,225 or 3.6 percent of all First Nations children aged fourteen and under were in foster care, compared with 15,345 or 0.3 percent of non-Aboriginal children.[9] The detrimental effects of the residential school experience, combined with prejudicial attitudes towards Aboriginal parenting skills and a tendency to see Aboriginal poverty as a symptom of neglect, contributed to these grossly disproportionate rates of child apprehension among Aboriginal people.

As was the case 100 years ago, Aboriginal children are being separated from their families and communities and placed in the care of agencies. Like the schools, Aboriginal child-welfare agencies are underfunded, and placements are often culturally inappropriate and, tragically, simply unsafe. The child-welfare system is the residential school system of our day.

EDUCATION

The residential school system failed as an educational system. Those who administered the system and many of its teachers assumed that Aboriginal children were unfit for anything more than a rudimentary elementary or vocational education. The staff handbook for the Presbyterian school in Kenora in the 1940s, for example, concluded that upon leaving the school, most students would "return to the Indian Reserves from which they had come." Only "a very small proportion of our total enrolment" was expected to go on to high school. Given this future, staff members were advised that "the best preparation we can give them is to teach them the Christian way of life."[10] The focus on elementary-level schooling and religious training amounted to a self-fulfilling prophecy. Most students left residential schools unprepared either to succeed in the market economy or to pursue more traditional activities such as hunting and fishing.

One of the most far-reaching and devastating legacies of residential schools has been their impact on the educational and economic success of Aboriginal people. The lack of role models and mentors, insufficient funds for the schools, inadequate teachers, and unsuitable curricula taught in a foreign language contributed to dismal success rates. The Commission has heard many examples of students who attended residential school for eight or more years, but who left with nothing more than Grade Three achievement, and sometimes without even the ability to read. According to Indian Affairs annual reports, into the early 1960s, only half of each year's enrolment got to Grade Six.[11]

Poor educational achievement has led to the chronic unemployment or underemployment, poverty, poor housing, substance abuse, family violence, and ill health that many former students of the schools have suffered as adults.

Governmental failure to meet the educational needs of Aboriginal children continues to the present day. Government funding is both inadequate and inequitably distributed. Educational achievement rates continue to be poor. Although secondary school graduation rates for all Aboriginal people have improved since the closure of the schools, considerable differences remain in comparison with the non-Aboriginal population. For example, according to the 2011 census, 29 percent of working-age Aboriginal people had not graduated from high school, compared with only 12 percent of their non-Aboriginal counterparts.[12]

Lower educational attainment for the children of Survivors has severely limited their employment and earning potential, just as it did for their parents. Aboriginal people have lower median after-tax income, are more likely to experience unemployment, and are more likely to collect employment insurance and social assistance benefits.[13] These statistics are true for all Aboriginal groups. For example, the unemployment rate for those living on reserves was 60 percent in 2006.[14] In 2009, the Métis unemployment rate for persons aged twenty-five to fifty-four was 9.4 percent, while the non-Aboriginal rate was 7.0 percent.[15] In 2006, the Inuit unemployment rate was 19 percent.[16]

Aboriginal people also have income well below their non-Aboriginal counterparts. The median income for Aboriginal people in 2006 was 30 percent lower than the median income for non-Aboriginal workers.[17] The gap narrows when Aboriginal people obtain a university degree—which they do at a far lower rate.[18] The rate of poverty for Aboriginal children is also very high—40 percent, compared with 17 percent for all children in Canada.[19] The income gap is pervasive: non-Aboriginal Canadians earn more than Aboriginal workers no matter whether they work on reserves or off reserves, or in urban, rural, or remote locations.[20] The poverty and attendant social problems that plague many Aboriginal communities can be traced back to the inadequacies of the residential schools. Overcoming this legacy will require an Aboriginal education system that meets the needs of Aboriginal students and respects Aboriginal parents, families, and cultures.

LANGUAGE AND CULTURE

In a study of the impact of residential schools, the Assembly of First Nations noted in 1994 that

> language is necessary to define and maintain a world view. For this reason, some First Nation elders to this day will say that knowing or learning the native language is basic to any deep understanding of a First Nation way of life, to being a First Nation person. For them, a First Nation world is quite simply not possible without its own language. For them, the impact of residential school silencing their language is equivalent to a residential school silencing their world.[21]

Residential schools were a systematic, government-sponsored attempt to destroy Aboriginal cultures and languages and to assimilate Aboriginal peoples so that they no longer existed as distinct peoples. English—and, to a lesser degree, French—were the only languages of instruction allowed in most residential schools.

Students were punished—often severely—for speaking their own languages. Michael Sillett, a former student at the North West River residential school in Newfoundland and Labrador, told the Commission, "Children at the dorm were not allowed to speak their mother tongue. I remember several times when other children were slapped or had their mouths washed out for speaking their mother tongue; whether it was Inuktitut or Innuaimun. Residents were admonished for just being Native."[22] As late as the 1970s, students at schools in northwestern Ontario were not allowed to speak their language if they were in the presence of a staff member who could not understand that language.[23] Conrad Burns, whose father attended the Prince Albert school, named this policy for what it was: "It was a cultural genocide. People were beaten for their language, people were beaten because ... they followed their own ways."[24]

By belittling Aboriginal culture, the schools drove a wedge between children and their parents. Mary Courchene recalled that in the 1940s at the Fort Alexander school in Manitoba she was taught that "my people were no good. This is what we were told every day: 'You savage. Your ancestors are no good. What did they do when they, your, your, your people, your ancestors you know what they used to do? They used to go and they, they would worship trees and they would, they would worship the animals.'"

She became so ashamed of being Aboriginal that when she went home one summer and looked at her parents, she concluded that she hated them:

> I just absolutely hated my own parents. Not because I thought they abandoned me; I hated their brown faces. I hated them because they were Indians; they were Indian. And here I was, you know coming from. So I, I looked at my dad and I challenged him and he, and I said, "From now on we speak only English in this house."

Her father's eyes filled with tears. Then he looked at her mother and said, in Ojibway, "I guess we'll never speak to this little girl again. Don't know her."[25] In other cases, on the basis of their residential school experiences, parents decided to speak only English in front of their children.[26]

The damage affected future generations, as former students found themselves unable or unwilling to teach their own children Aboriginal languages and cultural ways. As a result, many of the almost ninety surviving Aboriginal languages in Canada are under serious threat of disappearing. The United Nations Educational, Scientific and Cultural Organization (UNESCO) states that 70 percent of Canada's Aboriginal languages are endangered.[27] In the 2011 census, 14.5 percent of the Aboriginal population reported that their first language learned was an Aboriginal language.[28] In the previous 2006 census, 18 percent of those who identified as Aboriginal had reported an Aboriginal language as their first language learned, and a decade earlier, in the 1996 census, the figure was 26 percent. There are, however, variations among Aboriginal peoples. Nearly two-thirds of Inuit speak their Indigenous language, compared to 22.4 percent of First Nations people and only 2.5 percent of Métis people.[29] If the preservation of Aboriginal languages does not become a priority for both governments and Aboriginal communities, then what the residential schools failed to accomplish will come about through a process of systematic neglect.

HEALTH

Residential schools endangered the health and well-being of the children who attended them. Many students succumbed to infectious disease, particularly tuberculosis, at rates far in excess of non-Aboriginal children.[30] Children who had been poorly fed and raised in the unsanitary conditions that characterized most residential schools were susceptible to a myriad of health problems as adults. Many would later succumb to tuberculosis that they contracted in the schools.[31]

Sexual and physical abuse, as well as separation from families and communities, caused lasting trauma for many other students. Katherine Copenace, who attended the Roman Catholic school in Kenora, told the Commission about her struggles: "When I got older, I had thoughts of suicide, inflicting pain on myself which I did. I used to slash my arms, pierce my arms, my body and I destroyed myself with alcohol which the government introduced of course."[32]

In many cases, former students could find no alternatives to self destruction.[33] The effects of this trauma were often passed on to the children of residential school Survivors and sometimes to their grandchildren.

When reporting on First Nations health in 1905, Indian Affairs Chief Medical Officer Dr. Peter Bryce wrote that "the death-rate is wholly abnormal, amounting to, on an average, 34–70 per 1,000."[34] One hundred and ten years later, there continue to be troubling gaps in health outcomes between Aboriginal and non-Aboriginal Canadians. For example:

- The infant mortality rates for First Nations and Inuit children range from 1.7 to over 4 times the non-Aboriginal rate.[35]

- From 2004 to 2008, the "age-specific mortality rate" at ages one to nineteen in the Inuit homelands was 188.0 deaths per 100,000 person-years at risk, compared with only 35.3 deaths per 100,000 in the rest of Canada.[36]

- First Nations people aged forty-five and over have nearly twice the rate of diabetes as compared with the non-Aboriginal population.[37]

- First Nations people were six times more likely than the general population to suffer alcohol-related deaths, and more than three times more likely to suffer drug-induced deaths.[38]

The overall suicide rate among First Nation communities is about twice that of the total Canadian population. For Inuit, the rate is still higher: six to eleven times the rate for the general population. Aboriginal youth between the ages of ten and twenty-nine who are living on reserves are five to six times more likely to die by suicide than non-Aboriginal youth.[39]

Health disparities of such magnitude have social roots. They are stark evidence of federal policies that separated Aboriginal people from their traditional lands and livelihoods, confining them to cramped and inadequate housing on reserves that lacked the basic sanitary services. It was from these communities that residential schools recruited students, and it was to them that the students returned with their health further weakened.

JUSTICE

Residential schools inflicted profound injustices on Aboriginal people. Aboriginal parents were forced, often under pressure from the police, to give up their children to the schools. Children were taken far from their communities to live in frightening custodial institutions, which felt like prisons. The children who attended residential schools were often treated as if they were offenders, and yet they were the ones at risk of being physically and sexually abused.

The Canadian legal system failed to provide justice to Survivors who were abused. When, in the late 1980s, that system eventually did begin to respond to the abuse, it did so inadequately and in a way that often revictimized the Survivors. The Commission has been able to identify fewer than fifty convictions stemming from abuse at residential schools. This is a small fraction of the more than 38,000 claims of sexual and serious physical abuse that were submitted to the independent adjudication process that was established to assess and compensate residential school abuse claims.[40]

In many ways, the residential school experience lies at the root of the over-incarceration of Aboriginal people, which continues to this day. For Daniel Andre, the road from Grollier Hall in Inuvik in the Northwest Territories led, inevitably, to jail:

I knew that I needed help to get rid of what happened to me in
residential school. Like, everywhere I went, everything I did, all
the jobs I had, all the towns I lived in, all the people I met, always
brought me back to, to being in residential school, and being
humiliated, and beaten, and ridiculed, and told I was a piece of
garbage, I was not good enough, I was, like, a dog.... So, one of the
scariest things for me being in jail is being humiliated in front of
everybody, being made, laughed at, and which they do often 'cause
they're just, like, that's just the way they are. And a lot of them are,
like, survival of the fittest. And, like, if you show weakness, they'll,
they'll just pick on you even more and ... I had to, to survive. I
had to be strong enough to survive. I had to, I had to build up a
system where I became a jerk. I became a bad person. I became an
asshole. But I survived, and learnt all those things to survive.[41]

Andre's story was far too common. Traumatized by their
school experiences, many former students succumbed to addictions, and found themselves among the disproportionate number
of Aboriginal people who have come into conflict with the law.

Once Aboriginal persons are arrested, prosecuted, and convicted, they are more likely to be sentenced to prison than non-Aboriginal people. This overrepresentation is growing. In 1995–96, Aboriginal people made up 16 percent of all those sentenced to custody.
By 2011–12, that number had grown to 28 percent of all admissions
to sentenced custody, even though Aboriginal people make up only
4 percent of the Canadian adult population.[42] The over-incarceration
of women is even more disproportionate: in 2011–12, 43 percent of
admissions of women to sentenced custody were Aboriginal.[43] Aboriginal girls make up 49 percent of the youth admitted to custody,
and Aboriginal boys are 36 percent of those admitted to custody.[44]

There is another link between the substance abuse that
has plagued many residential school Survivors and the over-
incarceration of Aboriginal people. Studies from Canada and the
United States suggest that 15 percent to 20 percent of prisoners
have fetal alcohol spectrum disorder (FASD).[45] This is a permanent

brain injury caused when a woman's consumption of alcohol during pregnancy affects her fetus. The disabilities associated with FASD include memory impairments, problems with judgment and abstract reasoning, and poor adaptive functioning.[46] A recent Canadian study found that offenders with FASD had much higher rates of criminal involvement than those without FASD, including more juvenile and adult convictions.[47] Diagnosing FASD can be a long and costly process, and the lack of a confirmed diagnosis can result in the unjust imprisonment of Aboriginal people who are living with a disability. In this way, the traumas of residential school are quite literally passed down from one generation to another.[48]

As well as being more likely to be involved as offenders with the justice system, Aboriginal people are 58 percent more likely than non-Aboriginal people to be the victims of crime.[49] Aboriginal women report being victimized by violent crime at a rate almost three times higher than non-Aboriginal women—13 percent of Aboriginal women reported being victimized by violent crime in 2009.[50] The most disturbing aspect of this victimization is the extraordinary number of Aboriginal women and girls who have been murdered or are reported as missing. A 2014 Royal Canadian Mounted Police report found that between 1980 and 2012, 1,017 Aboriginal women and girls were killed and 164 were missing. Of these, 225 cases remain unsolved.[51]

Canada has acknowledged some aspects of the ongoing legacy and harms of residential schools. The Supreme Court has recognized that the legacy of residential schools should be considered when sentencing Aboriginal offenders. Although these have been important measures, they have not been sufficient to address the grossly disproportionate imprisonment of Aboriginal people, which continues to grow, in part because of a lack of adequate funding and support for culturally appropriate alternatives to imprisonment. There has been an increase in Aboriginal child-welfare agencies, but the disproportionate apprehension of Aboriginal children also continues to grow, in part because of a lack of adequate funding for culturally appropriate supports that would allow children to remain safely within their own families.

Many of the individual and collective harms have not yet been redressed, even after the negotiated out-of-court settlement of the residential school litigation in 2006, and Canada's apology in 2008. In fact, some of the damages done by residential schools to Aboriginal families, languages, education, and health may be perpetuated and even worsened as a result of current government policies. New policies may be based on a lack of understanding of Aboriginal people, similar to that which motivated the schools initially. For example, child-welfare and health policies may fail to take into account the importance of community in raising children. We must learn from the failure of the schools, to ensure that the mistakes of the past are not repeated in the future.

Understanding and redressing the legacy of residential schools will benefit all Canadians. Governments in Canada spend billions of dollars each year in responding to the symptoms of the intergenerational trauma of residential schools. Much of this money is spent on crisis interventions related to child welfare, family violence, ill health, and crime. Despite genuine reform efforts, the dramatic overrepresentation of Aboriginal children in foster care, and among the sick, the injured, and the imprisoned, continues to grow. The Commission is convinced that genuine reconciliation will not be possible until the broad legacy of the schools is both understood and addressed.

CHAPTER FOUR

RECONCILIATION

To some people, "reconciliation" is the re-establishment of a conciliatory state. However, this is a state that many Aboriginal people assert never has existed between Aboriginal and non-Aboriginal people. To others, "reconciliation," in the context of Indian residential schools, is similar to dealing with a situation of family violence. It is about coming to terms with events of the past in a manner that overcomes conflict and establishes a respectful and healthy relationship among people, going forward. It is in the latter context that the Truth and Reconciliation Commission of Canada has approached the question of reconciliation.

To the Commission, "reconciliation" is about establishing and maintaining a mutually respectful relationship between Aboriginal and non-Aboriginal peoples in this country. In order for that to happen, there has to be awareness of the past, acknowledgement of the harm that has been inflicted, atonement for the causes, and action to change behaviour.

We are not there yet. The relationship between Aboriginal and non-Aboriginal peoples is not a mutually respectful one. But, we believe we can get there, and we believe we can maintain it. Our ambition is to show how we can do that.

In 1996, the *Report of the Royal Commission on Aboriginal Peoples* urged Canadians to begin a national process of reconciliation that would have set the country on a bold new path, fundamentally changing the very foundations of Canada's relationship with Aboriginal peoples. Much of what the Royal Commission had to say has been ignored by government; a majority of its recommendations were never implemented. But the report and its findings opened people's eyes and changed the conversation about the reality for Aboriginal people in this country.

In 2015, as the Truth and Reconciliation Commission of Canada wraps up its work, the country has a rare second chance to seize a lost opportunity for reconciliation. We live in a twenty-first-century global world. At stake is Canada's place as a prosperous, just, and inclusive democracy within that global world. At the TRC's first National Event in Winnipeg, Manitoba, in 2010, residential school Survivor Alma Mann Scott said,

> The healing is happening—the reconciliation.... I feel that there's some hope for us not just as Canadians, but for the world, because I know I'm not the only one. I know that Anishinaabe people across Canada, First Nations, are not the only ones. My brothers and sisters in New Zealand, Australia, Ireland—there's different areas of the world where this type of stuff happened.... I don't see it happening in a year, but we can start making changes to laws and to education systems ... so that we can move forward.[1]

Reconciliation must support Aboriginal peoples as they heal from the destructive legacies of colonization that have wreaked such havoc in their lives. But it must do even more. Reconciliation must inspire Aboriginal and non-Aboriginal peoples to transform Canadian society so that our children and grandchildren can live together in dignity, peace, and prosperity on these lands we now share.

The urgent need for reconciliation runs deep in Canada. Expanding public dialogue and action on reconciliation beyond residential schools will be critical in the coming years. Although some progress has been made, significant barriers to reconciliation remain. The relationship between the federal government and Aboriginal peoples is deteriorating. Instead of moving towards reconciliation, there have been divisive conflicts over Aboriginal education, child welfare, and justice. The daily news has been filled with reports of controversial issues ranging from the call for a national inquiry on violence towards Aboriginal women and girls to the impact of the economic development of lands and resources on Treaties and Aboriginal title and rights.[2] The courts continue to hear Aboriginal rights cases, and new litigation has been filed by Survivors of day schools not covered under the Indian Residential Schools Settlement Agreement, as well as by victims of the "Sixties Scoop."[3] The promise of reconciliation, which seemed so imminent back in 2008 when the prime minister, on behalf of all Canadians, apologized to Survivors, has faded.

Too many Canadians know little or nothing about the deep historical roots of these conflicts. This lack of historical knowledge has serious consequences for First Nations, Inuit, and Métis peoples, and for Canada as a whole. In government circles, it makes for poor public policy decisions. In the public realm, it reinforces racist attitudes and fuels civic distrust between Aboriginal peoples and other Canadians.[4] Too many Canadians still do not know the history of Aboriginal peoples' contributions to Canada, or understand that by virtue of the historical and modern Treaties negotiated by our government, we are all Treaty people. History plays an important role in reconciliation; to build for the future, Canadians must look to, and learn from, the past.

As Commissioners, we understood from the start that although reconciliation could not be achieved during the TRC's lifetime, the country could and must take ongoing positive and concrete steps forward. Although the Commission has been a catalyst for deepening our national awareness of the meaning and potential of reconciliation, it will take many heads, hands, and hearts, working together, at all levels of society to maintain momentum in the years ahead. It will also take sustained political will at all levels of government and concerted material resources.

The thousands of Survivors who publicly shared their residential school experiences at TRC events in every region of this country have launched a much-needed dialogue about what is necessary to heal themselves, their families, communities, and the nation. Canadians have much to benefit from listening to the voices, experiences, and wisdom of Survivors, Elders, and Traditional Knowledge Keepers—and much more to learn about reconciliation. Aboriginal peoples have an important contribution to make to reconciliation. Their knowledge systems, oral histories, laws, and connections to the land have vitally informed the reconciliation process to date, and are essential to its ongoing progress.

At a Traditional Knowledge Keepers Forum sponsored by the TRC, Anishinaabe Elder Mary Deleary spoke about the responsibility for reconciliation that both Aboriginal and non-Aboriginal people carry. She emphasized that the work of reconciliation must continue in ways that honour the ancestors, respect the land, and rebalance relationships. She said,

> I'm so filled with belief and hope because when I hear your voices
> at the table, I hear and know that the responsibilities that our
> ancestors carried ... are still being carried ... even through all of
> the struggles, even through all of what has been disrupted ... we
> can still hear the voice of the land. We can hear the care and love
> for the children. We can hear about our law. We can hear about
> our stories, our governance, our feasts, [and] our medicines.... We
> have work to do. That work we are [already] doing as [Aboriginal]
> peoples. Our relatives who have come from across the water
> [non-Aboriginal people], you still have work to do on your road....
> The land is made up of the dust of our ancestors' bones. And so
> to reconcile with this land and everything that has happened,
> there is much work to be done ... in order to create balance.[5]

At the Victoria Regional Event in 2012, Survivor Archie Little said,

> [For] me reconciliation is righting a wrong. And how do we do
> that? All these people in this room, a lot of non-Aboriginals, a
> lot of Aboriginals that probably didn't go to residential school;
> we need to work together.... My mother had a high standing
> in our cultural ways. We lost that. It was taken away.... And

I think it's time for you non-Aboriginals ... to go to your
politicians and tell them that we have to take responsibility for what happened. We have to work together.[6]

The Reverend Stan McKay of the United Church, who is also a
Survivor, believes that reconciliation can happen only when everyone
accepts responsibility for healing in ways that foster respect. He said,

[There must be] a change in perspective about the way in which
Aboriginal peoples would be engaged with Canadian society
in the quest for reconciliation.... [We cannot] perpetuate the
paternalistic concept that only Aboriginal peoples are in need of
healing.... The perpetrators are wounded and marked by history in
ways that are different from the victims, but both groups require
healing.... How can a conversation about reconciliation take place
if all involved do not adopt an attitude of humility and respect?
... We all have stories to tell and in order to grow in tolerance
and understanding we must listen to the stories of others.[7]

Over the past five years, the Truth and Reconciliation Commission of Canada urged Canadians not to wait until its final report was issued before contributing to the reconciliation process.
We have been encouraged to see that across the country, many
people have been answering that call.

The youth of this country are taking up the challenge of reconciliation. Aboriginal and non-Aboriginal youth who attended TRC
National Events made powerful statements about why reconciliation matters to them. At the Alberta National Event in Edmonton
in March 2014, an Indigenous youth spoke on behalf of a national
Indigenous and non-Indigenous collaboration known as the "4Rs
Youth Movement." Jessica Bolduc said,

We have re-examined our thoughts and beliefs around colonialism, and have made a commitment to unpack our own baggage,
and to enter into a new relationship with each other, using
this momentum, to move our country forward, in light of the
150th anniversary of the Confederation of Canada in 2017.

At this point in time, we ask ourselves, "What does that anniversary mean for us, as Indigenous youth and non-Indigenous youth, and how do we arrive at that day with something we can celebrate together?"... Our hope is that, one day, we will live together, as recognized nations, within a country we can all be proud of.[8]

In 2013, at the British Columbia National Event in Vancouver, where over 5,000 elementary and secondary school students attended Education Day, several non-Aboriginal youth talked about what they had learned. Matthew Meneses said, "I'll never forget this day. This is the first day they ever told us about residential schools. If I were to see someone who's Aboriginal, I'd ask them if they can speak their language because I think speaking their language is a pretty cool thing." Antonio Jordao said, "It makes me sad for those kids. They took them away from their homes—it was torture, it's not fair. They took them away from their homes. I don't agree with that. It's really wrong. That's one of the worst things that Canada did." Cassidy Morris said, "It's good that we're finally learning about what happened." Jacqulyn Byers told us, "I hope that events like this are able to bring closure to the horrible things that happened, and that a whole lot of people now recognize that the crime happened and that we need to make amends for it."[9]

At the same National Event, TRC Honorary Witness Patsy George paid tribute to the strength of Aboriginal women and their contributions to the reconciliation process despite the oppression and violence they have experienced. She said,

> Women have always been a beacon of hope for me. Mothers and grandmothers in the lives of our children, and in the survival of our communities, must be recognized and supported. The justified rage we all feel and share today must be turned into instruments of transformation of our hearts and our souls, clearing the ground for respect, love, honesty, humility, wisdom, and truth. We owe it to all those who suffered, and we owe it to the children of today and tomorrow. May this day and the days ahead bring us peace and justice.[10]

Aboriginal and non-Aboriginal Canadians from all walks of life spoke to us about the importance of reaching out to one another in ways that create hope for a better future. Whether one is First Nations, Inuit, Métis, a descendant of European settlers, a member of a minority group that suffered historical discrimination in Canada, or a new Canadian, we all inherit both the benefits and obligations of Canada. We are all Treaty people who share responsibility for taking action on reconciliation.

Without truth, justice, and healing, there can be no genuine reconciliation. Reconciliation is not about "closing a sad chapter of Canada's past," but about opening new healing pathways of reconciliation that are forged in truth and justice. We are mindful that knowing the truth about what happened in residential schools in and of itself does not necessarily lead to reconciliation. Yet, the importance of truth telling in its own right should not be underestimated; it restores the human dignity of victims of violence and calls governments and citizens to account. Without truth, justice is not served, healing cannot happen, and there can be no genuine reconciliation between Aboriginal and non-Aboriginal peoples in Canada. Speaking to us at the Traditional Knowledge Keepers Forum in June of 2014, Elder Dave Courchene posed a critical question: "When you talk about truth, whose truth are you talking about?"[11]

The Commission's answer to Elder Courchene's question is that by *truth*, we mean not only the truth revealed in government and church residential school documents, but also the truth of lived experiences as told to us by Survivors and others in their statements to this Commission. Together, these public testimonies constitute a new oral history record, one based on Indigenous legal traditions and the practice of witnessing.[12] As people gathered at various TRC National Events and Community Hearings, they shared experiences of truth telling and offered expressions of reconciliation.

Over the course of its work, the Commission inducted a growing circle of TRC Honorary Witnesses. Their role has been to bear official witness to the testimonies of Survivors and their families, former school staff and their descendants, government and church officials, and any others whose lives have been affected by the residential schools. Beyond the work of the TRC, the Honorary Witnesses have pledged their commitment to the ongoing work of reconciliation between Aboriginal and non-Aboriginal peoples. We also encouraged everyone who attended TRC National Events or Community Hearings to see themselves as witnesses, with an obligation to find ways of making reconciliation a concrete reality in their own lives, communities, schools, and workplaces.

As Elder Jim Dumont explained at the Traditional Knowledge Keepers Forum in June 2014, "in Ojibwe thinking, to speak the truth is to actually speak from the heart."[13] At the Community Hearing in Key First Nation, Saskatchewan, in 2012, Survivor Wilfred Whitehawk told us he was glad that he disclosed his abuse:

> I don't regret it because it taught me something. It taught me to talk about truth, about me, to be honest about who I am.... I am very proud of who I am today. It took me a long time, but I'm there. And what I have, my values and belief systems are mine and no one is going to impose theirs on me. And no one today is going to take advantage of me, man or woman, the government or the RCMP, because I have a voice today. I can speak for me and no one can take that away.[14]

Survivor and the child of Survivors Vitaline Elsie Jenner said, "I'm quite happy to be able to share my story.... I want the people of Canada to hear, to listen, for it is the truth.... I also want my grandchildren to learn, to learn from me that, yes, it did happen."[15]

Another descendant of Survivors, Daniel Elliot, told the Commission,

> I think all Canadians need to stop and take a look and not look away. Yeah, it's embarrassing, yeah, it's an ugly part of our history. We don't want to know about it. What I want to see from the Commission is to rewrite the history books so that other generations will understand and not go through the same thing that we're going through now, like it never happened.[16]

President of the Métis National Council Clement Chartier
spoke to the Commission about the importance of truth to justice
and reconciliation. At the Saskatchewan National Event, he said,

> The truth is important. So I'll try to address the truth and a
> bit of reconciliation as well. The truth is that the Métis Nation,
> represented by the Métis National Council, is not a party to the
> Indian Residential Schools Settlement Agreement.... And the truth
> is that the exclusion of the Métis Nation or the Métis as a people
> is reflected throughout this whole period not only in the Indian
> Residential Schools Settlement Agreement but in the apology
> made by Canada as well....
>
> We are, however, the products ... of the same assimilationist
> policy that the federal government foisted upon the Treaty Indian
> kids. So there ought to be some solution.... The Métis boarding
> schools, residential schools, are excluded. And we need to ensure
> that everyone was aware of that and hopefully some point down the
> road, you will help advocate and get, you know, the governments or
> whoever is responsible to accept responsibility and to move forward
> on a path to reconciliation, because reconciliation should be for
> all Aboriginal peoples and not only some Aboriginal peoples.[17]

At the British Columbia National Event, the former lieutenant-
governor of British Columbia, the Honourable Steven Point, said,

> And so many of you have said today, so many of the witnesses that
> came forward said, "I cannot forgive. I'm not ready to forgive." And
> I wondered why. Reconciliation is about hearing the truth, that's for
> sure. It's also about acknowledging that truth. Acknowledging that
> what you've said is true. Accepting responsibility for your pain and
> putting those children back in the place they would have been, had
> they not been taken from their homes....
>
> What are the blockages to reconciliation? The continuing
> poverty in our communities and the failure of our government
> to recognize that, "Yes, we own the land." Stop the destruc-
> tion of our territories and for God's sake, stop the deaths of

so many of our women on highways across this country....
I'm going to continue to talk about reconciliation, but just as
important, I'm going to foster healing in our own people, so
that our children can avoid this pain, can avoid this destruction
and finally take our rightful place in this "Our Canada."[18]

When former residential school staff attended public TRC
events, some thought it was most important to hear directly from
Survivors, even if their own perspectives and memories of the
schools might differ from those of the Survivors. At a Community
Hearing in Thunder Bay, Ontario, Merle Nisley, who worked at the
Poplar Hill residential school in the early 1970s, said,

> I think it would be valuable for people who have been involved in
> the schools to hear stories personally. And I also think it would be
> valuable, when it's appropriate ... [for] former students who are on
> the healing path to ... hear some of our stories, or to hear some of our
> perspectives. But I know that's a very difficult thing to do.... Certainly
> this is not the time to try to ask all those former students to sit and
> listen to the rationale of the former staff because there's just too much
> emotion there ... and there's too little trust ... you can't do things like
> that when there's low levels of trust. So I think really a very important
> thing is for former staff to hear the stories and to be courageous
> enough just to hear them.... Where wrongs were done, where abuses
> happened, where punishment was over the top, and wherever sexual
> abuse happened, somehow we need to courageously sit and talk
> about that, and apologize. I don't know how that will happen.[19]

Nisley's reflections highlight one of the difficulties the Commission faced in trying to create a space for respectful dialogue between
former residential school students and staff. While, in most cases,
this was possible, in other instances, Survivors and their family
members found it very difficult to listen to former staff, particularly
if they perceived the speaker to be an apologist for the schools.

At the TRC Victoria Regional Event, Brother Tom Cavanaugh,
the district superior of the Oblates of Mary Immaculate for British

Columbia and the Yukon, spoke about his time as a supervisor at
the Christie residential school:

> What I experienced over the six years I was at Christie
> residential school was a staff, Native and non-Native alike,
> working together to provide as much as possible, a safe loving
> environment for the children attending Christie school. Was
> it a perfect situation? No, it wasn't a perfect situation ... but
> again, there didn't seem to be, at that time, any other viable
> alternative in providing a good education for so many children
> who lived in relatively small and isolated communities.

Survivors and family members who were present in the audience spoke out, saying, "Truth, tell the truth." Brother Cavanaugh
replied, "If you give me a chance, I will tell you the truth." When
TRC Chair Justice Murray Sinclair intervened to ask the audience
to allow Brother Cavanaugh to finish his statement, he was able
to do so without further interruption. Visibly shaken, Cavanaugh
then went on to acknowledge that children had also been abused
in the schools, and he condemned such actions, expressing his sor-
row and regret for this breach of trust:

> I can honestly say that our men are hurting too because of the abuse
> scandal and the rift that this has created between First Nations and
> church representatives. Many of our men who are still working
> with First Nations have attended various truth and reconciliation
> sessions as well as Returning to Spirit sessions, hoping to bring
> about healing for all concerned. The Oblates desire healing for
> the abused and for all touched by the past breach of trust. It is our
> hope that together we can continue to build a better society.[20]

Later that same day, Ina Seitcher, who attended the Christie
residential school, painted a very different picture of the school
from what Brother Cavanaugh had described:

> I went to Christie residential school. This morning I heard a priest
> talking about his Christie residential school. I want to tell him

[about] my Christie residential school. I went there for ten months.
Ten months that impacted my life for fifty years. I am just now on
my healing journey.... I need to do this, I need to speak out. I need to
speak for my mom and dad who went to residential school, for my
aunts, my uncles, all that are beyond now.... All the pain of our people, the hurt, the anger.... That priest that talked about how loving
that Christie residential school was—it was not. That priest was most
likely in his office not knowing what was going on down in the dorms
or in the lunchroom.... There were things that happened at Christie
residential school, and like I said, I'm just starting my healing journey. There are doors that I don't even want to open. I don't even want
to open those doors because I don't know what it would do to me.[21]

These two, seemingly irreconcilable, truths are a stark reminder
that there are no easy shortcuts to reconciliation. The fact that there
were few direct exchanges at TRC events between Survivors and
former school staff indicates that, for many, the time for reconciliation had not yet arrived. Indeed, for some, it may never arrive. At
the Manitoba National Event in 2010, Survivor Evelyn Brockwood
talked about why it is important to ensure that there is adequate time
for healing to occur in the truth and reconciliation process. She said,

When this came out at the beginning, I believe it was
1990, about residential schools, people coming out with
their stories, and ... I thought the term, the words they
were using, were truth, healing and reconciliation. But
somehow it seems like we are going from truth telling to
reconciliation, to reconcile with our white brothers and
sisters. My brothers and sisters, we have a lot of work to do
in the middle. We should really lift up the word healing....
Go slow, we are going too fast, too fast.... We have many tears
to shed before we even get to the word reconciliation.[22]

To determine the truth and to tell the full and complete story
of residential schools in this country, the TRC needed to hear from
Survivors and their families, former staff, government and church

officials, and all those affected by residential schools. Canada's national history in the future must be based on the truth about what happened in the residential schools. One hundred years from now, our children's children and their children must know and still remember this history, because they will inherit from us the responsibility of ensuring that it never happens again.

WHAT IS RECONCILIATION?

During the course of the Commission's work, it has become clear that the concept of reconciliation means different things to different people, communities, institutions, and organizations. The TRC mandate describes "reconciliation" as

> an ongoing individual and collective process, and will require commitment from all those affected including First Nations, Inuit and Métis former Indian Residential School (IRS) students, their families, communities, religious entities, former school employees, government and the people of Canada. Reconciliation may occur between any of the above groups.[23]

The Commission defines "reconciliation" as an ongoing process of establishing and maintaining respectful relationships. A critical part of this process involves repairing damaged trust by making apologies, providing individual and collective reparations, and following through with concrete actions that demonstrate real societal change. Establishing respectful relationships also requires the revitalization of Indigenous law and legal traditions. It is important that all Canadians understand how traditional First Nations, Inuit, and Métis approaches to resolving conflict, repairing harm, and restoring relationships can inform the reconciliation process.

Traditional Knowledge Keepers and Elders have long dealt with conflicts and harms using spiritual ceremonies and peacemaking practices, and by retelling oral history stories that reveal how their ancestors restored harmony to families and communities. These traditions and practices are the foundation of

Indigenous law; they contain wisdom and practical guidance for moving towards reconciliation across this land.[24]

As First Nations, Inuit, and Métis communities access and revitalize their spirituality, cultures, languages, laws, and governance systems, and as non-Aboriginal Canadians increasingly come to understand Indigenous history within Canada, and to recognize and respect Indigenous approaches to establishing and maintaining respectful relationships, Canadians can work together to forge a new covenant of reconciliation.

Despite the ravages of colonialism, every Indigenous nation across the country, each with its own distinctive culture and language, has kept its legal traditions and peacemaking practices alive in its communities. Although Elders and Knowledge Keepers across the land have told us that there is no specific word for "reconciliation" in their own languages, there are many words, stories, and songs, as well as sacred objects such as wampum belts, peace pipes, eagle down, cedar boughs, drums, and regalia, that are used to establish relationships, repair conflicts, restore harmony, and make peace. The ceremonies and protocols of Indigenous law are still remembered and practised in many Aboriginal communities.

At the TRC Traditional Knowledge Keepers Forum in June 2014, TRC Survivor Committee member and Elder Barney Williams told us that

> from sea to sea, we hear words that allude to ... what is reconciliation? What does healing or forgiveness mean? And how there's parallels to all those words that the Creator gave to all the nations.... When I listen and reflect on the voices of the ancestors, your ancestors, I hear my ancestor alluding to the same thing with a different dialect.... My understanding [of reconciliation] comes from a place and time when there was no English spoken ... from my grandmother who was born in the 1800s.... I really feel privileged to have been chosen by my grandmother to be the keeper of our knowledge.... What do we need to do? ... We need to go back to ceremony and embrace ceremony as part of moving forward. We need to understand the laws of our people.[25]

At the same Forum, Elder Stephen Augustine explained the roles of silence and negotiation in Mi'kmaq law. He said "silence" is a concept, and can be used as a consequence for a wrong action or to teach a lesson. Silence is employed according to proper procedures, and ends at a particular time too. Elder Augustine suggested that there is both a place for talking about reconciliation and a need for quiet reflection. Reconciliation cannot occur without listening, contemplation, meditation, and deeper internal deliberation. Silence in the face of residential school harms is an appropriate response for many Indigenous peoples. We must enlarge the space for respectful silence in journeying towards reconciliation, particularly for Survivors who regard this as key to healing. There is also a place for discussion and negotiation for those who want to move beyond silence. Dialogue and mutual adjustment are significant components of Mi'kmaq law. Elder Augustine suggested that other dimensions of human experience—our relationships with the earth and all living beings—are also relevant in working towards reconciliation. This profound insight is an Indigenous law that could be applied more generally.[26]

Elder Reg Crowshoe told the Commission that Indigenous peoples' worldviews, oral history traditions, and practices have much to teach us about how to establish respectful relationships among peoples and with the land and all living things. Learning how to live together in a good way happens through sharing stories and practising reconciliation in our everyday lives:

> When we talk about the concept of reconciliation, I think about some of the stories that I've heard in our culture and stories are important.... These stories are so important as theories but at the same time stories are important to oral cultures. So when we talk about stories, we talk about defining our environment and how we look at authorities that come from the land and how that land, when we talk about our relationship with the land, how we look at forgiveness and reconciliation is so important when we look at it historically.

We have stories in our culture about our superheroes, how
we treat each other, stories about how animals and plants give us
authorities and privileges to use plants as healing, but we also have
stories about practices. How would we practise reconciliation? How
would we practise getting together to talk about reconciliation
in an oral perspective? And those practices are so important.[27]

As Elder Crowshoe explained further, reconciliation requires
talking, but our conversations must be broader than Canada's
conventional approaches. Reconciliation between Aboriginal and
non-Aboriginal Canadians, from an Aboriginal perspective, also
requires reconciliation with the natural world. If human beings
resolve problems between themselves but continue to destroy the
natural world, then reconciliation remains incomplete. This is a
perspective that we as Commissioners have repeatedly heard: that
reconciliation will never occur unless we are also reconciled with
the earth. Mi'kmaq and other Indigenous laws stress that humans
must journey through life in conversation and negotiation with all
creation. Reciprocity and mutual respect help sustain our survival.
It is this kind of healing and survival that is needed in moving
forward from the residential school experience.

Over the course of its work, the Commission created space for
exploring the meanings and concepts of reconciliation. In public
Sharing Circles at National Events and Community Hearings, we
bore witness to powerful moments of truth sharing and humbling
acts of reconciliation. Many Survivors had never been able to tell
their own families the whole truth of what happened to them in the
schools. At hearings in Regina, Saskatchewan, Elder Kirby Littletent
said, "I never told, I just told my children, my grandchildren I went
to boarding school, that's all. I never shared my experiences."[28]

Many spoke to honour the memory of relatives who have
passed on. Simone, an Inuk Survivor from Chesterfield Inlet,
Nunavut, said,

I'm here for my parents—"Did you miss me when I went away?"
"Did you cry for me?"—and I'm here for my brother, who was a

victim, and my niece at the age of five who suffered a head injury
and never came home, and her parents never had closure. To this
day, they have not found the grave in Winnipeg. And I'm here
for them first, and that's why I'm making a public statement.[29]

Others talked about the importance of reconciling with family members, and cautioned that this process is just beginning.
Patrick Etherington, a Survivor from St. Anne's residential school
in Fort Albany, Ontario, walked with his son and others from Cochrane, Ontario, to the National Event in Winnipeg. He said that
the walk helped him to reconnect with his son, and that he "just
wanted to be here because I feel this process that we are starting,
we got a long ways to go."[30]

We saw the children and grandchildren of Survivors who,
in searching for their own identity and place in the world, found
compassion and gained new respect for their relatives who went to
the schools, once they heard about and began to understand their
experiences. At the Northern National Event in Inuvik, Northwest
Territories, Maxine Lacorne said,

> As a youth, a young lady, I talk with people my age because I have
> a good understanding. I talk to people who are residential school
> Survivors because I like to hear their stories, you know, and it gives
> me more understanding of my parents.... It is an honour to be here,
> to sit here among you guys, Survivors. Wow. You guys are strong
> people, you guys survived everything. And we're still going to be
> here. They tried to take us away. They tried to take our language
> away. You guys are still here, we're still here. I'm still here.[31]

We heard about children whose small acts of everyday resistance in the face of rampant abuse, neglect, and bullying in the
schools were quite simply heroic. At the TRC British Columbia National Event, Elder Barney Williams said that "many of us, through
our pain and suffering, managed to hold our heads up ... we were
brave children."[32] We saw old bonds of childhood friendship renewed
as people gathered and found each other at TRC-sponsored events.

Together, they remembered the horrors they had endured even as they recalled with pride long-forgotten accomplishments in various school sports teams, music, or art activities. We heard from resilient, courageous Survivors who, despite their traumatic childhood experiences, went on to become influential leaders in their communities and in all walks of Canadian life, including politics, government, law, education, medicine, the corporate world, and the arts.

We heard from officials representing the federal government that administered the schools. In a Sharing Circle at the Manitoba National Event, the Honourable Chuck Strahl (then minister of Indian Affairs and Northern Development Canada) said,

> Governments like to write ... policy, and they like to write
> legislation, and they like to codify things and so on. And
> Aboriginal people want to talk about restoration, reconciliation,
> forgiveness, about healing ... about truth. And those things
> are all things of the heart and of relationship, and not of
> government policy. Governments do a bad job of that.[33]

Church representatives spoke about their struggles to right the relationship with Aboriginal peoples. In Inuvik, Anglican Archbishop Fred Hiltz told us that

> as a church, we are renewing our commitment to work
> with the Assembly of First Nations in addressing long-
> standing, Indigenous justice issues. As a church, we are
> requiring anyone who serves the church at a national
> level to go through anti-racism training.... We have a lot to do
> in our church to make sure that racism is eliminated.[34]

Educators told us about their growing awareness of the inadequate role that post-secondary institutions played in training the teachers who taught in the schools. They have pledged to change educational practices and curriculum to be more inclusive of Aboriginal knowledge and history. Artists shared their ideas and feelings about truth and reconciliation through songs, paintings, dance, film, and other media. Corporations provided resources to bring Survivors to events, and, in some cases, some of their own staff and managers.

For non-Aboriginal Canadians who came to bear witness to Survivors' life stories, the experience was powerful. One woman said simply, "By listening to your story, my story can change. By listening to your story, I can change."[35]

RECONCILIATION AS RELATIONSHIP

In its 2012 *Interim Report*, the TRC recommended that federal, provincial, and territorial governments, and all parties to the Settlement Agreement, undertake to meet and explore the *United Nations Declaration on the Rights of Indigenous Peoples* as a framework for reconciliation in Canada. We remain convinced that the *United Nations Declaration* provides the necessary principles, norms, and standards for reconciliation to flourish in twenty-first-century Canada.

A reconciliation framework is one in which Canada's political and legal systems, educational and religious institutions, the corporate sector and civil society function in ways that are consistent with the *United Nations Declaration on the Rights of Indigenous Peoples*, which Canada has endorsed. The Commission believes that the following guiding principles of truth and reconciliation will assist Canadians moving forward:

1) The *United Nations Declaration on the Rights of Indigenous Peoples* is the framework for reconciliation at all levels and across all sectors of Canadian society.

2) First Nations, Inuit, and Métis peoples, as the original peoples of this country and as self-determining peoples, have Treaty, constitutional, and human rights that must be recognized and respected.

3) Reconciliation is a process of healing of relationships that requires public truth sharing, apology, and commemoration that acknowledge and redress past harms.

4) Reconciliation requires constructive action on addressing the ongoing legacies of colonialism that have had destructive impacts on Aboriginal peoples' education, cultures and languages, health, child welfare, the administration of justice, and economic opportunities and prosperity.

5) Reconciliation must create a more equitable and inclusive society by closing the gaps in social, health, and economic outcomes that exist between Aboriginal and non-Aboriginal Canadians.

6) All Canadians, as Treaty peoples, share responsibility for establishing and maintaining mutually respectful relationships.

7) The perspectives and understandings of Aboriginal Elders and Traditional Knowledge Keepers of the ethics, concepts, and practices of reconciliation are vital to long-term reconciliation.

8) Supporting Aboriginal peoples' cultural revitalization and integrating Indigenous knowledge systems, oral histories, laws, protocols, and connections to the land into the reconciliation process are essential.

9) Reconciliation requires political will, joint leadership, trust building, accountability, and transparency, as well as a substantial investment of resources.

10) Reconciliation requires sustained public education and dialogue, including youth engagement, about the history and legacy of residential schools, Treaties, and Aboriginal rights, as well as the historical and contemporary contributions of Aboriginal peoples to Canadian society.

Together, Canadians must do more than just *talk* about reconciliation; we must learn how to *practise* reconciliation in our everyday lives—within ourselves and our families, and in our communities, governments, places of worship, schools, and workplaces. To do so constructively, Canadians must remain committed to the ongoing work of establishing and maintaining respectful relationships.

For many Survivors and their families, this commitment is foremost about healing themselves, their communities, and nations, in ways that revitalize individuals as well as Indigenous cultures, languages, spirituality, laws, and governance systems. For governments, building a respectful relationship involves dismantling a centuries-old political and bureaucratic culture in which, all too often, policies and programs are still based on failed notions of assimilation. For churches, demonstrating long-term commitment requires atoning for actions within the residential schools, respecting Indigenous spirituality, and supporting Indigenous peoples' struggles for justice and equity. Schools must teach history in ways that foster mutual respect, empathy, and engagement. All Canadian children and youth deserve to know Canada's honest history, including what happened in the residential schools, and to appreciate the rich history and knowledge of Indigenous nations who continue to make such a strong contribution to Canada, including our very name and collective identity as a country. For Canadians from all walks of life, reconciliation offers a new way of living together.

CHAPTER FIVE

CALLS TO ACTION

In order to redress the legacy of residential schools and advance the process of Canadian reconciliation, the Truth and Reconciliation Commission makes the following calls to action:

LEGACY

CHILD WELFARE

1. We call upon the federal, provincial, territorial, and Aboriginal governments to commit to reducing the number of Aboriginal children in care by:

i.   Monitoring and assessing neglect investigations.

ii. Providing adequate resources to enable Aboriginal communities and child-welfare organizations to keep Aboriginal families together where it is safe to do so, and to keep children in culturally appropriate environments, regardless of where they reside.

iii. Ensuring that social workers and others who conduct child-welfare investigations are properly educated and trained about the history and impacts of residential schools.

iv. Ensuring that social workers and others who conduct child-welfare investigations are properly educated and trained

about the potential for Aboriginal communities and families
to provide more appropriate solutions to family healing.

v.   Requiring that all child-welfare decision makers
     consider the impact of the residential school
     experience on children and their caregivers.

2. We call upon the federal government, in collaboration with the
provinces and territories, to prepare and publish annual reports
on the number of Aboriginal children (First Nations, Inuit, and
Métis) who are in care, compared with non-Aboriginal children,
as well as the reasons for apprehension, the total spending on
preventive and care services by child-welfare agencies, and the
effectiveness of various interventions.

3. We call upon all levels of government to fully implement
Jordan's Principle.

4. We call upon the federal government to enact Aboriginal
child-welfare legislation that establishes national standards for
Aboriginal child apprehension and custody cases and includes
principles that:

i.   Affirm the right of Aboriginal governments to establish
      and maintain their own child-welfare agencies.

ii.   Require all child-welfare agencies and courts
      to take the residential school legacy into
      account in their decision-making.

iii. Establish, as an important priority, a requirement that
      placements of Aboriginal children into temporary
      and permanent care be culturally appropriate.

5. We call upon the federal, provincial, territorial, and
Aboriginal governments to develop culturally appropriate
parenting programs for Aboriginal families.

EDUCATION

6. We call upon the Government of Canada to repeal Section 43 of the *Criminal Code of Canada*.

7. We call upon the federal government to develop with Aboriginal groups a joint strategy to eliminate educational and employment gaps between Aboriginal and non-Aboriginal Canadians.

8. We call upon the federal government to eliminate the discrepancy in federal education funding for First Nations children being educated on reserves and those First Nations children being educated off reserves.

9. We call upon the federal government to prepare and publish annual reports comparing funding for the education of First Nations children on and off reserves, as well as educational and income attainments of Aboriginal peoples in Canada compared with non-Aboriginal people.

10. We call on the federal government to draft new Aboriginal education legislation with the full participation and informed consent of Aboriginal peoples. The new legislation would include a commitment to sufficient funding and would incorporate the following principles:

i. Providing sufficient funding to close identified educational achievement gaps within one generation.

ii. Improving education attainment levels and success rates.

iii. Developing culturally appropriate curricula.

iv. Protecting the right to Aboriginal languages, including the teaching of Aboriginal languages as credit courses.

v. Enabling parental and community responsibility, control, and accountability, similar to what parents enjoy in public school systems.

vi. Enabling parents to fully participate in the education of their children.

vii. Respecting and honouring Treaty relationships.

11. We call upon the federal government to provide adequate funding to end the backlog of First Nations students seeking a post-secondary education.

12. We call upon the federal, provincial, territorial, and Aboriginal governments to develop culturally appropriate early childhood education programs for Aboriginal families.

LANGUAGE AND CULTURE

13. We call upon the federal government to acknowledge that Aboriginal rights include Aboriginal language rights.

14. We call upon the federal government to enact an Aboriginal Languages Act that incorporates the following principles:

i.　Aboriginal languages are a fundamental and valued element of Canadian culture and society, and there is an urgency to preserve them.

ii.　Aboriginal language rights are reinforced by the Treaties.

iii.　The federal government has a responsibility to provide sufficient funds for Aboriginal-language revitalization and preservation.

iv.　The preservation, revitalization, and strengthening of Aboriginal languages and cultures are best managed by Aboriginal people and communities.

v.　Funding for Aboriginal language initiatives must reflect the diversity of Aboriginal languages.

15. We call upon the federal government to appoint, in consultation with Aboriginal groups, an Aboriginal Languages Commissioner. The commissioner should help promote Aboriginal languages and report on the adequacy of federal funding of Aboriginal-languages initiatives.

16. We call upon post-secondary institutions to create university and college degree and diploma programs in Aboriginal languages.

17. We call upon all levels of government to enable residential school Survivors and their families to reclaim names changed by the residential school system by waiving administrative costs for a period of five years for the name-change process and the revision of official identity documents, such as birth certificates, passports, driver's licenses, health cards, status cards, and social insurance numbers.

HEALTH

18. We call upon the federal, provincial, territorial, and Aboriginal governments to acknowledge that the current state of Aboriginal health in Canada is a direct result of previous Canadian government policies, including residential schools, and to recognize and implement the health-care rights of Aboriginal people as identified in international law, constitutional law, and under the Treaties.

19. We call upon the federal government, in consultation with Aboriginal peoples, to establish measurable goals to identify and close the gaps in health outcomes between Aboriginal and non-Aboriginal communities, and to publish annual progress reports and assess long-term trends. Such efforts would focus on indicators such as: infant mortality, maternal health, suicide, mental health, addictions, life expectancy, birth rates, infant and child health issues, chronic diseases, illness and injury incidence, and the availability of appropriate health services.

20. In order to address the jurisdictional disputes concerning Aboriginal people who do not reside on reserves, we call upon the federal government to recognize, respect, and address the distinct health needs of the Métis, Inuit, and off-reserve Aboriginal peoples.

21. We call upon the federal government to provide sustainable funding for existing and new Aboriginal healing centres to address the physical, mental, emotional, and spiritual harms caused by residential schools, and to ensure that the funding of healing centres in Nunavut and the Northwest Territories is a priority.

22. We call upon those who can effect change within the Canadian health-care system to recognize the value of Aboriginal healing practices and use them in the treatment of Aboriginal patients in collaboration with Aboriginal healers and Elders where requested by Aboriginal patients.

23. We call upon all levels of government to:

i.   Increase the number of Aboriginal professionals working in the health-care field.

ii. Ensure the retention of Aboriginal health-care providers in Aboriginal communities.

iii. Provide cultural competency training for all health- care professionals.

24. We call upon medical and nursing schools in Canada to require all students to take a course dealing with Aboriginal health issues, including the history and legacy of residential schools, the *United Nations Declaration on the Rights of Indigenous Peoples*, Treaties and Aboriginal rights, and Indigenous teachings and practices. This will require skills-based training in intercultural competency, conflict resolution, human rights, and anti-racism.

JUSTICE

25. We call upon the federal government to establish a written policy that reaffirms the independence of the Royal Canadian Mounted Police to investigate crimes in which the government has its own interest as a potential or real party in civil litigation.

26. We call upon the federal, provincial, and territorial governments to review and amend their respective statutes of limitations to ensure that they conform to the principle that governments and other entities cannot rely on limitation defences to defend legal actions of historical abuse brought by Aboriginal people.

27. We call upon the Federation of Law Societies of Canada to ensure that lawyers receive appropriate cultural competency training, which includes the history and legacy of residential schools, the *United Nations Declaration on the Rights of Indigenous Peoples*, Treaties and Aboriginal rights, Indigenous law, and Aboriginal–Crown relations. This will require skills-based training in intercultural competency, conflict resolution, human rights, and anti-racism.

28. We call upon law schools in Canada to require all law students to take a course in Aboriginal people and the law, which includes the history and legacy of residential schools, the *United Nations Declaration on the Rights of Indigenous Peoples*, Treaties and Aboriginal rights, Indigenous law, and Aboriginal–Crown relations. This will require skills-based training in intercultural competency, conflict resolution, human rights, and anti-racism.

29. We call upon the parties and, in particular, the federal government, to work collaboratively with plaintiffs not included in the Indian Residential Schools Settlement Agreement to have disputed legal issues determined expeditiously on an agreed set of facts.

30. We call upon federal, provincial, and territorial governments to commit to eliminating the overrepresentation of Aboriginal people in custody over the next decade, and to issue detailed annual reports that monitor and evaluate progress in doing so.

31. We call upon the federal, provincial, and territorial governments to provide sufficient and stable funding to implement and evaluate community sanctions that will provide realistic alternatives to imprisonment for Aboriginal offenders and respond to the underlying causes of offending.

32. We call upon the federal government to amend the Criminal Code to allow trial judges, upon giving reasons, to depart from mandatory minimum sentences and restrictions on the use of conditional sentences.

33. We call upon the federal, provincial, and territorial governments to recognize as a high priority the need to address and prevent Fetal Alcohol Spectrum Disorder (FASD), and to develop, in collaboration with Aboriginal people, FASD preventive programs that can be delivered in a culturally appropriate manner.

34. We call upon the governments of Canada, the provinces, and territories to undertake reforms to the criminal justice system to better address the needs of offenders with Fetal Alcohol Spectrum Disorder (FASD), including:

i.   Providing increased community resources and powers for courts to ensure that FASD is properly diagnosed, and that appropriate community supports are in place for those with FASD.

ii. Enacting statutory exemptions from mandatory minimum sentences of imprisonment for offenders affected by FASD.

iii. Providing community, correctional, and parole resources to maximize the ability of people with FASD to live in the community.

iv. Adopting appropriate evaluation mechanisms to measure the effectiveness of such programs and ensure community safety.

35. We call upon the federal government to eliminate barriers to the creation of additional Aboriginal healing lodges within the federal correctional system.

36. We call upon the federal, provincial, and territorial governments to work with Aboriginal communities to provide culturally relevant services to inmates on issues such as substance abuse, family and domestic violence, and overcoming the experience of having been sexually abused.

37. We call upon the federal government to provide more supports for Aboriginal programming in halfway houses and parole services.

38. We call upon the federal, provincial, territorial, and Aboriginal governments to commit to eliminating the overrepresentation of Aboriginal youth in custody over the next decade.

39. We call upon the federal government to develop a national plan to collect and publish data on the criminal victimization of Aboriginal people, including data related to homicide and family violence victimization.

40. We call on all levels of government, in collaboration with Aboriginal people, to create adequately funded and accessible Aboriginal-specific victim programs and services with appropriate evaluation mechanisms.

41. We call upon the federal government, in consultation with Aboriginal organizations, to appoint a public inquiry into the causes of, and remedies for, the disproportionate victimization of Aboriginal women and girls. The inquiry's mandate would include:

i. Investigation into missing and murdered Aboriginal women and girls.

ii. Links to the intergenerational legacy of residential schools.

42. We call upon the federal, provincial, and territorial governments to commit to the recognition and implementation of Aboriginal justice systems in a manner consistent with the Treaty and Aboriginal rights of Aboriginal peoples, the *Constitution*

Act, 1982, and the *United Nations Declaration on the Rights of Indigenous Peoples*, endorsed by Canada in November 2012.

RECONCILIATION

CANADIAN GOVERNMENTS AND THE *UNITED NATIONS DECLARATION ON THE RIGHTS OF INDIGENOUS PEOPLES*

43. We call upon federal, provincial, territorial, and municipal governments to fully adopt and implement the *United Nations Declaration on the Rights of Indigenous Peoples* as the framework for reconciliation.

44. We call upon the Government of Canada to develop a national action plan, strategies, and other concrete measures to achieve the goals of the *United Nations Declaration on the Rights of Indigenous Peoples*.

ROYAL PROCLAMATION AND COVENANT OF RECONCILIATION

45. We call upon the Government of Canada, on behalf of all Canadians, to jointly develop with Aboriginal peoples a Royal Proclamation of Reconciliation to be issued by the Crown. The proclamation would build on the Royal Proclamation of 1763 and the Treaty of Niagara of 1764, and reaffirm the nation-to-nation relationship between Aboriginal peoples and the Crown. The proclamation would include, but not be limited to, the following commitments:

i.   Repudiate concepts used to justify European sovereignty over Indigenous lands and peoples such as the Doctrine of Discovery and *terra nullius*.

ii.   Adopt and implement the *United Nations Declaration on the Rights of Indigenous Peoples* as the framework for reconciliation.

iii. Renew or establish Treaty relationships based on principles of mutual recognition, mutual respect, and shared responsibility for maintaining those relationships into the future.

iv.   Reconcile Aboriginal and Crown constitutional and legal orders to ensure that Aboriginal peoples are full partners in Confederation, including the recognition and integration of Indigenous laws and legal traditions in negotiation and implementation processes involving Treaties, land claims, and other constructive agreements.

46. We call upon the parties to the Indian Residential Schools Settlement Agreement to develop and sign a Covenant of Reconciliation that would identify principles for working collaboratively to advance reconciliation in Canadian society, and that would include, but not be limited to:

i.   Reaffirmation of the parties' commitment to reconciliation.

ii.   Repudiation of concepts used to justify European sovereignty over Indigenous lands and peoples, such as the Doctrine of Discovery and *terra nullius*, and the reformation of laws, governance structures, and policies within their respective institutions that continue to rely on such concepts.

iii. Full adoption and implementation of the *United Nations Declaration on the Rights of Indigenous Peoples* as the framework for reconciliation.

iv.   Support for the renewal or establishment of Treaty relationships based on principles of mutual recognition, mutual respect, and shared responsibility for maintaining those relationships into the future.

v.   Enabling those excluded from the Settlement Agreement to sign onto the Covenant of Reconciliation.

vi. Enabling additional parties to sign onto
the Covenant of Reconciliation.

47. We call upon federal, provincial, territorial, and municipal
governments to repudiate concepts used to justify European
sovereignty over Indigenous peoples and lands, such as the
Doctrine of Discovery and *terra nullius,* and to reform those
laws, government policies, and litigation strategies that continue
to rely on such concepts.

SETTLEMENT AGREEMENT PARTIES AND THE *UNITED NATIONS DECLARATION ON THE RIGHTS OF INDIGENOUS PEOPLES*

48. We call upon the church parties to the Settlement
Agreement, and all other faith groups and interfaith social
justice groups in Canada who have not already done so, to
formally adopt and comply with the principles, norms, and
standards of the *United Nations Declaration on the Rights of
Indigenous Peoples* as a framework for reconciliation. This would
include, but not be limited to, the following commitments:

i.   Ensuring that their institutions, policies, programs,
and practices comply with the *United Nations
Declaration on the Rights of Indigenous Peoples.*

ii. Respecting Indigenous peoples' right to self-
determination in spiritual matters, including the right
to practise, develop, and teach their own spiritual
and religious traditions, customs, and ceremonies,
consistent with Article 12:1 of the *United Nations
Declaration on the Rights of Indigenous Peoples.*

iii. Engaging in ongoing public dialogue and actions
to support the *United Nations Declaration
on the Rights of Indigenous Peoples.*

iv. Issuing a statement no later than March 31, 2016,
from all religious denominations and faith groups,

as to how they will implement the *United Nations Declaration on the Rights of Indigenous Peoples.*

49. We call upon all religious denominations and faith groups who have not already done so to repudiate concepts used to justify European sovereignty over Indigenous lands and peoples, such as the Doctrine of Discovery and *terra nullius.*

EQUITY FOR ABORIGINAL PEOPLE IN THE LEGAL SYSTEM

50. In keeping with the *United Nations Declaration on the Rights of Indigenous Peoples,* we call upon the federal government, in collaboration with Aboriginal organizations, to fund the establishment of Indigenous law institutes for the development, use, and understanding of Indigenous laws and access to justice in accordance with the unique cultures of Aboriginal peoples in Canada.

51. We call upon the Government of Canada, as an obligation of its fiduciary responsibility, to develop a policy of transparency by publishing legal opinions it develops and upon which it acts or intends to act, in regard to the scope and extent of Aboriginal and Treaty rights.

52. We call upon the Government of Canada, provincial and territorial governments, and the courts to adopt the following legal principles:

i. Aboriginal title claims are accepted once the Aboriginal claimant has established occupation over a particular territory at a particular point in time.

ii. Once Aboriginal title has been established, the burden of proving any limitation on any rights arising from the existence of that title shifts to the party asserting such a limitation.

NATIONAL COUNCIL FOR RECONCILIATION

53. We call upon the Parliament of Canada, in consultation and collaboration with Aboriginal peoples, to enact legislation to establish a National Council for Reconciliation. The legislation would establish the council as an independent, national, oversight body with membership jointly appointed by the Government of Canada and national Aboriginal organizations, and consisting of Aboriginal and non-Aboriginal members. Its mandate would include, but not be limited to, the following:

i. Monitor, evaluate, and report annually to Parliament and the people of Canada on the Government of Canada's post-apology progress on reconciliation to ensure that government accountability for reconciling the relationship between Aboriginal peoples and the Crown is maintained in the coming years.

ii. Monitor, evaluate, and report to Parliament and the people of Canada on reconciliation progress across all levels and sectors of Canadian society, including the implementation of the Truth and Reconciliation Commission of Canada's Calls to Action.

iii. Develop and implement a multi-year National Action Plan for Reconciliation, which includes research and policy development, public education programs, and resources.

iv. Promote public dialogue, public/private partnerships, and public initiatives for reconciliation.

54. We call upon the Government of Canada to provide multi-year funding for the National Council for Reconciliation to ensure that it has the financial, human, and technical resources required to conduct its work, including the endowment of a National Reconciliation Trust to advance the cause of reconciliation.

55. We call upon all levels of government to provide annual reports or any current data requested by the National Council

for Reconciliation so that it can report on the progress
towards reconciliation. The reports or data would include, but
not be limited to:

i.   The number of Aboriginal children—including Métis and
     Inuit children—in care, compared with non-Aboriginal
     children, the reasons for apprehension, and the total spending
     on preventive and care services by child-welfare agencies.

ii. Comparative funding for the education of First
     Nations children on and off reserves.

iii. The educational and income attainments of Aboriginal
     peoples in Canada compared with non-Aboriginal people.

iv. Progress on closing the gaps between Aboriginal and non-
     Aboriginal communities in a number of health indicators
     such as: infant mortality, maternal health, suicide, mental
     health, addictions, life expectancy, birth rates, infant and
     child health issues, chronic diseases, illness and injury
     incidence, and the availability of appropriate health services.

v.   Progress on eliminating the overrepresentation of
     Aboriginal children in youth custody over the next decade.

vi. Progress on reducing the rate of criminal victimization
     of Aboriginal people, including data related to homicide
     and family violence victimization and other crimes.

vii. Progress on reducing the overrepresentation of Aboriginal
     people in the justice and correctional systems.

56. We call upon the prime minister of Canada to formally
respond to the report of the National Council for Reconciliation
by issuing an annual "State of Aboriginal Peoples" report,
which would outline the government's plans for advancing the
cause of reconciliation.

PROFESSIONAL DEVELOPMENT AND
TRAINING FOR PUBLIC SERVANTS

57. We call upon federal, provincial, territorial, and municipal governments to provide education to public servants on the history of Aboriginal peoples, including the history and legacy of residential schools, the *United Nations Declaration on the Rights of Indigenous Peoples*, Treaties and Aboriginal rights, Indigenous law, and Aboriginal–Crown relations. This will require skills-based training in intercultural competency, conflict resolution, human rights, and anti-racism.

CHURCH APOLOGIES AND RECONCILIATION

58. We call upon the Pope to issue an apology to Survivors, their families, and communities for the Roman Catholic Church's role in the spiritual, cultural, emotional, physical, and sexual abuse of First Nations, Inuit, and Métis children in Catholic-run residential schools. We call for that apology to be similar to the 2010 apology issued to Irish victims of abuse and to occur within one year of the issuing of this Report and to be delivered by the Pope in Canada.

59. We call upon church parties to the Settlement Agreement to develop ongoing education strategies to ensure that their respective congregations learn about their church's role in colonization, the history and legacy of residential schools, and why apologies to former residential school students, their families, and communities were necessary.

60. We call upon leaders of the church parties to the Settlement Agreement and all other faiths, in collaboration with Indigenous spiritual leaders, Survivors, schools of theology, seminaries, and other religious training centres, to develop and teach curriculum for all student clergy, and all clergy and staff who work in Aboriginal communities, on the need to respect Indigenous spirituality in its own right, the history and legacy of residential

schools and the roles of the church parties in that system, the history and legacy of religious conflict in Aboriginal families and communities, and the responsibility that churches have to mitigate such conflicts and prevent spiritual violence.

61. We call upon church parties to the Settlement Agreement, in collaboration with Survivors and representatives of Aboriginal organizations, to establish permanent funding to Aboriginal people for:

i.   Community-controlled healing and reconciliation projects.

ii. Community controlled culture and language-revitalization projects.

iii. Community-controlled education and relationship-building projects.

iv. Regional dialogues for Indigenous spiritual leaders and youth to discuss Indigenous spirituality, self-determination, and reconciliation.

EDUCATION FOR RECONCILIATION

62. We call upon the federal, provincial, and territorial governments, in consultation and collaboration with Survivors, Aboriginal peoples, and educators, to:

i.   Make age-appropriate curriculum on residential schools, Treaties, and Aboriginal peoples' historical and contemporary contributions to Canada a mandatory education requirement for Kindergarten to Grade Twelve students.

ii. Provide the necessary funding to post-secondary institutions to educate teachers on how to integrate Indigenous knowledge and teaching methods into classrooms.

iii. Provide the necessary funding to Aboriginal schools to utilize Indigenous knowledge and teaching methods in classrooms.

iv. Establish senior-level positions in government
     at the assistant deputy minister level or higher
     dedicated to Aboriginal content in education.

63. We call upon the Council of Ministers of Education, Canada
to maintain an annual commitment to Aboriginal education
issues, including:

i.   Developing and implementing Kindergarten to
      Grade Twelve curriculum and learning resources
      on Aboriginal peoples in Canadian history, and
      the history and legacy of residential schools.

ii.   Sharing information and best practices on
      teaching curriculum related to residential
      schools and Aboriginal history.

iii. Building student capacity for intercultural
      understanding, empathy, and mutual respect.

iv.   Identifying teacher-training needs relating to the above.

64. We call upon all levels of government that provide public
funds to denominational schools to require such schools to
provide an education on comparative religious studies, which
must include a segment on Aboriginal spiritual beliefs and
practices developed in collaboration with Aboriginal Elders.

65. We call upon the federal government, through the
Social Sciences and Humanities Research Council, and
in collaboration with Aboriginal peoples, post-secondary
institutions and educators, and the National Centre for Truth
and Reconciliation and its partner institutions, to establish a
national research program with multi-year funding to advance
understanding of reconciliation.

YOUTH PROGRAMS

66. We call upon the federal government to establish multi-year
funding for community-based youth organizations to deliver

programs on reconciliation, and establish a national network to share information and best practices.

MUSEUMS AND ARCHIVES

67. We call upon the federal government to provide funding to the Canadian Museums Association to undertake, in collaboration with Aboriginal peoples, a national review of museum policies and best practices to determine the level of compliance with the *United Nations Declaration on the Rights of Indigenous Peoples* and to make recommendations.

68. We call upon the federal government, in collaboration with Aboriginal peoples, and the Canadian Museums Association to mark the 150th anniversary of Canadian Confederation in 2017 by establishing a dedicated national funding program for commemoration projects on the theme of reconciliation.

69. We call upon Library and Archives Canada to:

i.   Fully adopt and implement the *United Nations Declaration on the Rights of Indigenous Peoples* and the *United Nations Joinet-Orentlicher Principles*, as related to Aboriginal peoples' inalienable right to know the truth about what happened and why, with regard to human rights violations committed against them in the residential schools.

ii. Ensure that its record holdings related to residential schools are accessible to the public.

iii. Commit more resources to its public education materials and programming on residential schools.

70. We call upon the federal government to provide funding to the Canadian Association of Archivists to undertake, in collaboration with Aboriginal peoples, a national review of archival policies and best practices to:

i.   Determine the level of compliance with the *United Nations Declaration on the Rights of Indigenous Peoples* and the *United Nations Joinet-Orentlicher Principles*, as related to Aboriginal peoples' inalienable right to know the truth about what happened and why, with regard to human rights violations committed against them in the residential schools.

ii.   Produce a report with recommendations for full implementation of these international mechanisms as a reconciliation framework for Canadian archives.

MISSING CHILDREN AND BURIAL INFORMATION

71. We call upon all chief coroners and provincial vital statistics agencies that have not provided to the Truth and Reconciliation Commission of Canada their records on the deaths of Aboriginal children in the care of residential school authorities to make these documents available to the National Centre for Truth and Reconciliation.

72. We call upon the federal government to allocate sufficient resources to the National Centre for Truth and Reconciliation to allow it to develop and maintain the National Residential School Student Death Register established by the Truth and Reconciliation Commission of Canada.

73. We call upon the federal government to work with churches, Aboriginal communities, and former residential school students to establish and maintain an online registry of residential school cemeteries, including, where possible, plot maps showing the location of deceased residential school children.

74. We call upon the federal government to work with the churches and Aboriginal community leaders to inform the families of children who died at residential schools of the child's burial location, and to respond to families' wishes for appropriate commemoration ceremonies and markers, and reburial in home communities where requested.

75. We call upon the federal government to work with provincial, territorial, and municipal governments, churches, Aboriginal communities, former residential school students, and current landowners to develop and implement strategies and procedures for the ongoing identification, documentation, maintenance, commemoration, and protection of residential school cemeteries or other sites at which residential school children were buried. This is to include the provision of appropriate memorial ceremonies and commemorative markers to honour the deceased children.

76. We call upon the parties engaged in the work of documenting, maintaining, commemorating, and protecting residential school cemeteries to adopt strategies in accordance with the following principles:

i. The Aboriginal community most affected shall lead the development of such strategies.

ii. Information shall be sought from residential school Survivors and other Knowledge Keepers in the development of such strategies.

iii. Aboriginal protocols shall be respected before any potentially invasive technical inspection and investigation of a cemetery site.

NATIONAL CENTRE FOR TRUTH AND RECONCILIATION

77. We call upon provincial, territorial, municipal, and community archives to work collaboratively with the National Centre for Truth and Reconciliation to identify and collect copies of all records relevant to the history and legacy of the residential school system, and to provide these to the National Centre for Truth and Reconciliation.

78. We call upon the Government of Canada to commit to making a funding contribution of $10 million over seven years

to the National Centre for Truth and Reconciliation, plus an additional amount to assist communities to research and produce histories of their own residential school experience and their involvement in truth, healing, and reconciliation.

COMMEMORATION

79. We call upon the federal government, in collaboration with Survivors, Aboriginal organizations, and the arts community, to develop a reconciliation framework for Canadian heritage and commemoration. This would include, but not be limited to:

i.   Amending the Historic Sites and Monuments Act to include First Nations, Inuit, and Métis representation on the Historic Sites and Monuments Board of Canada and its Secretariat.

ii.   Revising the policies, criteria, and practices of the National Program of Historical Commemoration to integrate Indigenous history, heritage values, and memory practices into Canada's national heritage and history.

iii. Developing and implementing a national heritage plan and strategy for commemorating residential school sites, the history and legacy of residential schools, and the contributions of Aboriginal peoples to Canada's history.

80. We call upon the federal government, in collaboration with Aboriginal peoples, to establish, as a statutory holiday, a National Day for Truth and Reconciliation to honour Survivors, their families, and communities, and ensure that public commemoration of the history and legacy of residential schools remains a vital component of the reconciliation process.

81. We call upon the federal government, in collaboration with Survivors and their organizations, and other parties to the Settlement Agreement, to commission and install a publicly accessible, highly visible, Residential Schools National Monument in the city of Ottawa to honour Survivors and all the children who were lost to their families and communities.

82. We call upon provincial and territorial governments, in collaboration with Survivors and their organizations, and other parties to the Settlement Agreement, to commission and install a publicly accessible, highly visible, Residential Schools Monument in each capital city to honour Survivors and all the children who were lost to their families and communities.

83. We call upon the Canada Council for the Arts to establish, as a funding priority, a strategy for Indigenous and non-Indigenous artists to undertake collaborative projects and produce works that contribute to the reconciliation process.

MEDIA AND RECONCILIATION

84. We call upon the federal government to restore and increase funding to the CBC/Radio-Canada, to enable Canada's national public broadcaster to support reconciliation, and be properly reflective of the diverse cultures, languages, and perspectives of Aboriginal peoples, including, but not limited to:

i. Increasing Aboriginal programming, including Aboriginal-language speakers.

ii. Increasing equitable access for Aboriginal peoples to jobs, leadership positions, and professional development opportunities within the organization.

iii. Continuing to provide dedicated news coverage and online public information resources on issues of concern to Aboriginal peoples and all Canadians, including the history and legacy of residential schools and the reconciliation process.

85. We call upon the Aboriginal Peoples Television Network, as an independent non-profit broadcaster with programming by, for, and about Aboriginal peoples, to support reconciliation, including but not limited to:

i. Continuing to provide leadership in programming and
    organizational culture that reflects the diverse cultures,
    languages, and perspectives of Aboriginal peoples.

ii. Continuing to develop media initiatives that inform
    and educate the Canadian public, and connect
    Aboriginal and non-Aboriginal Canadians.

86. We call upon Canadian journalism programs and media
schools to require education for all students on the history
of Aboriginal peoples, including the history and legacy of
residential schools, the *United Nations Declaration on the
Rights of Indigenous Peoples*, Treaties and Aboriginal rights,
Indigenous law, and Aboriginal–Crown relations.

SPORTS AND RECONCILIATION

87. We call upon all levels of government, in collaboration with
Aboriginal peoples, sports halls of fame, and other relevant
organizations, to provide public education that tells the national
story of Aboriginal athletes in history.

88. We call upon all levels of government to take action to
ensure long-term Aboriginal athlete development and growth,
and continued support for the North American Indigenous
Games, including funding to host the games and for provincial
and territorial team preparation and travel.

89. We call upon the federal government to amend the Physical
Activity and Sport Act to support reconciliation by ensuring that
policies to promote physical activity as a fundamental element
of health and well-being, reduce barriers to sports participation,
increase the pursuit of excellence in sport, and build capacity in
the Canadian sport system, are inclusive of Aboriginal peoples.

90. We call upon the federal government to ensure that national
sports policies, programs, and initiatives are inclusive of
Aboriginal peoples, including, but not limited to, establishing:

i. In collaboration with provincial and territorial governments, stable funding for, and access to, community sports programs that reflect the diverse cultures and traditional sporting activities of Aboriginal peoples.

ii. An elite athlete development program for Aboriginal athletes.

iii. Programs for coaches, trainers, and sports officials that are culturally relevant for Aboriginal peoples.

iv. Anti-racism awareness and training programs.

91. We call upon the officials and host countries of international sporting events such as the Olympics, Pan Am, and Commonwealth games to ensure that Indigenous peoples' territorial protocols are respected and local Indigenous communities are engaged in all aspects of planning and participating in such events.

BUSINESS AND RECONCILIATION

92. We call upon the corporate sector in Canada to adopt the *United Nations Declaration on the Rights of Indigenous Peoples* as a reconciliation framework and to apply its principles, norms, and standards to corporate policy and core operational activities involving Indigenous peoples and their lands and resources. This would include, but not be limited to, the following:

i. Commit to meaningful consultation, building respectful relationships, and obtaining the free, prior, and informed consent of Indigenous peoples before proceeding with economic development projects.

ii. Ensure that Aboriginal peoples have equitable access to jobs, training, and education opportunities in the corporate sector, and that Aboriginal communities gain long-term sustainable benefits from economic development projects.

iii. Provide education for management and staff on the history of Aboriginal peoples, including the history and legacy of residential schools, the *United Nations Declaration on the Rights of Indigenous Peoples*, Treaties and Aboriginal rights, Indigenous law, and Aboriginal–Crown relations. This will require skills based training in intercultural competency, conflict resolution, human rights, and anti-racism.

NEWCOMERS TO CANADA

93. We call upon the federal government, in collaboration with the national Aboriginal organizations, to revise the information kit for newcomers to Canada and its citizenship test to reflect a more inclusive history of the diverse Aboriginal peoples of Canada, including information about the Treaties and the history of residential schools.

94. We call upon the Government of Canada to replace the Oath of Citizenship with the following:

i.   I swear (or affirm) that I will be faithful and bear true allegiance to Her Majesty Queen Elizabeth II, Queen of Canada, Her Heirs and Successors, and that I will faithfully observe the laws of Canada including Treaties with Indigenous Peoples, and fulfill my duties as a Canadian citizen.

GABEKANA

(AT THE END OF THE TRAIL)

For many generations, far too long by any estimation, knowledge about residential schools in Canada was hidden, repressed, disregarded, discounted, and discredited. In the last generation we have seen national attention, a class action lawsuit, a settlement agreement, and a truth and reconciliation process.

The reports of the Truth and Reconciliation Commission of Canada (TRC) provide an overall history of the system, and investigate, on a national scale, issues such as education, language, building quality, food and nutrition, discipline and abuse, sport and the arts, resistance, and the specifics of the student and staff experience. We can now be better informed of the history of residential schools.

Knowing the historical backdrop to the residential schools is essential to the ongoing work of reconciliation that is being undertaken in Canada. The TRC has documented the policy of cultural genocide directed at Indigenous people in order to do away with the government's legal and financial obligations and to assume control over Indigenous lands and resources. In partnership with the government, churches were involved in the administration of the schools and have assumed responsibility for some of the atrocities that took place in the schools. Both in philosophy and in practical terms, the schools operated on the premise that Indigenous people and cultures were lesser than their non-Indigenous counterparts. The law gave effect to these assumptions.

From reading this volume you will understand part of that history as it is now being researched, revisited, and retold. In its Summary of the Final Report, the TRC has provided us with a thematic overview of the legacy of the schools, thoughts on the challenges of reconciliation, and calls to action. These must be read as a whole: there is no reconciliation without an understanding of the history and legacy of residential schools. Conversely, we cannot understand our need for reconciliation, nor can we carve our path forward, without grounding it in the truths of the past. As the TRC report states:

> The Commission defines "reconciliation" as an ongoing process of establishing and maintaining respectful relationships. A critical part of this process involves repairing damaged trust by making apologies, providing individual and collective reparations, and following through with concrete actions that demonstrate real societal change. (see p. 154 in this volume)

We must rise to the challenge of knowing this history, and continue to acknowledge it while moving towards a new understanding of the relationships that we must rebuild.

THE ARCHIVE: OPENING THE DOOR

In its role of truth telling, the TRC was mandated to receive documents relating to residential schools from government and church archives. Throughout the process and while the TRC was completing its final report, documents were still being disclosed by parties that had agreed to provide them. These documents contain records of the schools and of more than 150,000 First Nations, Inuit, and Métis students who attended the schools. In addition, the TRC received 7,000 digitally recorded witness statements speaking about first-hand experiences of survivors, their descendants, church officials, and others whose lives were woven into the schools' history. The intent was that all of this information would form a more complete understanding of the truth relating to residential schools. The archive supports the re-telling of history from various and varied perspectives. The oral history created in *The Survivors Speak* (an interim report detailing personal statements to the TRC) provides an overview of the student experience as told by the Survivors themselves. Their testimonies are now preserved at the National Centre for Truth and Reconciliation (NCTR), along with statements of former staff of residential schools and intergenerational survivors.

The richness of the information received (documents, audio and visual recordings, and physical objects) should never be lost. The Indian Residential Schools Settlement Agreement (IRSSA) provided for the establishment of a permanent archive to hold the material received by the TRC. This archive is manifest in the form of the NCTR, which will foster dialogue and reconciliation and ensure that the permanent archive on residential schools is accessible, growing, and relevant to those who want and need to learn.

RESEARCH AT THE NATIONAL CENTRE FOR TRUTH AND RECONCILIATION (NCTR): THE DOOR WILL REMAIN OPEN FOREVER

This research centre has at its core the Survivor's experience, and it aims to ensure that a Survivor, their family, as well as community and academic researchers can continue to add to the truths that have been told and work to better understand the implications of those truths. By researching their residential school history, Survivors will have the opportunity to view documents that pertain to their experience. They will also have the opportunity to share their experience as part of the continuing collection of information for the archives. Families and communities will be able to view documents that relate to particular schools in their region and that were attended by their relatives.

Researchers will be able to mine the records for additional truths about the residential schools, and might be able to address some of the non-truths that have been perpetuated since the opening of the first residential schools and throughout generations. Research has revealed that some of the schools were engaged in nutritional and psychological experimentation. Further information will come to light as the records are reviewed, and additional research can be undertaken into the thousands of students who died while in residential schools and their burial locations. And there are many more paths of research that may be followed. As the layers of documents are peeled back, more research questions will arise. As records continue to be received into the archive, new information will be available.

New research will develop a variety of themes. Histories of particular schools may be compiled, which will deepen the scope of the national history. The recreational and cultural activities in schools may be studied. Issues such as educational attainment, discipline, and quality of institutional care need further contextualization on both a regional and national scale. The health of residential school students, for example, may be further considered in relation to the broader health of Indigenous peoples in Canada. There is also much more to be done in the way of comparative international study relating to boarding schools and institutions in other countries.

Research must have a purpose. Part of the purpose of further research in the archive is to uncover more truth about the residential school experience. Research will also play an important role in reconciliation. Key elements of the National Centre for Truth and Reconciliation's mandate are to ensure that the public can access historical records and other materials to help foster reconciliation and healing, and to encourage dialogue on the many issues that stand in the way of reconciliation. This mandate will also require us all to pay close attention to the calls to action of the TRC.

From the church, government, and school records, to the witness statements, art, and music, the archive constitutes an important step towards the development of a robust Indigenous archive. More records relating to residential schools will be sought out and added to the NCTR archive, including documents in the personal possession of public figures and individuals; provincial, territorial, and international archives; university and museum archives; and records of Indigenous education authorities and other Indigenous organizations.

Reconciliation cannot, however, be limited to the residential school system and its legacy. That legacy cannot be disentangled from the legacy of Canada's broader policies towards Indigenous people, which banned spiritual practices, placed them on agriculturally marginal land, failed to fulfill treaty obligations, and persecuted Indigenous political and spiritual leaders.

As part of the establishment of respectful relationships, the TRC has indicated that the revitalization of Indigenous laws and legal traditions is required. In the words of the Commissioners:

> It is important that all Canadians understand how traditional
> First Nations, Inuit, and Métis approaches to resolving conflict,
> repairing harm, and restoring relationships can inform
> the reconciliation process. (see p. 154 in this volume)

A significant effort must be made to ensure that Indigenous legal principles and processes of decision-making are guiding the process of reconciliation, including in the interpretation and implementation of historic treaties.

Canadians must also learn about the rich contributions that Indigenous peoples have made to the history of Canada. Further materials related to Crown–Aboriginal relations, Treaties and Aboriginal Rights, and other themes identified by Indigenous people may also form part of this archive in the future. The NCTR archive is not closed or finite. And the work on reconciliation will build on what we have been able to learn about the residential school experience and its legacy to consider further steps in maintaining respectful relationships. The TRC emphasized that more research is needed to fully understand how the reconciliation process itself may work to repair broken trust and establish more constructive relationships between Indigenous and non-Indigenous peoples in Canada.

FOR THE NEXT GENERATIONS: MIKINAAK (THE PATH OF THE TURTLE)

The NCTR is physically located at the University of Manitoba, in Treaty One territory and the homeland of the Métis Nation, in a building ceremonially named One Feather (bezhig miigwan). A turtle rock formation guards the entranceway to the building and hosts the sacred fire of the centre. It is a home for the archive, a hub for research, and a place of commemoration.

Based on the vision of a network of partners in all regions of the country, the centre also exists wherever you are. It is in the searchable database online, it is in the education initiatives and opportunities provided in your places of learning, it is in regional initiatives and partner institutions, it is with the Survivors, intergenerational survivors, and their families.

A door has been opened, and some truth has been able to enter the national consciousness. We must collectively ensure that the doors that lead to truth will never be closed again. We must also ensure that our understanding of the history of residential schools continues to grow. Finally, we must ensure that our understanding engages action in a process of reconciliation.

Histories and legacies should not be forgotten. The reconciliation that flows from them should be honoured.

The doors to the NCTR are open to you, forever.

Aimée Craft

DIRECTOR OF RESEARCH,
NATIONAL CENTRE FOR TRUTH AND RECONCILIATION

A NOTE ON THE TEXT

This book is dedicated to the Survivors of Canada's residential school system. Their courage to speak of their experiences is at the heart of the work of the Truth and Reconciliation Commission that inspired this volume.

The tremendous commitment and efforts of hundreds of people, led by Commissioners Justice Murray Sinclair, Chief Wilton Littlechild, and Dr. Marie Wilson, ensured that the Survivors who wished to speak were heard and their words documented for all Canadians to listen and to learn.

With this abridged edition of the TRC report, University of Manitoba Press hopes to make the history of residential schools and the findings of the TRC more accessible to more people. While some will want to read the report in its entirety, this essential edition offers a less daunting starting point for students and interested Canadians.

In the course of its work, the TRC produced a number of reports leading up to the release of its final report in six volumes. This edition consists primarily of the text of *What We Have Learned: Principles of Truth and Reconciliation*—which features the History from *Honouring the Truth, Reconciling for the Future* (the Executive Summary of the TRC report) and shorter versions of its Introduction, Reconciliation, and Legacy chapters. This edition also contains the ninety-four Calls to Action and new materials that help to contextualize the report and inspire further action and education.

The Press is especially honoured that Phil Fontaine agreed to write a foreword for this edition. A residential school survivor and TRC honorary witness, Phil Fontaine's efforts have been critical in bringing the issue of residential schools to the attention of governments and the public. He first placed the issue on the national agenda in 1990 when he spoke publicly about the abuse that he and his fellow students had experienced. In 2005, as National Chief of the Assembly of First Nations, he launched a class-action lawsuit against the Government of Canada over the legacy of residential schools and then secured Prime Minster Paul Martin's commitment to a settlement, leading to the successful negotiation of the Indian Residential Schools Settlement Agreement in 2006. It is questionable whether the work of the TRC that made this book possible would have yet happened without Phil Fontaine's staunch dedication to seeking acknowledgment of and redress for the history and legacy of residential schools.

The Press is also grateful for the support and collaboration of Ry Moran, Aimée Craft, and the staff of the National Centre for Truth and Reconciliation (NCTR). We hope that Aimée Craft's afterword will inspire readers to explore the resources at the NCTR, to learn about a family's or community's experience of residential schooling or to carry out research that will interrogate the structures of government and society that allowed such a system to exist in the way it did for so long. The NCTR is a rich archive and a resource for reconciliation for all Canadians.

A portion of all proceeds from the sale of this book will be donated to the NCTR to assist with its ongoing educational and research activities.

NOTES

FOREWORD

1. Michael Ignatieff, "Articles of Faith," *Index on Censorship* 25, no. 5 (Sept. 1996): 113.

INTRODUCTION

1. For coercion, see: Ray, *Illustrated History*, 151–152. For fraud, see: Upton, "Origins of Canadian Indian Policy," 56. For failure to implement Treaties, see: Sprague, *Canada's Treaties with Aboriginal People*, 13. For taking land without Treaty, see Fisher, *Contact and Conflict*.

2. For examples from Saskatchewan, see: Miller, *Skyscrapers Hide the Heavens*, 222; Stonechild, "Indian View," 263; Wiebe, "Mistahimaskwa," http://www.biographi.ca/en/bio/mistahimaskwa_11E.html (accessed 14 July 2014).

3. Barron, "Indian Pass System."

4. For an example, see: *An Act to amend and consolidate the laws respecting Indians*, Statutes of Canada 1880, chapter 28, section 72, reproduced in Venne, *Indian Acts*, 75.

5. For examples, see Brown. "Economic Organization and the Position of Women"; Fiske, "Fishing Is Women's Business"; Klein, "Mother as Clanswoman."

6. *An Act for the gradual enfranchisement of Indians*, Statutes of Canada 1869, chapter 42, reproduced in Venne, *Indian Acts*, 11.

7. For an example, see: *An Act further to amend "The Indian Act, 1880,"* Statutes of Canada 1884, chapter 27, section 3, reproduced in Venne, *Indian Acts*, 93.

8. Canada, House of Commons Debates (9 May 1883), 1107–1108.

9. Library and Archives Canada, RG10, volume 6810, file 470-2-3, volume 7, Evidence of D. C. Scott to the Special Committee of the House of Commons Investigating the Indian Act amendments of 1920, (L-2)(N-3).

10. Canada, "Statement of the Government of Canada on Indian Policy," page 20 of 24-page portable document format file.

11. Canada, *Annual Report of the Department of Indian Affairs, 1931*, 60.

12. Indian Residential Schools Settlement – Official Court Website, http://www.residentialschoolsettlement.ca/schools.html (accessed 5 February 2015).

13. Prime Minister Stephen Harper, Statement of Apology – to former students of Indian Residential Schools, 11 June 2008, http://www.aadnc-aandc.gc.ca/eng/1100100015644/1100100015649.

14. TRC, NRA, Library and Archives Canada, RG10, volume 7936, file 32-104, J. W. House to G. H. Gooderham, 26 January 1942. [OLD-004156-0001]

15. Canada, Special Joint Committee, 1947, 1474.

16. Canada, Special Joint Committee, 1947, 1508–1509.

17. TRC, NRA, The Presbyterian Church in Canada Archives, Toronto, ON, Acc. 1988-7004, box 46, file 1, "Cecilia Jeffrey Indian Residential School," J. C. E. Andrews, 1953, 36. [NCA-009046]

18. TRC, NRA, INAC – Resolution Sector – IRS Historical Files Collection – Ottawa, GRS Files, box 1A, file 43, Albert Southard, 8 March 1957. [IRC-040039]

19. Renaud, "Indian Education Today," 30.

CHAPTER ONE: THE HISTORY

1. TRC, AVS, Frederick Ernest Koe, Statement to the Truth and Reconciliation Commission of Canada, Inuvik, Northwest Territories, 30 June 2011, Statement Number: SC091.

2. TRC, AVS, Marlene Kayseas, Statement to the Truth and Reconciliation Commission of Canada, Regina, Saskatchewan, 16 January 2012, Statement Number: SP035.

3. TRC, AVS, Larry Beardy, Statement to the Truth and Reconciliation Commission of Canada, Thompson, Manitoba, 25 September 2012, Statement Number: SP082.

4. TRC, AVS, Florence Horassi, Statement to the Truth and Reconciliation Commission of Canada, Tulita, Northwest Territories, 10 May 2011, Statement Number: 2011-0394.

5. TRC, AVS, Lily Bruce, Statement to the Truth and Reconciliation Commission of Canada, Alert Bay, British Columbia, 4 August 2011, Statement Number: 2011-3285.

6. TRC, AVS, Vitaline Elsie Jenner, Statement to the Truth and Reconciliation Commission of Canada, Winnipeg, Manitoba, 16 June 2010, Statement Number: 02-MB-16JU10-131. (Translated words confirmed by Translation Bureau, Public Works and Government Services Canada [8817169_TG_Kinugus_EN_CP].)

7. TRC, AVS, Nellie Ningewance, Statement to the Truth and Reconciliation Commission of Canada, Sault Ste. Marie, Ontario, 1 July 2011, Statement Number: 2011-0305.

8. TRC, AVS, Bernice Jacks, Statement to the Truth and Reconciliation Commission of Canada, Victoria, British Columbia, 13 April 2012, Statement Number: 2011-3971.

9. TRC, AVS, Marthe Basile-Coocoo, Statement to the Truth and Reconciliation Commission of Canada (translated from French), Montréal, Québec, 26 April 2013, Statement Number: 2011-6103.

10. TRC, AVS, Pauline St-Onge, Statement to the Truth and Reconciliation Commission of Canada (translated from French), Montréal, Québec, 25 April 2013, Statement Number: 2011-6134.

11. TRC, AVS, Campbell Papequash, Statement to the Truth and Reconciliation Commission of Canada, Key First Nation, Saskatchewan, 20 January 2012, Statement Number: SP038.

12. TRC, AVS, Roy Denny, Statement to the Truth and Reconciliation Commission

of Canada, Eskasoni First Nation, Nova Scotia, 14 October 2011, Statement Number: 2011-2678.

13. TRC, AVS, Calvin Myerion, Statement to the Truth and Reconciliation Commission of Canada, Winnipeg, Manitoba, 16 June 2010, Statement Number: 02-MB-16JU10-122.

14. TRC, AVS, Archie Hyacinthe, Statement to the Truth and Reconciliation Commission of Canada, Kenora, Ontario, 15 March 2011, Statement Number: 2011-0279.

15. TRC, AVS, Margo Wylde, Statement to the Truth and Reconciliation Commission of Canada, Val d'Or, Québec, 5 February 2012, Statement Number: SP100.

16. TRC, AVS, Murray Crowe, Statement to the Truth and Reconciliation Commission of Canada, Sault Ste. Marie, Ontario, 1 July 2011, Statement Number: 2011-0306.

17. TRC, AVS, Wilbur Abrahams, Statement to the Truth and Reconciliation Commission of Canada, Terrace, British Columbia, 30 November 2011, Statement Number: 2011-3301.

18. TRC, AVS, Martin Nicholas, Statement to the Truth and Reconciliation Commission of Canada, Grand Rapids, Manitoba, 24 February 2010, Statement Number: 07-MB-24FB10-001.

19. TRC, AVS, Lorna Morgan, Statement to the Truth and Reconciliation Commission of Canada, Winnipeg, Manitoba, 17 June 2010, Statement Number: 02-MB-16JU10-041.

20. TRC, AVS, Gilles Petiquay, Statement to the Truth and Reconciliation Commission of Canada (translated from French), La Tuque, Québec, 6 March 2013, Statement Number: 2011-6001.

21. TRC, AVS, Wilbur Abrahams, Statement to the Truth and Reconciliation Commission of Canada, Terrace, British Columbia, 30 November 2011, Statement Number: 2011-3301.

22. TRC, AVS, Peter Ross, Statement to the Truth and Reconciliation Commission of Canada, Tsiigehtchic, Northwest Territories, 8 September 2011, Statement Number: 2011-0340.

23. TRC, AVS, Daniel Nanooch, Statement to the Truth and Reconciliation Commission of Canada, High Level, Alberta, 4 July 2013, Statement Number: 2011-1868.

24. TRC, AVS, Bernice Jacks, Statement to the Truth and Reconciliation Commission of Canada, Victoria, British Columbia, 13 April 2012, Statement Number: 2011-3971.

25. TRC, AVS, Helen Kakekayash, Statement to the Truth and Reconciliation Commission of Canada, Ottawa, Ontario, 5 February 2011, Statement Number: 01-ON-05FE11-002.

26. TRC, AVS, Bernard Catcheway, Statement to the Truth and Reconciliation Commission of Canada, Skownan First Nation, Manitoba, 12 October 2011, Statement Number: 2011-2510.

27. TRC, AVS, Julianna Alexander, Statement to the Truth and Reconciliation Com-

mission of Canada, Enderby, British Columbia, 12 October 2011, Statement Number: 2011-3286.

28. TRC, AVS, William Herney, Statement to the Truth and Reconciliation Commission of Canada, Halifax, Nova Scotia, 29 October 2011, Statement Number: 2011-2923.

29. TRC, AVS, Raymond Cutknife, Statement to the Truth and Reconciliation Commission of Canada, Hobbema, Alberta, 25 July 2013, Statement Number: SP125.

30. TRC, AVS, Timothy Henderson, Statement to the Truth and Reconciliation Commission of Canada, Winnipeg, Manitoba, 28 June 2011, Statement Number: 2011-0291.

31. TRC, AVS, Shirley Waskewitch, Statement to the Truth and Reconciliation Commission of Canada, Saskatoon, Saskatchewan, 24 June 2012, Statement Number: 2011-3521.

32. TRC, AVS, Patrick Bruyere, Statement to the Truth and Reconciliation Commission of Canada, Winnipeg, Manitoba, 16 June 2010, Statement Number: 02-MB-16JU10-157.

33. TRC, AVS, Ernest Barkman, Statement to the Truth and Reconciliation Commission of Canada, Garden Hill First Nation, Manitoba, 30 March 2011, Statement Number: 2011-0123. (Translated from Oji-Cree to English by Translation Bureau, Public Works and Government Services Canada, 8956124.)

34. TRC, AVS, Paul Dixon, Statement to the Truth and Reconciliation Commission of Canada, Val d'Or, Québec, 6 February 2012, Statement Number: SP101.

35. TRC, AVS, Betsy Annahatak, Statement to the Truth and Reconciliation Commission of Canada, Halifax, Nova Scotia, 28 October 2011, Statement Number: 2011-2896.

36. TRC, AVS, Rick Gilbert, Statement to the Truth and Reconciliation Commission of Canada, Vancouver, British Columbia, 20 September 2013, Statement Number: 2011-2389.

37. TRC, AVS, Nick Sibbeston, Statement to the Truth and Reconciliation Commission of Canada, Inuvik, Northwest Territories, 30 June 2011, Statement Number: NNE202.

38. TRC, AVS, [Name redacted], Statement to the Truth and Reconciliation Commission of Canada, Prince Albert, Saskatchewan, 1 February 2012, Statement Number: 2011-3879. (Translated from Woodland Cree to English by Translation Bureau, Public Works and Government Services Canada, 8956130.)

39. TRC, AVS, Jack Anawak, Statement to the Truth and Reconciliation Commission of Canada, Inuvik, Northwest Territories, 30 June 2011, Statement Number: NNE202.

40. TRC, AVS, Lydia Ross, Statement to the Truth and Reconciliation Commission of Canada, Winnipeg, Manitoba, 16 June 2010, Statement Number: 02-MB-16JU10-029.

41. TRC, AVS, Stephen Kakfwi, Statement to the Truth and Reconciliation Commission of Canada, Inuvik, Northwest Territories, 30 June 2011, Statement Number: NNE202.

42. TRC, AVS, Victoria McIntosh, Statement to the Truth and Reconciliation Commission of Canada, Winnipeg, Manitoba, 16 June 2010, Statement Number: 02-MB-16JU10-123.

43. TRC, AVS, Shirley Flowers, Statement to the Truth and Reconciliation Commission of Canada, Goose Bay, Newfoundland and Labrador, 20 September 2011, Statement Number: SP025.

44. Howe, *Empire*, 21–22.

45. Howe, *Empire*, 57.

46. For East Africa, see: Thiong'o, *Dreams in a Time of War*. For Australia, see: Australia, "'Bringing Them Home,' National Inquiry," www.humanrights.gov.au/ sites/default/files/content/pdf/social_justice/bringing_them_home_report.pdf [25]. For Siberia, see: Bartels and Bartels, *When the North Was Red*, 12; Bloch, *Red Ties*, 38.

47. Diffie and Winnius, *Foundations*, 78–83; Pagden, *Peoples and Empires*, 56.

48. Howe, *Empire*, 62–63.

49. Hobsbawm, *On Empire*, 67.

50. Wood, *Empire of Capital*, 74–87.

51. Wolfe, "Settler Colonialism," 388.

52. Wolfe, "Settler Colonialism," 388, 391, 399.

53. Address of C. C. Painter to the 1886 Lake Mohonk Conference, "Proceedings of the Lake Mohonk Conference," in *Eighteenth Annual Report of the Board of Indian Commissioners, 1886*, 61–62.

54. Howe, *Empire*, 80–81.

55. Howe, *Empire*, 62.

56. Wood, *Empire of Capital*, 40–41.

57. For examples, see: Diffie and Winius, *Foundations*, 65–66, 94–95; Pagden, *Peoples and Empires*, 54; Williams, *American Indian*, 72–73.

58. Elliott, *Empires of the Atlantic*, 11, 23; Pagden, *Spanish Imperialism*, 14.

59. Pagden, *Lords of All the World*, 47.

60. Elliott, *Empires of the Atlantic*, 11–12; Frichner, "Preliminary Study," 11; Seed, *Ceremonies of Possession*, 17–18.

61. H. Verelst, "Some Observations on the Right of the Crown of Great Britain to the North West Continent of America," PRC co 5/283, f. 5, quoted in Armitage, *Ideological Origins*, 192.

62. Banner, "Why Terra Nullius," 95. The court case is referred to as *Mabo v. Queensland (No. 2)*.

63. Wood, *Origin of Capitalism*, 111.

64. Howe, *Empire*, 86–87.

65. Speech quoted in: *Archibald Philip Primrose (5th earl of Rosebery) ... Australian speechlets, 1883–84 [by A. P. Primrose]*, http://books.google.ca/books?id=CncI-AAAAQAAJ&printsec=frontcover&dq=Australian+speechlets,+1883-84+[by

+A.P.+Primrose.].&hl=en&sa=X-&ei=zN2IUuGdMOTA2gW0vIHYDA&ved
=0CDkQ6AEwAA#v=onepage&q=Australian percent20speechlets percent2C
percent201883-84 percent20[by percent20A.P. percent20Primrose.].&f=false
(accessed 17 November 2013).

66. Canada, *Annual Report of the Department of Indian Affairs, 1884*, 154.

67. Usher, *William Duncan*, 41. See also: Choquette, *Oblate Assault*; Huel, *Proclaiming the Gospel*; Hyam, *Britain's Imperial Century*.

68. Howe, *Empire*, 85.

69. Howe, *Empire*, 90; Perry, "Metropolitan Knowledge," 109–111.

70. Huel, *Proclaiming the Gospel*, 1–6; Choquette, *Oblate Assault*, 1–20; Choquette, *Canada's Religions*, 173–176.

71. For example, see: Usher, *William Duncan*, 8, 11.

72. Moorhouse, *Missionaries*, 274.

73. Moorhouse, *Missionaries*, 33; Rompkey, *Story of Labrador*, 34, 36–39.

74. For Canada, see, for example: McMillan and Yellowhorn, *First Peoples*. For a global perspective, see: Coates, *A Global History*.

75. Jaenen, "Education for Francization," 54–55; Trudel, *Beginnings of New France*, 134–135.

76. Jaenen, *Friend and Foe Aspects*, 96, 163, 166.

77. Magnuson, *Education in New France*, 47–50; Trudel, *Beginnings of New France*, 231; Axtell, *Invasion Within*, 56–58; Jaenen, "Education for Francization," 56; Jaenen, *Friend and Foe Aspects*, 95, 168.

78. Hamilton, *Federal Indian Day Schools*, 4–5; Fingard, "New England Company," 30–32.

79. Stevenson, "Red River Indian Mission School," 141.

80. Graham, *Mush Hole*, 7.

81. TRC, NRA, Library and Archives Canada, RG10, Acc. 1984-85/112, box 47, file 451/25-1, Newspaper article, "Mohawk Institute May Close after 139 Years," no date; [TAY-001133] TRC, NRA, Diocese of Huron Archives, Anglican Church of Canada, Huron University College, London, ON, Luxton Papers, box 27, Indian Reserves, Richard Isaac, Six Nations Council To Whom It May Concern, 13 March 1970; [TAY-001432] TRC, NRA, INAC – Resolution Sector – IRS Historical Files Collection – Ottawa, file 479/25-13-001, volume 3, G. D. Cromb to Deputy Minister, 20 March 1970. [TAY-003053-0001]

82. Ryerson, "Report on Industrial Schools," 76.

83. Ryerson, "Report on Industrial Schools," 73.

84. *Report of the Special Commissioners 1858*, n.p.

85. TRC, NRA, Library and Archives Canada, RG10, volume 6210, file 468-10, part 5, Samuel Devlin to Indian Affairs, 20 May 1946. [MER-003806-0001]

86. Gresko, "Paul Durieu," http://www.biographi.ca/en/bio/durieu_paul_12E.html (accessed 31 August 2014). McNally gives the opening as 1862: McNally, *Lord's Distant Vineyard*, 67.

87. McCarthy, *From the Great River*, 160; Carney, "Grey Nuns and Children," 291; Duchaussois, *Grey Nuns*, 148.

88. Miller, *Compact, Contract, Covenant*, 156; Davin, *Report on Industrial Schools*, 10. Population figures for this period are only estimates. James Miller cites 12,000 mixed-blood people in 1870, and, in his 1879 report, Nicholas Flood Davin stated that 28,000 people were under Treaty. Miller, *Compact, Contract, Covenant*, 199; Davin, *Report on Industrial Schools*, 10.

89. Great Britain, *Rupert's Land and North-Western Territory Order* (Schedule A), 23 June 1870, http://www.justice.gc.ca/eng/rp-pr/csj-sjc/constitution/lawreg-loireg/p1t32.html.

90. Getty and Lussier, *Long as the Sun Shines*, 35.

91. Banner, *How Indians Lost Their Land*, 85.

92. Tobias, "Protection, Civilization, Assimilation," 128.

93. Miller, *Compact, Contract, Covenant*, 156.

94. Miller, *Compact, Contract, Covenant*, 154.

95. Friesen, "Magnificent Gifts," 205, 212.

96. Erasmus, *Buffalo Days*, 250.

97. Ray, *Illustrated History*, 212; Taylor, "Canada's Northwest Indian Policy," 3.

98. Sprague, *Canada's Treaties with Aboriginal People*, 13.

99. For an example of a request for a day school on a reserve, see: McCullough, "Peyasiw-awasis," http://www.biographi.ca/en/bio/peyasiw_awasis_15E.html (accessed 6 June 2014).

100. Miller, *Compact, Contract, Covenant*, 164–165.

101. Morris, *Treaties of Canada*, 202.

102. In Canada, the *Indian Act* had been preceded by the 1868 *Act to provide for the organization of the Department of the Secretary of State of Canada and for the Administration of the Affairs of the Indians*, and the 1869 *An Act for the gradual enfranchisement of Indians*.

103. *An Act to amend and consolidate the laws respecting Indians*, Statutes of Canada 1876, chapter 18.

104. Miller, *Skyscrapers Hide the Heavens*, 255.

105. Library and Archives Canada, RG10, volume 6810, file 470-2-3, volume 7, Evidence of D. C. Scott to the Special Committee of the House of Commons Investigating the Indian Act amendments of 1920 (L-2)(N-3).

106. For the banning of the Potlatch, see: LaViolette, *Struggle for Survival*, 41–42; Cole and Chaikin, *Iron Hand*, 16–17, 95. For the banning of the Thirst Dance, see: Pettipas, *Severing the Ties*, 53–54, 95–96.

107. For examples, see: LaViolette, *Struggle for Survival*, 41–42; Cole and Chaikin, *Iron Hand*, 16–17, 95; TRC, NRA, Library and Archives Canada, RG10, volume 3825, file 60511-1, J. Hugonard to Indian Commissioner, 23 November 1903. [RCA-011007-0001]

108. Canada, Sessional Papers 1885, number 116. F., 95–96, J. S. Dennis to Sir John A. Macdonald, 20 December 1878.

109. Davin, *Report on Industrial Schools*, 14.

110. Driver, "Discipline Without Frontiers?," 282.

111. Parker, *Uprooted*, 190.

112. Sutherland, *Children in English-Canadian Society*, 100.

113. Sutherland, *Children in English-Canadian Society*, 138.

114. Fear-Segal, *White Man's Club*, 186; Standing Bear, *My People the Sioux*, 123–133.

115. Canada, *Annual Report of the Department of Indian Affairs, 1884* (for High River, 76; for Battleford, 154; for Qu'Appelle, 161).

116. Canada, House of Commons Debates (22 May 1883), 1376.

117. Library and Archives Canada, RG10, volume 3647, file 8128, Andsell Macrae, 18 December 1886.

118. Canada, *Annual Report of the Department of Indian Affairs, 1910*, 273.

119. Canada, *Annual Report of the Department of Indian Affairs, 1883*, 104.

120. Library and Archives Canada, RG10, volume 3924, file 116823, L. Vankoughnet to Sir John A. Macdonald, 15 March 1886.

121. TRC, NRA, Library and Archives Canada, RG10, volume 6001, file 1-1-1, part 1, Privy Council Order Number 1278, 7 June 1888; [PLD-007312] Library and Archives Canada, RG10, volume 3819, file 58418, J. Hugonnard to Hayter Reed, 11 May 1889; [PLD-009475] Library and Archives Canada, RG10, volume 3675, file 11422-4, J. Hugonnard to E. Dewdney, 5 May 1891. [PLD-009435]

122. TRC, NRA, Library and Archives Canada, RG10, volume 3879, file 91833, Order-in-Council, 22 October 1892. [RIS-000354]

123. For the admission of infected children, see: TRC, NRA, Library and Archives Canada, RG10, volume 4037, file 317021, T. Ferrier to the editor, 23 November 1907. [RCA-000315]

124. For details, see: Canada, *Annual Report of the Department of Indian Affairs, 1904*, xxvii–xxviii; TRC, NRA, Library and Archives Canada, MG17, B2, Class 'G' C.1/P.2, Church Missionary Society, "Resolutions Regarding the Administration of the North-West Canada Missions," 7 April 1903; [PAR-003622] Blake, *Don't you hear*; TRC, NRA, Library and Archives Canada, RG10, volume 3928, file 117004-1, "Report on Indian Missions and Schools," Presented to the Diocesan Synod, Diocese of Calgary, J. W. Tims, August 1908; [OLD-008159] The United Church of Canada Archives, Toronto, Acc. No. 1979.199C, box 5, file 68, "Report of the Synod's Commission on Indian Affairs," 5 December 1904; [RIS-000246] TRC, NRA, Library and Archives Canada, RG10, volume 6039, file 160-1, part 1, Frank Pedley to Reverend and dear sirs, 21 March 1908; [AEMR-120155] TRC, NRA, Anglican Church of Canada, General Synod Archives, ACC-MSCC-GS 75-103, series 3:1, box 48, file 3, Frank Pedley to Norman Tucker, 26 March 1909; [AAC-090228] Archives of Saskatchewan, MacKay Papers, Frank Oliver, "Letter to S. H. Blake, 28 January, 1908," quoted in Wasylow, "History of Battleford Industrial School," 225–226; Anglican Church General Synod Archives, 75-103, series 2-14, Frank Oliver to A. G. G., 28 Janu-

ary 1908, quoted in Gull, "'Indian Policy,'" 15; TRC, NRA, Anglican Church of
Canada, General Synod Archives, ACC-MSCC-GS 75-103, series 3:1, box 48,
file 3, Letter signed by S. H. Blake, Andrew Baird, Hamilton Cassels, T. Ferrier,
R. F. MacKay, 22 May 1908; [AAC-090192] TRC, NRA, Library and Archives
Canada, RG10, volume 6039, file 160-1, part 1, Frank Pedley to Frank Oliver, 9
April 1908; [AEMR-120157] TRC, NRA, Anglican Church of Canada, General
Synod Archives, ACC-MSCC-GS 75-103, series 3:1, box 48, file 3, "Report of
the Sub-Committee of the Advisory Board On Indian Education," n.d.; [AAC-
090231] TRC, NRA, Library and Archives Canada, RG10, volume 3919, file
116751-1A, J. B. Magnan to D. Laird, 12 December 1902; [SBR-003409] TRC,
NRA, Library and Archives Canada, RG10, volume 3919, file 116751-1A, Clif-
ford Sifton to Governor General in Council, 23 December 1903; [FAR-000095]
TRC, NRA, Library and Archives Canada, RG10, volume 6039, file 160-1, part 1,
Frank Pedley to Mr. Oliver, 30 May 1908; [120.00294] TRC, NRA, Library and
Archives Canada, RG10, volume 6327, file 660-1, part 1, J. Hugonnard to Frank
Oliver, 28 March 1908; [PLD-007334] TRC, NRA, Library and Archives Canada,
RG10, volume 6039, file 160-1, part 1, Superintendent General of Indian Affairs
to T. Ferrier, 18 July 1908; [AEMR-016328] TRC, NRA, Library and Archives
Canada, RG10, volume 6039, file 160-1, part 1, Heron to Frank Oliver, 16 Febru-
ary 1909; [AEMR-120164] TRC, NRA, Library and Archives Canada, RG10,
volume 6039, file 160-4, part 1, Association of Indian Workers to Frank Oliver,
19 February 1909; [AEMR-016332] TRC, NRA, Library and Archives Canada,
RG10, FA 10-17, volume 6041, file 160-5, part 1, 1905–1934, Emile Legal to
Frank Pedley, 20 July 1908; [AEMR-254243] TRC, NRA, Anglican Church of
Canada, General Synod Archives, ACC-MSCC-GS 75-103, series 3:1, box 48,
file 3, Arthur Barner to S. H. Blake, 16 February 1909. [AAC-090206]

125. For the initial improvement, see: TRC, NRA, Library and Archives Canada,
RG10, volume 6032, file 150-40A, part 1, Headquarters – Compulsory Attendance of Pupils – Indian Schools, 1904–1933, Microfilm reel C-8149, FA 10-17,
"Re: Per Capita Grants at Indian Residential Schools," Russell Ferrier, 5 April 1932.
[120.18050] For an example of the impact of inflation, see: TRC, NRA, Library
and Archives Canada, RG10, volume 6468, file 890-1, part 1, J. Welch to D. C.
Scott, 28 July 1916. [MIS-001473] For cuts in the 1930s, see: TRC, NRA, Anglican Church of Canada, General Synod Archives, ACC-MSCC-GS 75-103, series
2.15, box 27, file 1, The Joint Delegation and Interview with the Prime Minister,
20 December 1934; [AAC-087280] TRC, NRA, Library and Archives Canada,
RG10, volume 7185, file 1/25-1-7-1, part 1, Harold McGill to Church Officers,
Principals of Indian Residential Schools, 22 February 1933. [AEMR-255373]

126. TRC, NRA, Library and Archives Canada, RG10, volume 7185, file 1/25-1-7-?,
part 1, R. A. Hoey to Dr. McGill, 4 November 1938. [AEMR-120432]

127. For staffing, see: Canada, *Annual Report of the Department of Indian Affairs,
1955*, 51; Canada, *Annual Report of the Department of Indian Affairs, 1957*, 56.
As an experiment in 1949, Indian Affairs had taken on responsibility for directly
employing the teaching staff in schools at Shubenacadie, the Mohawk Institute,
and Port Alberni. TRC, NRA, DIAND HQ, file 1/25-1-5-2, volume 1, 1952–
1969, Laval Fortier to J. P. Mulvihill, 26 October 1953. [AEMR-120563] For diet,
see: TRC, NRA, Library and Archives Canada, RG55, FA 55-19, volume 20784,
Treasury Board Submission 559690, Req. Authority for the Recommendation
and Establishment of Domestic Staff, Laval Fortier to Secretary, Treasury Board,
22 January 1960. [120.04620]

128. TRC, NRA, Canadian Welfare Council and Caldwell 1967, 89. [AEMR-019759]

129. TRC, NRA, Canadian Welfare Council and Caldwell 1967, 92. [AEMR-019759]

130. TRC, NRA, Library and Archives Canada, RG10, volume 6032, file 150-40A, part 1, Regulations Relating to the Education of Indian Children, Ottawa: Government Printing Bureau, 1894. [AGA-001516-0000]

131. For example, see: TRC, NRA, Library and Archives of Canada, RG10, volume 6374, file 764-10, part 1, S. H. Middleton to J. E. Pugh, 26 April 1940. [PUL-071183]

132. TRC, NRA, Library and Archives Canada – Burnaby, RG10, FA 10-136, volume 11466, 987/18-24, part 1, Truancy, 1952–1969, NAC, Burnaby, R. Sedgewick to Acting Deputy Superintendent General Indian Affairs, 11 October 1891; [SQU-001298-0001] RG10, volume 1575, C-14851, 1898–1899, NAC, Application for Admission, 30 November 1898. [BQL-008267-0001]

133. TRC, NRA, Library and Archives Canada, RG10, FA 10-379, 1999-01431-6, box 405, 987/25-1-018, part 1, Indian Education – Squamish Students Residence, Fraser District, 1950–1969, NAC, Ottawa, P. Phelan to Legal Adviser, 17 November 1952; [SQU-000595] Burnaby, RG10, FA 10-136, volume 11466, 987/18-24, part 1, Truancy, 1952–1969, NAC, Burnaby, P. Phelan to W. S. Arneil, 22 November 1952. [SQU-001297] For an example of a father who successfully went to court to have his children, who had been voluntarily enrolled in a residential school, returned to him, see: Library and Archives Canada, RG10, volume 2552, file 112-220-1, Martin Benson to Deputy Superintendent General of Indian Affairs, 25 September 1903.

134. TRC, NRA, Library and Archives Canada, RG10, volume 7184, file 1/25-1-5-7, part 1, W. M. Graham to Secretary, 19 February 1926. [NCA-014626]

135. Canada, *Annual Report of the Department of Indian Affairs, 1945*, 168, 183.

136. TRC, NRA, Library and Archives Canada, RG10, volume 6039, file 160-1, part 1, Martin Benson, Memorandum, 13, 15 July 1897. [100.00108]

137. For *Indian Act*, see: *An Act respecting Indians*, Statutes of Canada 1951, chapter 29, sections 113–122, 169–172. For regulations, see: TRC, NRA, INAC – Resolution Sector – IRS Historical Files Collection – Ottawa, file 1/25-1-5-2, volume 1, "Regulations With Respect to Teaching, Education, Inspection, and Discipline for Indian Residential Schools, Made and Established for the Superintendent General of Indian Affairs Pursuant to Paragraph (a) of Section 114 of the Indian Act," 20 January 1953. [PAR-001203-0001]

138. The *Public Schools Act*, Revised Statutes of Manitoba 1954, chapter 215, 923–1,114.

139. *The Manitoba Gazette*, April 9, 1955, 509–510.

140. TRC, NRA, Library and Archives Canada, RG10, volume 6032, file 150-40A, part 1, Headquarters – Compulsory Attendance of Pupils – Indian Schools, 1904–1933, Microfilm reel C-8149, FA 10-17, Indian Agent, Hagersville to Secretary, Indian Affairs, 20 February 1922; [AEMR-255312] *An Act respecting Indians*, Statutes of Canada 1919–1920, chapter 50, section 1, amending Revised Statutes of Canada 1906, chapter 81, section 10, reproduced in Venne, *Indian Acts*, 178–179.

141. TRC, NRA, Library and Archives Canada, RG10, volume 6309, file 654-1, part 1,

J. K. Irwin to Indian Affairs, 22 October 1926. [GDC-006528]

142. TRC, NRA, Library and Archives Canada, RG10, volume 6309, file 654-1, part 1, J. D. McLean to J. K. Irwin, 29 October 1926. [GDC-006529]

143. TRC, NRA, DIAND HQ, file 1/25-1, volume 19, 1968, J. A. MacDonald to the Minister, 9 October 1968. [AEMR-121636]

144. Canada, *Annual Report of the Department of Indian Affairs, 1956*, 76–77; TRC, ASAGR, Department of Northern Affairs and National Resources, *Annual Report Fiscal Year 1957–1958*, 115. [AANDC-452773]

145. Canada, *Annual Report of the Department of Indian Affairs, 1931*, 60.

146. TRC, NRA, Anglican Church of Canada, General Synod Archives, ACC-MSCC-GS 75-103, series 3:2, box 55, file 6, S. Gould to D. C. Scott, Ottawa, 18 December 1931; [AAC-090271] TRC, NRA, Anglican Church of Canada, General Synod Archives, Triennial Report of the Board of Management to the Board of Missions, M.S.C.C. 07/1934, Accession GS 75-2A, Archibald [Fleming], Bishop of the Arctic, "The Arctic," in S. Gould, General Secretary, Board of Management, M.S.C.C., "Triennial Report of the Board of Management, M.S.C.C.," 4 July 1934, 353. [AGS-000185]

147. TRC, NRA, Library and Archives Canada, RG10, volume 6112, file 350-10, part 1, W. L. Tyrer to Sutherland, 8 February 1934. [FGA-001100] Although no trace of the decision to award funds to the Catholic school has been found in the archives, by April 1937, the Oblates had begun submitting official Indian Affairs paperwork with regard to the student population at St. Joseph's. See, for example: TRC, NRA, Library and Archives Canada, RG10, volume 6113, file 351-10, part 1, D. Couture, "Application for Admission to the Ste. Theresa Fort George Catholic Residential School for Louise Jolly," 1 April 1937. [FTG-003180-0000]

148. For the Carcross, Yukon, fire, see: Canada, *Annual Report of the Department of Indian Affairs, 1940*, 186. For the Ahousaht, British Columbia, fire, see: Canada, *Annual Report of the Department of Indian Affairs, 1940*, 186. For the Alberni, British Columbia, fire, see: Canada, *Annual Report of the Department of Indian Affairs, 1941*, 166. For the File Hills, Saskatchewan, fire, see: TRC, NRA, Library and Archives Canada, volume 6303, file 653-5, part 6, E. S. Jones to The Secretary, Indian Affairs Branch, Department of Mines and Resources, 10 April 1943; [FHR-000252] Canada, *Annual Report of the Department of Indian Affairs, 1942*, 136. For the Fort George, Québec (the Anglican school), fire, see: TRC, NRA, Library and Archives Canada, RG10, volume 6112, file 350-5, part 1, Thomas Orford to Secretary, Indian Affairs, 3 February 1943. [FGA-001026] For the Onion Lake, Saskatchewan (the Anglican school), fire, see: Canada, *Annual Report of the Department of Indian Affairs, 1944*, 155. For the Wabasca, Alberta, fire, see: TRC, NRA, Library and Archives Canada, RG10, volume 6378, file 767-5, part 3, H. A. Alderwood to R. A. Hoey, 3 January 1945; [JON-003675] Canada, Annual Report of the Department of Indian Affairs, 1945, 169. For the Norway House, Manitoba, fire, see: TRC, NRA, Library and Archives Canada, RG10, volume 6268, file 581-1, part 2, R. A. Hoey to Acting Deputy Minister, 29 May 1946. [NHU-000117] For the Lac La Ronge, Saskatchewan, fire, see: TRC, NRA, Provincial Archives of Alberta, Anglican Diocese of Athabasca Fonds, Edmonton, AB, Acc. PR1970.0387/1641, box 41, Anglican Diocese of Athabasca Fonds, file A320/572, Indian Schools – General, Official Correspondence of Bishop Sovereign, 1941–1947, Report of Fire at All Saints' School, Lac la Ronge, Sask.,

2 February 1947. [PAR-123539] For the Delmas, Saskatchewan, fire, see: TRC, NRA, Library and Archives Canada, RG10, volume 8756, file 671/25-1-010, J. P. B. Ostrander to Indian Affairs Branch, 19 January 1948. [THR-000266-0001]

149. See, for example: TRC, NRA, Library and Archives Canada, RG85, volume 229, file 630/158-9, part 1, Government Hostel – Chesterfield Inlet, 1929–1953, Extracts from S. J. Bailey's Report, Eastern Arctic Patrol, 27 July 1948. [CIU-000189]

150. See, for example: Davin, *Report on Industrial Schools*, 9.

151. For an example of Métis children at a church-run boarding school, see: Erickson, "'Bury Our Sorrows in the Sacred Heart,'" 34–35.

152. For an example of the Métis being viewed as 'dangerous,' see: Library and Archives Canada, RG10, volume 6031, "Extract from a letter dated the 19th July, 1899, from the Rev. Father Hugonard."

153. For an example, see: TRC, NRA, Library and Archives Canada, R776-0-5 (RG55), volume 562, T.B. #252440, Clifford Sifton to Mr. Smart, 18 October 1899. [NPC-523981c]

154. For an early example of this view, see: Canada, Sessional Papers 1885, number 116, 81, Memo: Hugh Richardson, 1 December 1879.

155. For an example, see: Library and Archives Canada, RG10, volume 6323, file 658-10, part 3, W. M. Graham to the Secretary of the Department of Indian Affairs, 5 December 1929.

156. For example, it was estimated in 1936 that 80 percent of Métis children in Alberta received no education. Chartrand, "Métis Residential School Participation," 41.

157. Quiring, *CCF Colonialism in Northern Saskatchewan*; Barron, *Walking in Indian Moccasins*.

158. For detailed treatment of the issue, see: Chartrand, Logan, and Daniels, *Métis History and Experience*.

159. For examples, see: TRC, NRA, National Capital Regional Service Centre – LAC – Ottawa, volume 2, file 600-1, locator #062-94, Education of Eskimos (1949–1957), Department of Northern Affairs and National Resources to Northern Administration and Lands Branch, 8 April 1958; [NCA-016925] TRC, NRA, Library and Archives Canada – Ottawa, RG85, volume 1506, file 600-1-1, part 2A, J. G. Wright to Mr. Gibson, 19 November 1946. [NCA-005728]

160. For a 1940 assessment of building conditions, see: TRC, NRA, Library and Archives Canada, RG10, volume 6012, file 1-1-5A, part 2, R. A. Hoey to Dr. McGill, 31 May 1940. [BIR-000248]

161. Canada, Special Joint Committee, 1946, 3, 15.

162. Canada, *Annual Report of the Department of Indian Affairs, 1945*, 168, 183; Canada, *Annual Report of the Department of Indian Affairs, 1955*, 70, 76–78.

163. Canada, *Annual Report of the Department of Indian Affairs, 1949*, 199.

164. *An Act respecting Indians*, Statutes of Canada 1951, chapter 29, section 113, reproduced in Venne, *Indian Acts*, 350.

165. Canada, *Annual Report of the Department of Indian Affairs, 1961*, 57.

166. Canada, *Annual Report of the Department of Indian Affairs, 1961*, 63.

167. See, for example: TRC, NRA, No document location, no document file source, The Canadian Catholic Conference, "A Brief to the Parliamentary Committee on Indian Affairs," May 1960, 8. [GMA-001642-0000]

168. Newman, *Indians of the Saddle Lake Reserve*, 81–87.

169. For a discussion that places both child welfare and residential schools in the context of the ongoing colonization of Aboriginal people, see: McKenzie and Hudson, "Native Children."

170. For an example of this assessment, see: TRC, NRA, Canadian Welfare Council and Caldwell 1967, 89. [AEMR-019759]

171. For examples of the link between the closure of residential schools and the increase in children in care, see: TRC, NRA, Library and Archives Canada, RG10, box 98, Acc., 1999-01431-6, file 274/25-1-010, part 1, P. L. McGillvray to Indian Affairs Branch, 17 November 1964; [NCA-010544] TRC, NRA, INAC – Resolution Sector – IRS Historical Files Collection – Ottawa, file 211/6-1-010, volume 6, R. F. Davey to Michael Kearney, 12 June 1967; [SRS-000175] TRC, NRA, Library and Archives Canada, RG10, Acc. 1984-85/112, box 47, file 451/25-1, Newspaper article, "Mohawk Institute May Close after 139 Years," no date; [TAY-001133] TRC, NRA, Diocese of Huron Archives, Anglican Church of Canada, Huron University College, London, ON, Luxton Papers, box 27, Indian Reserves, Richard Isaac, Six Nations Council To Whom It May Concern, 13 March 1970; [TAY-001432] TRC, NRA, INAC – Resolution Sector – IRS Historical Files Collection – Ottawa, file 479/25-13-001, volume 3, G. D. Cromb to Deputy Minister, 20 March 1970; [TAY-003053-0001] TRC, NRA, National Capital Regional Service Centre – LAC – Ottawa, file 671/6-2-025, volume 4, Onion Lake Band Council Resolution, 31 July 1974. [ORC-008733-0002]

172. McKenzie and Hudson, "Native Children," 126.

173. See, for example: TRC, NRA, INAC – Resolution Sector – IRS Historical Files Collection – Ottawa, RCAP [89-22], file E4974-2031, St. Mary's Student Residence, BC Region, part 1, 1981–1989, B, "Benefit to Children," undated notes from 1982. [MIS-008082-0001]

174. TRC, NRA, DIAND, file 1/25-13, volume 13, R. F. Battle to Deputy Minister, 2 February 1968; [AEMR-014646] TRC, NRA, INAC – Resolution Sector – IRS Historical Files Collection – Ottawa, 1/25-13, 01/68–07/68, volume 13, R. F. Davey to Regional Superintendent of Schools, 13 June 1968. [LOW-016591]

175. Canada, *Annual Report of the Department of Indian Affairs, 1969–1970*, 128.

176. TRC, NRA, DIAND HQ, file 1/25-13-2, volume 2, 06/1968–03/1969, J. A. MacDonald to J. J. Carson, 8 November 1968. [AEMR-121640]

177. TRC, NRA, Government of Northwest Territories – Education, Culture and Employment, Miscellaneous Hostel Reports RIMS ID# 1209, box 9, "Student Residences (Hostels)," undated. [RCN-007183]

178. Canada, *Annual Report of the Department of Indian Affairs, 1968–1969*, 139; Canada, *Annual Report of the Department of Indian Affairs, 1970–1971*, 19.

179. Canada, "Statement of the Government of Canada on Indian Policy," 1969, pages 7, 8, and 22 of 24-page portable document format file.

180. Canada, "Statement of the Government of Canada on Indian Policy," 1969, pages 8 and 20 of 24-page portable document format file.

181. National Indian Brotherhood, "Statement on the Proposed New Indian Policy," Ottawa, 26 June 1969, quoted in Weaver, *Making Canadian Indian Policy*, 174.

182. Indian Chiefs of Alberta 1970, page 16 of 95-page portable document file. [Citizens Plus "Red Paper"]

183. Weaver, *Making Canadian Indian Policy*, 187.

184. For an example of local dissatisfaction, see: TRC, NRA, No document location, no document file source, Jos Houle to G.-M. Latour, 24 July 1966. [OGP-417032]

185. TRC, NRA, INAC – Resolution Sector – IRS Historical Files Collection – Ottawa, file 779/25-2-009, volume 1 (Ctrl #55-4), Dennis Bell, "Indian School," CP [Canadian Press], 15 September 1970. [NCA-007310-0001]

186. "Indians Will Operate Blue Quills School," *Edmonton Journal*, 1 August 1970. [Blue Quills clippings.pdf]

187. TRC, NRA, Library and Archives Canada – Burnaby, file 951/6-1-030, volume 9, New Christie Student Residence, 1974–1977, FA 10-138, Archival Acc. V1985-86/397, Archival box 2, R. C. Telford to L. E. Wight, 6 May 1974; [CST-001710-0000] INAC – Main Records Office – Ottawa 901/16-2, volume 5, Audit Reports – B.C. Regional Office, 07/1974–06/1978, locator #L362, DIAND – Ottawa Central Registry, [illegible] for R. C. Pankhurst to Director, Finance and Management, 29 January 1975. [CST-009455]

188. All these schools were in Saskatchewan. The Beauval school closed in 1995, see: TRC, NRA, INAC – Resolution Sector – IRS Historical Files Collection – Ottawa, file E4965-2013, volume 3, Beauval Residential School, box 1, file 1-5, Memorandum of Understanding and Agreement Re: The Beauval Indian Education Centre, 6 June 1995. [BVL-001306] The Duck Lake and the Gordon's residences both closed in 1996, see: TRC, NRA, INAC – Resolution Sector – IRS Historical Files Collection – Ottawa, file E4974-10474, volume 2, Ray Gamracy to Dana Commercial Credit Canada, 6 June 1996; [SMD-000651-0000] Gordon's School, Anglican Indian and Eskimo Residential Schools, Anglican Church of Canada, www.anglican.ca/relationships/histories/gordons-school-punnichy (accessed 5 May 2014). The Lestock, Marieval, and Prince Albert residences all closed in 1997, see: TRC, NRA, INAC – Resolution Sector – IRS Historical Files Collection – Ottawa, Muskowekwan Residential School, box 67, file 1, Muskowekwan Education Centre Board of Directors, Minutes 16 July 1997; [MDD-007310-0001] INAC – Resolution Sector – IRS Historical Files Collection – Ottawa, file E4971-361, volume 3, Myler Savill to Lionel Sparvier, 21 July 1997; [MRS-000002-0001] INAC – Resolution Sector – IRS Historical Files Collection – Ottawa, file E4974-1355, volume 8, "Education Centre Set to Re-open," *Prince Albert Herald*, Carrie Hunter, 15 October 1997 [PAR-003103-0001]

189. Canada, *Annual Report of the Department of Indian Affairs, 1984–1985*, 54.

190. Thompson, "Dehcho Hall to Close its Doors," *Northern News Services online*, 26 January 2009, http://www.nnsl.com/frames/newspapers/2009-01/jan26_09h.html.

191. TRC, NRA, No document location, no document file source, B. Pusharenko, Inuvik, NWT, "Demolition of Former Residential School Called for to Put Bad Memories to Rest," *Edmonton Journal*, 13 August 1998. [GNN-000298-0026]

CHAPTER TWO: THE SCHOOL EXPERIENCE

1. TRC, NRA, Library and Archives Canada, RG10, volume 6040, file 160-4, part 1, R. B. Heron to Regina Presbytery, April 1923. [AEMR-016371]

2. Canada, *Annual Report of the Department of Indian Affairs, 1941*, 189; Canada, *Annual Report of the Department of Indian Affairs, 1942*, 154; Canada, *Annual Report of the Department of Indian Affairs, 1943*, 168; Canada, *Annual Report of the Department of Indian Affairs, 1944*, 177; Canada, *Annual Report of the Department of Indian Affairs, 1945*, 190; Canada, *Annual Report of the Department of Indian Affairs, 1946*, 231; Canada, *Annual Report of the Department of Indian Affairs, 1947*, 236; Canada, *Annual Report of the Department of Indian Affairs, 1948*, 234; Canada, *Annual Report of the Department of Indian Affairs, 1949*, 215, 234; Canada, *Annual Report of the Department of Indian Affairs, 1950*, 86–87; Canada, *Annual Report of the Department of Indian Affairs, 1951*, 34–35; Canada, *Annual Report of the Department of Indian Affairs, 1952*, 74–75; Canada, *Annual Report of the Department of Indian Affairs, 1953*, 82–83; Canada, *Annual Report of the Department of Indian Affairs, 1954*, 88–89; Canada, *Annual Report of the Department of Indian Affairs, 1955*, 78–79; Canada, *Annual Report of the Department of Indian Affairs, 1956*, 76–77; Canada, *Annual Report of the Department of Indian Affairs, 1956–57*, 88–89; Canada, *Annual Report of the Department of Indian Affairs, 1958*, 90–91; Canada, *Annual Report of the Department of Indian Affairs, 1959*, 94; Canada, *Annual Report of the Department of Indian Affairs, 1960*,.94; Canada, *Annual Report of the Department of Indian Affairs, 1961*, 103.

3. Canada, *Annual Report of the Department of Indian Affairs, 1942*, 154; Canada, *Annual Report of the Department of Indian Affairs, 1943*, 168; Canada, *Annual Report of the Department of Indian Affairs, 1944*, 177; Canada, *Annual Report of the Department of Indian Affairs, 1945*, 190; Canada, *Annual Report of the Department of Indian Affairs, 1946*, 231; Canada, *Annual Report of the Department of Indian Affairs, 1947*, 236; Canada, *Annual Report of the Department of Indian Affairs, 1948*, 234; Canada, *Annual Report of the Department of Indian Affairs, 1949*, 215; Canada, *Annual Report of the Department of Indian Affairs, 1950*, 86–87; Canada, *Annual Report of the Department of Indian Affairs, 1951*, 34–35; Canada, *Annual Report of the Department of Indian Affairs, 1952*, 74–75; Canada, *Annual Report of the Department of Indian Affairs, 1953*, 82–83; Canada, *Annual Report of the Department of Indian Affairs, 1954*, 88–89; Canada, *Annual Report of the Department of Indian Affairs, 1955*, 78–79; Canada, *Annual Report of the Department of Indian Affairs, 1956*, 76–77; Canada, *Annual Report of the Department of Indian Affairs, 1956–57, 88–89; Canada, Annual Report of the Department of Indian Affairs, 1958*, 91; Canada, *Annual Report of the Department of Indian Affairs, 1959*, 94; Canada, *Annual Report of the Department of Indian Affairs, 1960*, 94; Canada, *Annual Report of the Department of Indian Affairs, 1961*, 102; Canada, *Annual Report of the Department of Indian Affairs, 1962*, 73; Canada, *Annual Report of the Department of Indian Affairs, 1963*, 62.

4. Canada, *Annual Report of the Department of Indian Affairs, 1883*, 96.

5. TRC, NRA, Library and Archives Canada, RG10, volume 6323, file 658-6, part 1, Department of Indian Affairs Inspector's Report for the St. Barnabas, Indian Residential school, D. Hicks, 25 September 1928. [PAR-003233]

6. Library and Archives Canada, RG10, volume 6205, file 468-1, part 2, S. R. McVitty to Secretary, Indian Affairs, 30 January 1928. [McVittie to Secretary, Jan 30 1928]

7. TRC, NRA, Library and Archives Canada, RG10, volume 6342, file 750-1, part 1, Microfilm reel C-8699, J. D. McLean to Reverend E. Ruaux, 21 June 1915. [MRY-001517] For a similar report from the Battleford, Saskatchewan, school, see: Canada, *Annual Report of the Department of Indian Affairs, 1909*, 349–350. For a Manitoba example, see: TRC, NRA, Library and Archives Canada, RG10, volume 6267, file 580-5, part 4, Joseph Hamilton Inspection Report, not dated. [DRS-000570]

8. TRC, NRA, INAC – Resolution Sector – IRS Historical Files Collection – Ottawa, file 673/23-5-038, volume 1, H. L. Winter to Indian Affairs, 9 September 1932. [MRS-000138-0001]

9. TRC, NRA, Library and Archives Canada, RG10, volume 6327, file 660-1, part 1, J. D. McLean to Rev. J. Hugonard, 30 May 1911. [PLD-007442]

10. TRC, NRA, Library and Archives Canada, RG10, volume 6422, file 869-1, part 2, R. H. Cairns, inspector to J. D. McLean, 5 January 1915. [COQ-000390]

11. TRC, NRA, Library and Archives Canada, RG10, volume 6431, file 877-1, part 2, "Extract from Report of Mr. Inspector Cairns dated September 5th and 6th, 1928 on the Alberni Indian Residential School." [ABR-001591]

12. TRC, NRA, Library and Archives Canada, RG10, volume 6001, file 1-1-1, part 3, "Department of Indian Affairs, Schools Branch," 31 March 1935. [SRS-000279]

13. For a British Columbia example, see: TRC, NRA, Library and Archives Canada, RG10, volume 6431, file 877-1, part 1, A. W. Neill to A. W. Vowell, 8 July 1909. [ABR-007011-0001] For a Manitoba example, see: TRC, NRA, Library and Archives Canada, RG10, volume 6262, file 578-1, part 4, W. M. Graham to Secretary, Indian Affairs, 4 February 1922. [ELK-000299]

14. For example, a 1936 United Church document on First Nations education policy stated that the staff of all United Church schools should be composed of people who had a "Christian motive, or, in other words, a missionary purpose coupled with skill in some particular field to teach his specialty to the Indians." Staff members were expected to be "closely related to and actively interested in the work of the nearest United Church," and be acquainted with, and sympathetic to, "the religious education programme of the United Church." Having laid out these fairly specific requirements, the policy document added that "some minimum educational qualifications for staff members should be outlined." TRC, NRA, United Church Archives, Acc. 83.050C, box 144-21, "Statement of Policy Re Indian Residential Schools," June 1936. [UCC-050004]

15. For an example of the link between low pay and unqualified teachers, see: TRC, NRA, Library and Archives Canada, RG10, volume 6039, file 160-1, part 1, Martin Benson, Memorandum, 15 July 1897, 4, 25. [100.00108]

16. TRC, NRA, Library and Archives Canada, RG10, volume 4041, file 334503, F. H. Paget to Frank Pedley, 25 November 1908, 55. [RCA-000298]

17. TRC, NRA, Library and Archives Canada, RG10, volume 6431, file 877-1, part 1, A. W. Vowell to Secretary, Indian Affairs, 14 July 1909. [ABR-007011-0000]

18. Canada, *Annual Report of the Department of Indian Affairs, 1955*, 51.

19. TRC, NRA, DIAND, file 1/25-1, volume 22, R. F. Davey to Bergevin, 15 September 1959, 3. [AEMR-019616]

20. Canada, *Annual Report of the Department of Indian Affairs, 1903*, 342–343. For other examples of the emphasis on religious training in the schools, see: Canada, *Annual Report of the Department of Indian Affairs, 1887*, 27–28; Canada, *Annual Report of the Department of Indian Affairs, 1910*, 433–434; Canada, *Annual Report of the Department of Indian Affairs, 1890*, 119; Canada, *Annual Report of the Department of Indian Affairs, 1900*, 323. Canada, *Annual Report of the Department of Indian Affairs, 1901*, 317, 320.

21. Moine, *My Life in a Residential School*, n.p.

22. TRC, NRA, The Presbyterian Church in Canada Archives, Toronto, ON, Tyler Bjornson File, 'Presbyterian Research,' "Presbyterian Indian Residential School Staff Handbook," 1. [IRC-041206]

23. For Kelly, see: Morley, *Roar of the Breakers*, 57, 158. For Ahenakew, see: Ahenakew, *Voices of the Plains Cree*, 14–24. For Kennedy, see: Canada, *Annual Report of the Department of Indian Affairs, 1902*, 194. For Dion, see: Dion, *My Tribe the Crees*, 156–163. For Johnson, see: Johnston, *Buckskin & Broadcloth*, 46. For Lickers, see: "Norman Lickers First Ontario Indian Lawyer," *Brantford Expositor*, November 18, 1938, quoted in Briggs, "Legal Professionalism," 2.

24. Canada, Special Joint Committee, 1947, 747.

25. TRC, AVS, David Charleson, Statement to the Truth and Reconciliation Commission of Canada, Deroche, British Columbia, 20 January 2010, Statement Number: 2011-5043.

26. TRC, AVS, Isabelle Whitford, Statement to the Truth and Reconciliation Commission of Canada, Keeseekoowenin First Nation, Manitoba, 28 May 2010, Statement Number: S-KFN-MB-01-004.

27. TRC, AVS, Betsy Olson, Statement to the Truth and Reconciliation Commission of Canada, Saskatoon, Saskatchewan, 21 June 2012, Statement Number: 2011-4378.

28. TRC, AVS, Leona Agawa, Statement to the Truth and Reconciliation Commission of Canada, Sault Ste. Marie, Ontario, 6 November 2010, Statement Number: 01-ON-4-6NOV10-006.

29. Canada, *Annual Report of the Department of Indian Affairs, 1921*, 28.

30. TRC, NRA, Library and Archives Canada, RG10, volume 6014, file 1-1-6 MAN, part 1, Duncan Campbell Scott to Mr. Meighen, 1 June 1920. [NCA-002403]

31. Canada, Special Joint Committee, *Minutes of Evidence*, D. F. Brown Presiding, 15 April 1947, 483–484.

32. Canada, Special Joint Committee, *Minutes of Evidence*, D. F. Brown Presiding, 17 April 1947, 505.

33. TRC, NRA, Library and Archives Canada, RG85, volume 1338, file 600-1-1, part 19, D. W. Hepburn, "Northern Education: Facade for Failure," *Variables: The Journal of the Sociology Club* (University of Alberta) 2, no. 1 (February 1963): 16. [NCA-005960]

34. TRC, NRA, Library and Archives Canada, RG85, volume 1338, file 600-1-1, part

19, D. W. Hepburn, "Northern Education: Facade for Failure." *Variables: The Journal of the Sociology Club* (University of Alberta) 2, no. 1 (February 1963): 17. [NCA-005960]

35. TRC, NRA, Library and Archives Canada, RG85, volume 1338, file 600-1-1, part 19, D. W. Hepburn, "Northern Education: Facade for Failure." *Variables: The Journal of the Sociology Club* (University of Alberta) 2, no. 1 (February 1963): 18. [NCA-005960]

36. TRC, NRA, National Archives of Canada, RG10, volume 8760, file 901/25-1, part 2, R. F. Davey to Director, 14 March 1956, 4. [AEMR-120651]

37. See, for example: TRC, NRA, DIAND, file 1/25-1 (E.10), "Report on Textbooks," 6–9; [AEMR- 019193A] Commission Parent, *Rapport de la Commission royale d'enquête sur l'enseignement dans la province de Québec*, volume 3, *L'administration de l'enseignement*, part B, "Diversité religieuse, culturelle, et unité de l'administration," http://classiques.uqac.ca/contemporains/quebec_commission_parent/rapport_parent_4/rapport_parent_vol_4.pdf, paragraph 210 (accessed 7 August 2012); TRC, NRA, DIAND, file 1/25-1 (E.10), "Report on Textbooks," 6–9; [AEMR-019193A] Vanderburgh, *The Canadian Indian*.

38. TRC, NRA, DIAND, file 1/25-1 (E.10), "Report on Textbooks," 1–6. [AEMR-019193A]

39. TRC, AVS, Mary Courchene, Statement to the Truth and Reconciliation Commission of Canada, Pine Creek First Nation, Manitoba, 28 November 2011, Statement Number: 2011-2515.

40. TRC, AVS, Lorna Cochrane, Statement to the Truth and Reconciliation Commission of Canada, Winnipeg, Manitoba, 18 June 2010, Statement Number: SC110.

41. Elias, "Lillian Elias," 51.

42. See, for example: TRC, AVS, Victoria McIntosh, Statement to the Truth and Reconciliation Commission of Canada, Winnipeg, Manitoba, 16 June 2010, Statement Number: 02-MB-16JU10-123.

43. TRC, AVS, Walter Jones, Statement to the Truth and Reconciliation Commission of Canada, Victoria, British Columbia, 14 April 2012, Statement Number: 2011-4008.

44. Pigott, "The Leadership Factory," B3.

45. Blondin-Andrew, "New Ways of Looking for Leadership," 64.

46. John Amagoalik, quoted in McGregor, *Inuit Education*, 110.

47. Amagoalik, *Changing the Face of Canada*, 43–46.

48. TRC, AVS, David Simailak, Statement to the Truth and Reconciliation Commission of Canada, Baker Lake, Nunavut, 15 November 2011, Statement Number: SP032.

49. TRC, AVS, Roddy Soosay, Statement to the Truth and Reconciliation Commission of Canada, Hobbema, Alberta, 25 July 2013, Statement Number: 2011-2379.

50. TRC, AVS, Martha Loon, Statement to the Truth and Reconciliation Commission of Canada, Thunder Bay, Ontario, 25 November 2010, Statement Number: 01-ON-24NOV10-021.

51. TRC, AVS, Frederick Ernest Koe, Statement to the Truth and Reconciliation Commission of Canada, Inuvik, Northwest Territories, 30 June 2011, Statement Number: SC091.

52. TRC, AVS, Madeleine Dion Stout, Statement to the Truth and Reconciliation Commission of Canada, Winnipeg, Manitoba, 18 June 2010, Statement Number: 02-MB-18JU10-059.

53. TRC, NRA, Library and Archives Canada, RG10, volume 6191, file 462-1, part 1, Russell T. Ferrier to George Prewer, 8 February 1922. [CRS-001015]

54. Canada, *Annual Report of the Department of Indian Affairs, 1887*, 126.

55. Canada, *Annual Report of the Department of Indian Affairs, 1884*, 155.

56. Canada, *Annual Report of the Department of Indian Affairs, 1886*, 139.

57. Library and Archives Canada, RG10, volume 3930, file 117377-1 A, H. Reed to Bishop of Rupert's Land, 31 May 1893.

58. Wasylow, "History of Battleford Industrial School," 467.

59. Elias, "Lillian Elias," 54–55.

60. For laundry example, see: TRC, NRA, Library and Archives Canada, RG10, volume 6207, file 468-5, part 6, S. R. McVitty to Secretary Indian Affairs, 3 January 1929. [MER-000751] For kitchen example, see: TRC, NRA, Library and Archives Canada, RG10, volume 6058, file 265- 13, part 1, J. P. Mackey to A. F. MacKenzie, 20 May 1930. [SRS-000252] For workshop example, see: TRC, NRA, Library and Archives Canada, RG10, volume 6219, file 471-13, part 1, Russell T. Ferrier to J. Howitt, 13 June 1932. [AGA-000069]

61. For an example, see: TRC, NRA, Library and Archives Canada, RG10, volume 6327, file 660-1, part 3, A. F. MacKenzie to G. Leonard, 6 May 1936. [PLD-006119]

62. TRC, NRA, Library and Archives Canada, RG10, volume 6327, file 660-1, part 3, A. F. MacKenzie to William Hall, 18 May 1936. [PLD-000750]

63. TRC, NRA, Library and Archives Canada, RG10, volume 6327, file 660-1, part 3, William Hall to Indian Affairs, 30 April 1936. [PLD-000746]

64. TRC, NRA, Library and Archives Canada, RG10, volume 6255, file 576-1, part 4, R. T. Chapin to A. G. Hamilton, 10 September 1941. [BRS-000461-0001] For the boy's age, see: TRC, NRA, Library and Archives Canada, RG10, volume 6258, file 576-10, part 8, "Application for Admission," Kenneth Smith, 1 July 1938. [BRS-002184-0007]

65. TRC, NRA, Library and Archives Canada, RG10, volume 6259, file 576-23, part 1, G. C. Elwyn to RCMP, 20 April 1949. [BRS-000332]

66. TRC, NRA, Library and Archives Canada, RG10, volume 6352, file 753-23, part 1, 1935–1944, Microfilm reel C-8709, Acting Director to J. T. Faunt, 18 December 1944. [EDM-003369]

67. TRC, NRA, Library and Archives Canada, RG10, volume 6251, file 575-1, part 3, R. A. Hoey to A. G. Smith, 24 September 1942. [BIR-000272]

68. For ending of half-day system, see: TRC, NRA, INAC – Resolution Sector – IRS Historical Files Collection – Ottawa, file 1/25-1-5-2, volume 1, Superintendent

General DIAND, "Regulations with respect to teaching, education, inspection, and discipline for Indian Residential Schools, Made and Established by the Superintendent General of Indian Affairs Pursuant to Paragraph (a) of Section 114 of the Indian Act," 20 January 1953; [PAR-001203-0001] H. M. Jones to Deputy Minister. [PAR-001203-0000]

69. TRC, NRA, INAC – Resolution Sector – IRS Historical Files Collection – Ottawa, file 128/25-2- 575, volume 1, J. R. Bell to R. D. Ragan, 17 February 1959. [IRC-041312]

70. TRC, NRA, Library and Archives Canada, RG10, volume 3674, file 11422, E. Dewdney to Thomas Clarke, 31 July 1883. [120.06668]

71. TRC, NRA, Library and Archives Canada, RG10, volume 6452, file 884-1, part 1, Microfilm reel 8773, "Rules and Regulations, Kootenay Industrial School." [AEMR-011621A]

72. Library and Archives Canada, RG10, volume 3836, file 68557, H. Reed, Suggestions for the Government of Indian schools, 27 January 1890.

73. Canada, *Annual Report of the Department of Indian Affairs, 1894*, 248–249.

74. Canada, *Annual Report of the Department of Indian Affairs, 1887*, 128.

75. Canada, *Annual Report of the Department of Indian Affairs, 1898*, 345.

76. Canada, *Annual Report of the Department of Indian Affairs, 1898*, 355.

77. Canada, *Annual Report of the Department of Indian Affairs, 1898*, 302.

78. Canada, *Annual Report of the Department of Indian Affairs, 1903*, 457.

79. TRC, NRA, St. Paul's Archives, Acts of Canonical Visitation, 1883–1966, Stacks 2L, Acte Général de Visite des Missions Indiennes du Nord-Ouest Canadien par le T.R.P. Théodore Labouré, O.M.I., Supérieur Général, Rome Maison Générale, 45. [OMI-034614]

80. Wasylow, "History of Battleford Industrial School," 449.

81. Moran, *Stoney Creek Woman*, 58.

82. Callahan, "On Our Way to Healing," 68.

83. Graham, *Mush Hole*, 368.

84. Provincial Archives of British Columbia, Transcript Disc #182, Mary Englund, interviewed by Margaret Whitehead, 31 July 1980, PABC No. 3868.

85. Graham, *Mush Hole*, 449.

86. TRC, AVS, Arthur Ron McKay, Statement to the Truth and Reconciliation Commission of Canada, Winnipeg, Manitoba, 18 June 2010, Statement Number: 02-MB-18JU10-044.

87. TRC, AVS, Peter Nakogee, Statement to the Truth and Reconciliation Commission of Canada, Timmins, Ontario, 9 November 2010, Statement Number: 01-ON-4-6NOV10-023. (Translated from Swampy Cree to English by Translation Bureau, Public Works and Government Services Canada, 8961944_002.)

88. TRC, AVS, Meeka Alivaktuk (translated from Inuktitut), Statement to the Truth and Reconciliation Commission of Canada, Pangnirtung, Nunavut, 13 February 2012, Statement Number: SP045.

89. TRC, AVS, Sam Kautainuk (translated from Inuktitut), Statement to the Truth and Reconciliation Commission of Canada, Pond Inlet, Nunavut, 7 February 2012, Statement Number: SP044.

90. TRC, AVS, Greg Ranville, Statement to the Truth and Reconciliation Commission of Canada, Saskatoon, Saskatchewan, 22 June 2012, Statement Number: 2011-1752.

91. TRC, AVS, William Herney, Statement to the Truth and Reconciliation Commission of Canada, Halifax, Nova Scotia, 29 October 2011, Statement Number: 2011-2923.

92. TRC, AVS, Alphonsine McNeely, Statement to the Truth and Reconciliation Commission of Canada, Fort Good Hope, Northwest Territories, 13 July 2010, Statement Number: 01-NWT-JY10-002.

93. TRC, AVS, Pierrette Benjamin, Statement to the Truth and Reconciliation Commission of Canada, La Tuque, Québec, 6 March 2013, Statement Number: SP105.

94. TRC, AVS, John Kistabish (translated from French), Statement to the Truth and Reconciliation Commission of Canada, Montréal, Québec, 26 April 2013, Statement Number: 2011-6135.

95. Snow, *These Mountains Are Our Sacred Places*, 110.

96. TRC, AVS, Andrew Bull Calf, Statement to the Truth and Reconciliation Commission of Canada, Lethbridge, Alberta, 10 October 2013, Statement Number: 2011-0273.

97. TRC, AVS, Evelyn Kelman, Statement to the Truth and Reconciliation Commission of Canada, Lethbridge, Alberta, 10 October 2013, Statement Number: SP128.

98. TRC, AVS, Marilyn Buffalo, Statement to the Truth and Reconciliation Commission of Canada, Hobbema, Alberta, 25 July 2013, Statement Number: SP125.

99. TRC, AVS, Sarah McLeod, Statement to the Truth and Reconciliation Commission of Canada, Kamloops, British Columbia, 8 August 2009, Statement Number: 2011-5009.

100. TRC, NRA, Library and Archives Canada, RG10, volume 7936, file 32-104, J. W. House to G. H. Gooderham, 26 January 1942. [OLD-004156-0001]

101. TRC, NRA, Library and Archives Canada, 875-1, part 4, volume 6426, 1937–1947, NAC, F. E. Anfield to Ex-Pupils & Graduates of the Kwawkewlth Agency, 6 April 1943. [MIK-002742-0001]

102. Thaddee Andre (translated from French), Statement to the Truth and Reconciliation Commission of Canada, Montréal, Québec, 25 April 2013, Statement Number: 2011-6068.

103. See, for example, the brief that the Canadian Catholic Conference submitted to the Joint Committee of the Senate and House of Commons on Indian Affairs in 1960. TRC, NRA, No document source, no document location, "CCC Brief on Indian Welfare and Education," *Indian Record*, June 1960, 3. [BVT-001818]

104. TRC, AVS, Alex Alikashuak, Statement to the Truth and Reconciliation Commission of Canada, Winnipeg, Manitoba, 16 June 2010, Statement Number: 02-MB-16JU10-137.

105. Canadian Welfare Council, *Indian Residential Schools*, 100.

106. TRC, NRA, Provincial Archives of Alberta, PAA 71.220 B56 2429, J. Weitz, "Report on the use of the language, history and customs of the Blood Indians in the classes of Level I, during the school year 1968–69," 30 June 1969. [OGP-023347]

107. For an example from British Columbia, see: TRC, NRA, No document location, no document file source, 958/25-13, volume 3, J. A. Andrews to R. F. Davey, 28 June 1966. [ABR-000402]

108. Canada, *Annual Report of the Department of Indian Affairs, 1974–1975*, 32–33.

109. TRC, AVS, Rose Dorothy Charlie, Statement to the Truth and Reconciliation Commission of Canada, Whitehorse, Yukon, 27 May 2011, Statement Number: 2011-1134.

110. TRC, AVS, Joline Huskey, Statement to the Truth and Reconciliation Commission of Canada, Behchoko, Northwest Territories, 15 April 2011, Statement Number: 2011-0231.

111. TRC, AVS, Bruce R. Dumont, Statement to the Truth and Reconciliation Commission of Canada, Batoche, Saskatchewan, 23 July 2010, Statement Number: 01-SK-18-25JY10-013.

112. Canada, House of Commons Debates (22 May 1888), 1681.

113. Library and Archives Canada, RG10, volume 6816, file 486-2-5, part 1, H. Reed to J. Hugonnard, 13 June 1890.

114. Canada, *Annual Report of the Department of Indian Affairs, 1896*, xxxviii.

115. See, for examples: Canada, *Annual Report of the Department of Indian Affairs, 1894*, 151; Canada, *Annual Report of the Department of Indian Affairs, 1894*, 193–194; Canada, *Annual Report of the Department of Indian Affairs, 1897*, 284.

116. TRC, NRA, Library and Archives Canada, RG10, volume 1347, Microfilm reel C-13916, P. Claessen to W. R. Robertson, 17 August 1909. [KUP-004235]

117. Canada, *Annual Report of the Department of Indian Affairs, 1909*, 420.

118. Library and Archives Canada, RG10, volume 3881, file 934189, M. Begg to A. Forget, 23 February 1895.

119. TRC, NRA, Library and Archives Canada, RG10, volume 6318, file 657-1, part 1, A. E. Forget to Indian Agent, Touchwood Hills, 31 January 1896. [MDD-000851]

120. TRC, NRA, Library and Archives Canada, RG10, volume 6326, file 659-10, part 1, J. E. Pratt to Philip Phelan, 15 June 1936. [ORC-006021]

121. Library and Archives Canada, RG10, volume 6816, file 486-2-5, part 1, Extract Presbytery of Winnipeg, Committee on Indian Work, R. J. MacPherson, 9 September 1922.

122. Montour, *Brown Tom's School Days*, 26.

123. Brass, *I Walk in Two Worlds*, 25.

124. Brass, *I Walk in Two Worlds*, 25–26.

125. Moran, *Stoney Creek Woman*, 53–54.

126. Quoted in Krech, "Nutritional Evaluation," 186.

127. Quoted in Krech, "Nutritional Evaluation," 186.

128. Canada, *Annual Report of the Department of Indian Affairs, 1895*, 114.

129. TRC, NRA, Library and Archives Canada, RG10, volume 3918, file 116659-1, John F. Smith to Assistant Deputy and Secretary, Indian Affairs, 29 March 1918. [AEMR-255360]

130. TRC, NRA, Library and Archives Canada, RG10, FA 10-13, volume 3918, Microfilm reel C-10161, file 116.659-1, 1892–1920, Spec. Claims Kamloops Agency: General Correspondence Pertaining to Kamloops Industrial School, F. V. Agnew to Indian Affairs, 4 June 1918. [KAM-009763]

131. TRC, NRA, Library and Archives Canada, RG10, volume 6039, file 160-1, part 1, Martin Benson, to J. D. McLean, 15 July 1897. [100.00109]

132. TRC, NRA, Library and Archives Canada, RG10, volume 6187, file 461-1, part 3, Frank Edwards to the Secretary, Indian Affairs Branch, 26 June 1939. [IRC-048013]

133. For examples just from the 1920s, see: TRC, NRA, Library and Archives Canada, RG10, volume 3933, file 117657-1, Microfilm reel C-10164, W. M. Graham to Duncan C. Scott, 1 October 1914; [AEMR-013533] TRC, NRA, Library and Archives Canada, RG10, volume 6348, file 752-1, part 1, 1894–1936, Microfilm reel 8705, "Extract from Nurse Ramage's report, November 1921"; [CFT-000156-0001] TRC, NRA, Library and Archives Canada, RG10, volume 6348, file 752-1, part 1, 1894–1936, Microfilm reel 8705, "Extract of report of G. H. Gooderham, for month of October 1921"; [CFT-000148] TRC, NRA, Library and Archives Canada, RG10, volume 6337, file 663-1, part 1, Russell T. Ferrier to Reverend A. Watelle, 31 January 1922; [THR-000149] TRC, NRA, Library and Archives Canada, RG10, volume 6337, file 663-1, part 1, Russell T. Ferrier to Reverend A. Watelle, 16 February 1922; [THR-000151] TRC, NRA, Library and Archives Canada, RG10, volume 6327, file 660-1, part 2, "Memorandum for File," Russell T. Ferrier, 17 March 1922; [PLD-007242] TRC, NRA, Library and Archives Canada, RG10, volume 6444, file 881-5, part 2, 1922–1924, Microfilm reel C-8767, "Extract from Inspector's Report on the Fraser Lake Residential School, dated April 23rd and 24th, 1923"; [LEJ-003751] TRC, NRA, Library and Archives Canada, RG10, volume 6443, file 881-1, part 1, N. Coccola to J. D. McLean, 22 June 1923; [LEJ-001012] TRC, NRA, Library and Archives Canada, RG10, volume 6318, file 657-1, part 1, A. F. MacKenzie to J. B. Hardinge, 21 September 1923; [MDD-000731] TRC, NRA, Library and Archives Canada, RG10, volume 6324, file 659-5, part 2, "Onion Lake R.C. Boarding School," 1926; [ORC-000346-0001] TRC, NRA, Library and Archives Canada, RG10, volume 6252, file 575-5, part 2, A. G. Hamilton to Mr. Graham, 23 June 1927; [BIR-000079] TRC, NRA, Library and Archives Canada, RG10, volume 6252, file 575-5, part 2, W. Murison to W. Graham, 17 November 1927; [BIR-000093] TRC, NRA, Library and Archives Canada, RG10, volume 6268, file 580-14, part 1, A. F. MacKenzie to J. W. Waddy, 25 April 1927; [DRS-000574] TRC, NRA, Library and Archives Canada, volume 6268, file 580-14, part 1, J. W. Waddy to Assistant Deputy and Secretary, 6 May 1927; [DRS-000575] TRC, NRA, Library and Archives Canada, RG10, volume 6267, file 580-1, part 2, J. Waddy to Indian Affairs, 24 November 1928; [DRS-000564] TRC, NRA, Library and Archives Canada, RG10, volume 6267, file 580-1, part 2, Inspection report, 31 October 1929. [DRS-000566]

134. TRC, NRA, No document location, no document file source, T. M. Kennedy to Reverend Father Provincial, 2 December 1937. [OKM-000248]

135. TRC, NRA, Library and Archives Canada, RG10, volume 6455, file 884-14, part 1, Microfilm reel C-8777, "Extract from report of Inspector Cairns, Dated Nov. 9, 1922, on the Kuper Island Industrial School." [KUP-003836-0000]

136. TRC, NRA, Library and Archives Canada, RG10, volume 6262, file 578-1, part 4, W. Murison to Indian Affairs, 2 June 1925. [ELK-000330]

137. Health Canada, Food and Nutrition, Canada's Food Guides from 1942 to 1992, http://www.hc-sc.gc.ca/fn-an/food-guide-aliment/context/fg_history-histoire_ga-eng.php#fnb9 (accessed 14 December 2013).

138. TRC, NRA, Library and Archives Canada, RG10, volume 6306, file 652-5, part 6, L. B. Pett to P. E. Moore, 8 December 1947. [SMD-001897-0000]

139. TRC, NRA, Library and Archives Canada, RG10, 8796, file 1/25-13, part 4, L. B. Pett to H. M. Jones, 21 March 1958. [NPC-400776]

140. TRC, NRA, Headquarters, 1/25-1-4-1, Indian Education – Dietary Scale, Residential Schools, K. A. Feyrer, G. C. Butler, 22 December 1966. [LOW-002326-0004]

141. TRC, NRA, Unknown document location, file 901/25-13, Gerald Michaud, 1 April 1969. [120.08100C]

142. TRC, NRA, Library and Archives Canada, RG29, volume 2990, file 851-6-4, part 5a, L. Leclerc to A/Regional Director, Manitoba Region, 26 November 1970. [NPC-605542]

143. TRC, AVS, Daisy Diamond, Statement to the Truth and Reconciliation Commission of Canada, Winnipeg, Manitoba, 18 June 2010, Statement Number: SC110.

144. TRC, AVS, Dora Fraser, Statement to the Truth and Reconciliation Commission of Canada, Winnipeg, Manitoba, 19 June 2010, Statement Number: 02-MB-19JU10-012.

145. TRC, AVS, Ellen Okimaw, Statement to the Truth and Reconciliation Commission of Canada, Timmins, Ontario, 8 November 2010, Statement Number: 01-ON-4-6NOV10-022.

146. TRC, AVS, Bernard Catcheway, Statement to the Truth and Reconciliation Commission of Canada, Skownan First Nation, Manitoba, 12 October 2011, Statement Number: 2011-2510.

147. TRC, AVS, Bernard Sutherland, Statement to the Truth and Reconciliation Commission of Canada, Fort Albany, Ontario, 29 January 2013, Statement Number: 2011-3180. (Translated from Cree to English by Translation Bureau, Public Works and Government Services Canada, 8961944_003.)

148. "Nun Forced Native Students to Eat Their Own Vomit," Edmonton Journal, 25 June 1999.

149. TRC, AVS, Simon Awashish, Statement to the Truth and Reconciliation Commission of Canada, La Tuque, Québec, 5 March 2013, Statement Number: SP104.

150. TRC, AVS, Woodie Elias, Statement to the Truth and Reconciliation Commis-

sion of Canada, Fort McPherson, Northwest Territories, 12 September 2012, Statement Number: 2011-0343.

151. TRC, AVS, Dorothy Nolie, Statement to the Truth and Reconciliation Commission of Canada, Alert Bay, British Columbia, 20 October 2011, Statement Number: 2011-3294.

152. TRC, AVS, Nellie Trapper, Statement to the Truth and Reconciliation Commission of Canada, Winnipeg, Manitoba, 18 June 2010, Statement Number: 02-MB-16JU10-086.

153. TRC, AVS, Inez Dieter, Statement to the Truth and Reconciliation Commission of Canada, Regina, Saskatchewan, 16 January 2012, Statement Number: SP035.

154. TRC, AVS, Gladys Prince, Statement to the Truth and Reconciliation Commission of Canada, Brandon, Manitoba, 13 October 2011, Statement Number: 2011-2498. (Translated from Ojibway to English by Translation Bureau, Public Works and Government Services Canada, 8956132.)

155. TRC, AVS, Frances Tait, Statement to the Truth and Reconciliation Commission of Canada, Victoria, British Columbia, 13 April 2012, Statement Number: 2011-3974.

156. TRC, AVS, Hazel Bitternose, Statement to the Truth and Reconciliation Commission of Canada, Regina, Saskatchewan, 17 January 2012, Statement Number: SP036.

157. Sadowski, "Preliminary Report on the Investigation," 7–8.

158. TRC, LACAR, Library and Archives Canada, Ottawa, RG29, Department of Health fonds, Medical Services sous-fonds, Medical Services Branch Central Registry File series, Administrative Records from Blocks 800 to 849 sub-series, finding aid 29-143, Perm. volume 2622, file 800-4-9, file volume 1, file dates 09/1952 to 11/1976, file name "Records Retirement," *Indian and Northern Health Services Administrative Circular 57-66*, Destruction and Retention of Documents, P. E. Moore, 7 August 1957. [46a-c000301-d0008-001]

159. For an example, see: Canada, *Annual Report of the Department of Indian Affairs, 1893*, 91–97.

160. TRC, NRA, Library and Archives Canada, RG10, volume 6016, file 1-1-23, part 1, A. F. MacKenzie to Indian Agents, Principals of Indian Residential Schools, 17 April 1935. [SBR-001147-0000] Under this policy, the principal was to inform the Indian agent of the death of a student. The agent was then to convene and chair a three-person board of inquiry. The two other members of the board were to be the principal and the physician who attended the student. The board was to complete a form provided by Indian Affairs that requested information on the cause of death and the treatment provided to the child. Parents were to be notified of the inquiry and given the right to attend or have a representative attend the inquiry to make a statement. However, an inquiry was not to be delayed for more than seventy-two hours to accommodate parents. TRC, NRA, Library and Archives Canada, RG10, volume 6016, file 1-1-23, part 1, Indian Affairs Memorandum, 17 April 1935. [SBR-001147-0001]

161. See, for examples: TRC, NRA, Anglican Church of Canada, General Synod Archives, Anglican Church of Canada, GS-75-103, B17, Minutes of meeting of Indian and Eskimo Commission Held on Tuesday, January 11th, 1927, 11;

[AAC-083001] St. Boniface Historical Society, Archives Deschâtelets, L 541 M27L 266, Brachet to père provincial, 20 October 1928.

162. TRC, NRA, Library and Archives Canada, RG10, volume 6302, file 650-23, part 2, Inspector, Commanding Prince Albert Sub-Division to The Officer in Charge, RCMP, Regina, Saskatchewan, 10 September 1942. [BVL-000822]

163. For discussions of the health conditions on the Prairies and the federal government's failure to meet its Treaty commitments, see: Carter, *Lost Harvests*; Daschuk, *Clearing the Plains*; and Lux, *Medicine that Walks*. For food and Treaties, see: Miller, *Skyscrapers Hide the Heavens*, 228–230.

164. TRC, NRA, Library and Archives Canada, RG10, volume 6039, file 160-1, part 1, Martin Benson, to J. D. McLean, 15 July 1897. [100.00109]

165. Canada, *Annual Report of the Department of Indian Affairs, 1904*, 204.

166. TRC, NRA, Library and Archives Canada, RG10, volume 6012, file 1-1-5A, part 2, R. A. Hoey to Dr. McGill, 31 May 1940. [BIR-000248] For date of Hoey's appointment, see: Manitoba Historical Society, Memorable Manitobans: Robert Alexander Hoey (1883–1965), http://www.mhs.mb.ca/docs/people/hoey_ra.shtml (accessed 21 December 2013).

167. TRC, NRA, INAC – Resolution Sector – IRS Historical Files Collection – Ottawa, file 6-21-1, volume 4, control 25-2, The National Association of Principals and Administrators of Indian Residences Brief Presented to the Department of Indian Affairs and Northern Development as requested by Mr. E. A. Cote, Deputy Minister, prepared in 1967, presented 15 January 1968. [NCA-011495]

168. TRC, NRA, Library and Archives Canada, RG10, volume 13033, file 401/25-13, volume 1, R. F. Davey to H. B. Rodine, 5 February 1968. [AEMR-014634]

169. For Beauval fire, see: TRC, NRA, Library and Archives Canada, RG10, volume 6300, file 650-1, part 1, Louis Mederic Adam to Indian Affairs, 22 September 1927. [BVL-000879] For Cross Lake fire, see: TRC, NRA, Library and Archives Canada, RG10, volume 6260, file 577-1, part 1, J. L. Fuller to A. MacNamara, 8 March 1930; [CLD-000933-0000] TRC, NRA, Library and Archives Canada, RG10, volume 6260, file 577-1, part 1, William Gordon to Assistant Deputy and Secretary, Indian Affairs, 10 March 1930. [CLD-000934]

170. For deaths, see: Stanley, "Alberta's Half-Breed Reserve," 96–98; Library and Archives Canada, RG10, volume 6300, file 650-1, part 1, O. Charlebois to Duncan Scott, 21 September 1927; [BVL-000874] Louis Mederic Adam to Indian Affairs, 22 September 1927; [BVL-000879] TRC, NRA, Library and Archives Canada, RG10, volume 6260, file 577-1, part 1, J. L. Fuller to A. McNamara, 8 March 1930; [CLD-000933-0000] William Gordon to Assistant Deputy and Secretary, Indian Affairs, 10 March 1930; [CLD-000934] TRC, NRA, INAC – Resolution Sector – IRS Historical Files Collection – Ottawa, file 675/6-2-018, volume 2, D. Greyeyes to Indian Affairs, 22 June 1968. [GDC-005571]

171. Canada, *Annual Report of the Department of Indian Affairs, 1906*, 274–275.

172. Bryce, *Report on the Indian Schools*, 18.

173. Bryce, *Report on the Indian Schools*, 17.

174. Bryce, *Report on the Indian Schools*, 18.

175. For details, see: Canada, *Annual Report of the Department of Indian Affairs, 1904*,

xxvii–xxviii; TRC, NRA, Library and Archives Canada, MG17, B2, Class 'G' C.1/P.2, Church Missionary Society, "Resolutions Regarding the Administration of the North-West Canada Missions," 7 April 1903; [PAR-003622] Blake, *Don't you hear*; TRC, NRA, Library and Archives Canada, RG10, volume 3928, file 117004-1, "Report on Indian Missions and Schools," Presented to the Diocesan Synod, Diocese of Calgary, J. W. Tims, August 1908; [OLD-008159] The United Church of Canada Archives, Toronto, Acc. No. 1979.199C, box 5, file 68, "Report of the Synod's Commission on Indian Affairs," 5 December 1904; [RIS-000246] TRC, NRA, Library and Archives Canada, RG10, volume 6039, file 160-1, part 1, Frank Pedley to Reverend and dear sirs, 21 March 1908; [AEMR-120155] TRC, NRA, Anglican Church of Canada, General Synod Archives, ACC-MSCC-GS 75-103, series 3:1, box 48, file 3, Frank Pedley to Norman Tucker, 26 March 1909; [AAC-090228] Archives of Saskatchewan, MacKay Papers, Frank Oliver, "Letter to S. H. Blake, 28 January, 1908," quoted in Wasylow, "History of Battleford Industrial School," 225–226; Anglican Church General Synod Archives, 75-103, series 2-14, Frank Oliver to A. G. G., 28 January 1908, quoted in Gull, "'Indian Policy,'" 15; TRC, NRA, Anglican Church of Canada, General Synod Archives, ACC-MSCC-GS 75-103, series 3:1, box 48, file 3, Letter signed by S. H. Blake, Andrew Baird, Hamilton Cassels, T. Ferrier, R. F. MacKay, 22 May 1908; [AAC-090192] TRC, NRA, Library and Archives Canada, RG10, volume 6039, file 160-1, part 1, Frank Pedley to Frank Oliver, 9 April 1908; [AEMR-120157] TRC, NRA, Anglican Church of Canada, General Synod Archives, ACC-MSCC-GS 75-103, series 3:1, box 48, file 3, "Report of the Sub-Committee of the Advisory Board On Indian Education," n.d.; [AAC-090231] TRC, NRA, Library and Archives Canada, RG10, volume 3919, file 116751-1A, J. B. Magnan to D. Laird, 12 December 1902; [SBR-003409] TRC, NRA, Library and Archives Canada, RG10, volume 3919, file 116751-1A, Clifford Sifton to Governor General in Council, 23 December 1903; [FAR-000095] TRC, NRA, Library and Archives Canada, RG10, volume 6039, file 160-1, part 1, Frank Pedley to Mr. Oliver, 30 May 1908; [120.00294] TRC, NRA, Library and Archives Canada, RG10, volume 6327, file 660-1, part 1, J. Hugonnard to Frank Oliver, 28 March 1908; [PLD-007334] TRC, NRA, Library and Archives Canada, RG10, volume 6039, file 160-1, part 1, Superintendent General of Indian Affairs to T. Ferrier, 18 July 1908; [AEMR-016328] TRC, NRA, Library and Archives Canada, RG10, volume 6039, file 160-1, part 1, Heron to Frank Oliver, 16 February 1909; [AEMR-120164] TRC, NRA, Library and Archives Canada, RG10, volume 6039, file 160-4, part 1, Association of Indian Workers to Frank Oliver, 19 February 1909; [AEMR-016332] TRC, NRA, Library and Archives Canada, RG10, FA 10-17, volume 6041, file 160-5, part 1, 1905–1934, Emile Legal to Frank Pedley, 20 July 1908; [AEMR-254243] TRC, NRA, Anglican Church of Canada, General Synod Archives, ACC-MSCC-GS 75-103, series 3:1, box 48, file 3, Arthur Barner to S. H. Blake, 16 February 1909. [AAC 090206]

176. Library and Archives Canada, RG10, volume 6039, file 160-1, part 1, *Correspondence and Agreement Relating to the Maintenance and Management of Indian Boarding Schools* (Ottawa: Government Printing Bureau, 1911). [AEMR-120208A]

177. For examples, see: TRC, NRA, Library and Archives Canada, RG10, volume 6113, file 350-23, part 1, H. A. Alderwood to Percy Moore, 25 January 1946; [FGA-001121] TRC, NRA, No document location, no file source, 988/23-9, p. 2, 1947–48, R. H. Moore to Indian Affairs Branch, 30 June 1948; [KUP-001240] TRC, NRA, Library and Archives Canada, RG10, volume 6279, file 584-10,

part 4, R. S. Davies to Indian Affairs, 3 October 1951; [SBR-004545-0000] TRC, NRA, Library and Archives Canada, RG10, volume 6445, file 881-10, part 5, P. E. Moore to Superintendent, Welfare and Training Division, 23 December 1940. [LEJ-002117]

178. Canada, *Annual Report of the Department of Indian Affairs, 1893*, 173.

179. Library and Archives Canada, RG10, volume 3674, file 11422-5, H. Reed to Deputy Superintendent General of Indian Affairs, 13 May 1891.

180. TRC, NRA, Library and Archives Canada, RG10, volume 3920, file 116818, H. J. Denovan, 1 May 1901. [EDM-009805]

181. For Regina, see: TRC, NRA, Library and Archives Canada, RG10, volume 3927, file 116836-1A, J. A. Graham to J. A. Sinclair, 2 February 1904. [RIS-000075] For Onion Lake, see: TRC, NRA, Library and Archives Canada, RG29, volume 2915, file 851-1-A671, part 1a, Lang Turner to Secretary, Indian Affairs, 31 October 1921. [NPC-602633] For Mission, see: TRC, NRA, Library and Archives Canada, RG10, volume 6470, file 890-5, part 2, A. O'N. Daunt, 18 December 1924. [MIS-004992] For Muncey, see: TRC, NRA, Library and Archives Canada, RG10, volume 6207, file 468-5, part 7, A. F. MacKenzie to K. J. Beaton, 9 July 1935. [MER-000845]

182. TRC, NRA, Library and Archives Canada, RG10, volume 6305, file 652-1, part 1, J. McArthur to Secretary, Indian Affairs, 5 July 1909; [SMD-001186] 6 July 1909. [SMD-001187]

183. TRC, NRA, Library and Archives Canada, RG10, volume 3921, file 116818-1B, J. F. Woodsworth to Secretary, Indian Affairs, 25 November 1918. [EDM-000956]

184. TRC, NRA, Library and Archives Canada, RG10, volume 6041, file 160-5, part 1, "Memorandum of the Convention of the Catholic Principals of Indian Residential Schools held at Lebret, Saskatchewan, August 28 and 29, 1924." [200.4.00016]

185. For an example from the Sarcee Reserve school, see: TRC, NRA, Library and Archives Canada, RG29, volume 3403, file 823-1-A772, T. J. Fleetham to Secretary, Indian Affairs, 4 March 1915. [NPC-604045a] For an example from the High River school, see: Provincial Archives of Alberta, Oblates of Mary Immaculate, école Dunbow, Boîte 80, #3381, Journal quotidien de l'école Dunbow, 18 January 1916, quoted in Pettit, "'To Christianize and Civilize,'" 254.

186. For concerns about hospitals from the 1940s, see: TRC, NRA, Library and Archives Canada, RG29, volume 2905, file 851-1-A486, part 1, P. E. Moore to B. T. McGhie, 19 February 1942. [NPC-620532] For overall concerns regarding care in British Columbia school infirmaries in 1960, see: TRC, NRA, Library and Archives Canada – Ottawa, RG10, volume 8697, file 957/6-1, part 3, P. E. Moore to H. M. Jones, 22 July 1960. [MIS-000240]

187. For complaints from the Winnipeg, Manitoba, school, see: TRC, NRA, Library and Archives Canada, RG10, volume 8797, file 1/25-13, part 10, André Renaud to R. F. Davey, 10 August 1959. [NRD-300276] For complaints from the Roman Catholic school in The Pas, Manitoba, see: TRC, NRA, Library and Archives Canada, RG29, volume 2915, file 851-1-A578, part 3, P. E. Moore to Regional Superintendent, Central Region, INHS, 15 May 1961. [NPC-602638] For complaints from the La Tuque, Québec, school, see: TRC, NRA, Quebec Regional Service Centre – LAC – Québec City, Acc. 81-116, box 303441, file

377/17-1, J. E. DeWolf to R. L. Boulanger, 21 January 1965. [LTR-001513-0005] For concerns from the Roman Catholic school in Cardston, Alberta, see: TRC, NRA, Provincial Archives – Alberta, PAA 71.220 B161 2419, J. F. Y. Levaque to Mr. Tully, 19 November 1967. [OGP-023087]

188. Waldram, Herring, and Young, *Aboriginal Health in Canada*, 188–198; Wherrett, *Miracle of the Empty Beds*, 109–110.

189. Library and Archives Canada, Canadian Tuberculosis Association, quoted in Wherrett, *Miracle of the Empty Beds*, 111.

190. Library and Archives Canada, RG10, volume 3940, file 121698-13, Summary of statements made at meeting attached to correspondence, H. R. Halpin to Secretary, Indian Affairs, 16 November 1897. For Kah-pah-pah-mah-am-wa-ko-we-kochin's name and his being deposed from office, see: Library and Archives Canada, RG10, volume 3940, file 121698-13, Extract of a report of a Committee of the Honourable Privy Council Approved his Excellency on the 20 September 1897.

191. Moine, *My Life in a Residential School*.

192. Dion, *My Tribe the Crees*, 129.

193. Baker, *Khot-La-Cha*, 46.

194. TRC, AVS, Ray Silver, Statement to the Truth and Reconciliation Commission of Canada, Mission, British Columbia, 17 May 2011, Statement Number: 2011-3467.

195. TRC, AVS, [Name redacted], Statement to the Truth and Reconciliation Commission of Canada, Deline, Northwest Territories, 2 March 2010, Statement Number: 07-NWT-02MR1-002.

196. Canada, *Annual Report of the Department of Indian Affairs, 1888*, xiv.

197. Fraser River Heritage Park, The OMI Cemetery, http://www.heritagepark-mission.ca/omicemetery.html (accessed 4 November 2014).

198. Father Allard's diary, quoted in Cronin, *Cross in the Wilderness*, 219.

199. TRC, NRA, Library and Archives Canada, RG10, volume 3921, file 116818-1B, J. F. Woodsworth to Secretary, Indian Affairs, 25 November 1918. [EDM-000956]

200. Shanahan, *Jesuit Residential School at Spanish*, 4.

201. TRC, NRA, Library and Archives Canada, RG10, volume 6016, file 1-1-12, part 1, "Burial Expenses," J. D. McLean, no date. [PAR-008816]

202. For examples from the Spanish, Ontario, school, see: Library and Archives Canada, RG10, volume 6217, file 471-1, part 1, N. Dugas to Dear Sir, 25 August 1913; [Story no 1.1.jpg] Library and Archives Canada, RG10, volume 6217, file 471-1, part 1, N. Dugas to Secretary, Indian Affairs, 2 September 1913. [Story no 1.1.6.jpg]

203. Brass, *I Walk in Two Worlds*, 26.

204. TRC, LACAR, Department of Indian Affairs and Northern Development, Indian and Inuit Affairs Program, 133619, Yukon Regional Office, Accession 89-476 VFRC, box 7, file volume 1, file number 29-3, J. H. Gordon to Superintendent, Indian Affairs, Yukon, 16 July 1958; [46b-c009024-d0015-001] TRC, LACAR, Department of Indian Affairs and Northern Development, Indian and

Inuit Affairs Program, 133619, Yukon Regional Office, Accession 89-476 VFRC, box 7, file volume 1, file number 29-3, M. Matas to Gordon Harris, 16 April 1958; [46a-c001040-d0010-005] TRC, LACAR, Department of Indian Affairs and Northern Development, Indian and Inuit Affairs Program, 133619, Yukon Regional Office, Accession 89-476 VFRC, box 7, file volume 1, file number 29-3, M. Matas to W. L. Falconer, 22 July 1958; [46a-c001040-d0010-002] TRC, LACAR, Department of Indian Affairs and Northern Development, Indian and Inuit Affairs Program, 133619, Yukon Regional Office, Accession 89-476 VFRC, box 7, file volume 1, file number 29-3, W. L. Falconer to Director, Indian and Northern Health Services, 24 July 1958; [46a-c001040-d0010-001] TRC, LACAR, Department of Indian Affairs and Northern Development, Indian and Inuit Affairs Program, 133619, Yukon Regional Office, Accession 89-476 VFRC, box 7, file volume 1, file number 29-3, M. G. Jutras to Indian Commissioner, British Columbia, 26 August 1958. [46b-c009024-d0010-001]

205. TRC, NRA, The Presbyterian Church in Canada Archives, Toronto, ON, Acc. 1988-7004, box 17, file 4, Colin Wasacase to Giollo Kelly, 17 November 1966. [CJC-007910] For Wenjack's age, see: Adam, "The Lonely Death of Charlie Wenjack," 30.

206. TRC, NRA, National Capital Regional Service Centre – LAC – Ottawa, file 486/18-2, volume 2, box V-24-83, 06/26/1946–09/23/1975, M. J. Pierce to Indian Affairs, 23 October 1974; [FTA-001096] Edwards, "This Is about Reuniting a Family, Even in Death," *Toronto Star*, 4 March 2011, http://www.thestar.com/news/gta/2011/03/04/this_is_about_reuniting_a_family_even_in_death.html; Edwards, "Star Gets Action: Charlie Hunter Headed Home," *Toronto Star*, 24 March 2011, http://www.thestar.com/news/gta/2011/03/24/star_gets_action_charlie_hunter_headed_home.html.

207. Wasylow, "History of Battleford Industrial School," 268.

208. TRC, NRA, Library and Archives Canada, RG10, volume 3920, file 116818, D. L. Clink to Indian Commissioner, June 4 1895. [EDM-003380]

209. TRC, NRA, Library and Archives Canada, RG10, volume 3920, file 116818, H. Reed to Assistant Commissioner, 28 June 1895. [EDM-003376]

210. TRC, NRA, Library and Archives Canada, RG10, volume 6358, file 758-1, part 1, Reverend Canon Gould to Duncan Campbell Scott, 26 January 1920. [IRC-041334]

211. TRC, NRA, Library and Archives Canada, RG10, volume 8542, file 51/25-1, part 2, Philip Phelan, 14 April 1953. [FAR-000067]

212. Library and Archives Canada, RG10, volume 3558, file 64, part 39, David Laird to Superintendent of Indian Affairs, 13 March 1899.

213. TRC, NRA, Library and Archives Canada, RG10, volume 1346, Microfilm reel C-13916, G. Donckele to W. H. Lomas, 29 December 1896. [KUP-004264]

214. Audette, "Report on the Commission," 2–7.

215. Library and Archives Canada, RG10, volume 3880, file 92499, Memorandum, Hayter Reed, undated; T. Clarke, "Report of Discharged Pupils," in Canada, Sessional Papers 1894, Paper 13, 103.

216. TRC, NRA, Library and Archives Canada, RG10 (Red), volume 2771, file

154845, part 1, J. G. Ramsden to J. D. McLean, 23 December 1907. [TAY-003542]

217. "Damages for Plaintiff in Miller Vs. Ashton Case," *Brantford Expositor*, 1 April 1914.

218. TRC, NRA, Anglican Church of Canada, General Synod Archives, Accession GS 75-403, series 2:15[a], box 16, [Illegible] Chairman, Indian and Eskimo Commission, Westgate, T. B. R., Field Secretary, Indian and Eskimo Commission, "Minutes of the Meeting of the Indian Residential School Commission held on March 18th, 1921." [AGS-000014]

219. TRC, NRA, Library and Archives Canada, RG10, School Files, volume 6358, file 758-1, part 1, 20 August 1919 [OLD-000497]; TRC, NRA, Library and Archives Canada, RG10, volume 6358, file 758-1, part 1, "Statement taken by Constable Wright, RNWMP, 27 November 1919"; [IRC- 041330] TRC, NRA, Library and Archives Canada, RG10, School Files, volume 6358, file 758-1, part 1, 20 August 1919; [OLD-000497] TRC, NRA, Library and Archives Canada, RG10, volume 6358, file 758-1, part 1, Thomas Graham to W. M. Graham, 1 December 1919; [IRC-041328] TRC, NRA, Library and Archives Canada, RG10, volume 6358, file 758-1, part 1, P. H. Gentleman to Canon Gould, 12 January 1920. [IRC-041335]

220. TRC, NRA, Library and Archives Canada, RG10, volume 6436, file 878-1, part 1, Microfilm reel C-8762, 1890–1912, Statement of Johnny Sticks, 28 February 1902. [JOE-060004]

221. TRC, NRA, Library and Archives Canada, RG10, volume 6267, file 580-1, part 2, J. W. Waddy to W. M. Graham, 5 October 1925. [DRS-000543-0001]

222. TRC, AVS, Isabelle Whitford, Statement to the Truth and Reconciliation Commission of Canada, Keeseekoowenin First Nation, Manitoba, 28 May 2010, Statement Number: S-KFN-MB-01-004.

223. TRC, AVS, Rachel Chakasim, Statement to the Truth and Reconciliation Commission of Canada, Timmins, Ontario, 9 November 2010, Statement Number: 01-ON-4-6NOV10-019.

224. TRC, AVS, Fred Brass, Statement to the Truth and Reconciliation Commission of Canada, Key First Nation, Saskatchewan, 21 January 2012, Statement Number: SP039.

225. TRC, AVS, Geraldine Bob, Statement to the Truth and Reconciliation Commission of Canada, Fort Simpson, Northwest Territories, 23 November 2011, Statement Number: 2011-2685.

226. TRC, AVS, William Antoine, Statement to the Truth and Reconciliation Commission of Canada, Little Current, Ontario, 12 May 2011, Statement Number: 2011-2002.

227. TRC, AVS, Eva Simpson, Statement to the Truth and Reconciliation Commission of Canada, Norway House First Nation, Manitoba, 10 May 2011, Statement Number: 2011-0290.

228. TRC, AVS, Dorothy Ross, Statement to the Truth and Reconciliation Commission of Canada, Thunder Bay, Ontario, 25 November 2010, Statement Number: 01-ON-24NOV10-014.

229. TRC, AVS, Archie Hyacinthe, Statement to the Truth and Reconciliation Commission of Canada, Kenora, Ontario, 15 March 2011, Statement Number: 2011-0279.

230. TRC, AVS, Jonas Grandjambe, Statement to the Truth and Reconciliation Commission of Canada, Fort Good Hope, Northwest Territories, 15 July 2010, Statement Number: 01-NWT-JY10-024.

231. TRC, AVS, Delores Adolph, Statement to the Truth and Reconciliation Commission of Canada, Mission, British Columbia, 19 May 2011, Statement Number: 2011-3458.

232. TRC, AVS, Joseph Wabano, Statement to the Truth and Reconciliation Commission of Canada, Fort Albany, Ontario, 29 January 2013, Statement Number: SP099.

233. TRC, AVS, Noel Starblanket, Statement to the Truth and Reconciliation Commission of Canada, Regina, Saskatchewan, 16 January 2012, Statement Number: 2011-3314.

234. TRC, AVS, Mervin Mirasty, Statement to the Truth and Reconciliation Commission of Canada, Saskatoon, Saskatchewan, 21 June 2012, Statement Number: 2011-4391.

235. TRC, AVS, Nellie Trapper, Statement to the Truth and Reconciliation Commission of Canada, Winnipeg, Manitoba, 18 June 2010, Statement Number: 02-MB-16JU10-086.

236. TRC, AVS, Wendy Lafond, Statement to the Truth and Reconciliation Commission of Canada, Batoche, Saskatchewan, 24 July 2010, Statement Number: 01-SK-18-25JY10-015.

237. TRC, AVS, Don Willie, Statement to the Truth and Reconciliation Commission of Canada, Alert Bay, British Columbia, 3 August 2011, Statement Number: 2011-3284.

238. Adams, "The Indians."

239. TRC, NRA, Library and Archives Canada, "Native Mission School Shut Down over Discipline Controversy," by Margaret Loewen Reimer, *Mennonite Reporter*, Volume 19, Number 22, 13 November 1989. [PHD-000143]

240. TRC, NRA, INAC – Resolution Sector – IRS Historical Files Collection – Ottawa, file 372/25-13-024, volume 1, C. T. Blouin and L. Poulin, to A. R. Jolicoeur, 13 October 1970. [LTR-001178-0001]

241. TRC, NRA, INAC – Resolution Sector – IRS Historical Files Collection – Ottawa, GRS Files, box R2, [Name redacted], Ronald J. Pratt and Herman Blind to [Name redacted], 8 December 1993. [IRC-047202-0002]

242. Library and Archives Canada, Hayter Reed Papers MG29, E 106, volume 18, Personnel H-L, J. W. Tims to Indian Commissioner, October 27, 1891.

243. Library and Archives Canada, Hayter Reed Papers MG29, E 106, volume 18, Personnel H-L, L. Vankoughnet to H. Reed, 7 December 1891.

244. For example, see: Library and Archives Canada, Sifton Papers, volume 19, 12129-39; 12123, J. H. Fairlie to A. Forget, 23 August 1897; A. Forget to Sifton, 30 October 1897; TRC, NRA, Library and Archives Canada, RG10, volume 6211,

file 469-1, part 3, Duncan C. Scott to B. P. Fuller, 16 November 1916. [SWK-001406]

245. TRC, NRA, Library and Archives Canada, RG10, volume 13356, "Investigation – Kuper Island School 1939, Police report regarding runaways from Kuper Island School," 10 January 1939; [IRC-040001] TRC, NRA, Library and Archives Canada, RG10, volume 13356, "Investigation – Kuper Island School 1939," D. M. MacKay to Secretary, Indian Affairs Branch, Ottawa, 12 January 1939; [IRC-040007-0001] TRC, NRA, Library and Archives Canada, RG10, volume 13356, "Investigation – Kuper Island School 1939, Cpl S. Service, 13 January 1939; [IRC-040003] TRC, NRA, Library and Archives Canada, RG10, volume 13356, "Investigation – Kuper Island School 1939, Confidential Notes," Gerald H. Barry, 13 January 1939. [IRC-040010]

246. TRC, NRA, Library and Archives Canada, RG10, volume 13356, "Investigation – Kuper Island School 1939," G. H. Barry to Major D. M. MacKay, 17 January 1939; [IRC-040014] TRC, NRA, Library and Archives Canada, RG10, volume 13356, "Investigation – Kuper Island School 1939," Harold McGill to Major D. M. MacKay, 27 January 1939. [IRC-040021]

247. For example, see: TRC, NRA, INAC – Archival Unit – Ottawa, file 772/3-1, volume 2, 10/11– 05/66, C. Pant Schmidt to Harold McGill, 17 August 1944; [IRC-047003] T. R. L. MacInnes to Director, Indian Affairs, 25 August 1944; [IRC-047005] Sarah Elizabeth Brown, "Ex-residential School Student Files Suit," Whitehorse Star, 21 April 2003; Elizabeth Asp, Jackie McLaren, Jim Sheldon, Michelle Tochacek, and Ruby Van Bibber, "Bishop's comments invalided any apology," Letter to the Editor, Whitehorse Star, 11 August 1999.

248. TRC, NRA, Library and Archives Canada, RG10, volume 6309, file 645-1, part 3, R. S. Davis, excerpt from Quarterly Report Ending March, 1945, on Touchwood Agency. [IRC-047128]

249. TRC, NRA, INAC – Resolution Sector – IRS Historical Files Collection – Ottawa, GRS Files, box 1A, file 22, Head Teacher [Illegible] to My Lord Bishop, 10 January 1956. [IRC-040120]

250. For examples, see: TRC, NRA, Library and Archives Canada, 709/25-1-001, 1951–1961, part 2, L. C. Hunter to R. F. Davey, 30 November 1960; [IRC-040054] TRC, NRA, United Church of Canada/Victoria University Archives, Acc. No. 8[Illegible].050C, box 112, file 17, Edmonton IRS – Correspondence 1958–60/UCC Docs Toronto, Dwight Powell to E. E. M. Joblin, 25 November 1960. [UCA-080215] It was not until 1968 that Indian Affairs began requiring school schools superintendents to submit the names of all who had been dismissed because they had "created problems." TRC, NRA, National Archives of Canada, Acc. E1996-97/312, Vol. 2, File 672/25-1, R.F. Davey to All School Superintendents, 7 May 1968; [120.07885] TRC, NRA, Library and Archives Canada – Burnaby Vol. 11500, File 901/1-13, pt. 1, School Establishment, 1968-1972, FA 10-138, A. H. Friesen to All District School Superintendents, 1 June 1968. [120.07891]

251. TRC, NRA, Library and Archives Canada – Burnaby Vol. 11500, File 901/1-13, pt. 1, School Establishment, 1968-1972, FA 10-138, A. H. Friesen to All District School Superintendents, 1 June 1968. [120.07891]

252. The details of these convictions will be outlined in a forthcoming TRC report.

253. Indian Residential Schools Adjudication Secretariat, Adjudication Secretariat Statistics, from September 19, 2007, to January 31, 2015, http://iap-pei.ca/information/stats-eng.php (accessed 20 February 2015).

254. Joseph Jean Louis Comeau worked there from 1958 to 1965, *R. v. Comeau*, 1988 CanLII 3839 (AB QB). Martin Houston worked there from 1960 to 1962, TRC, ASAGR, Aboriginal Affairs and Northern Development Canada, Walter Rudnicki to Director, Indian Affairs, 17 August 1962; [AANDC-234696] Aboriginal Affairs and Northern Development Canada, Royal Canadian Mounted Police Report, Western Arctic Division, Division file number 628-626-1, code 0559, re: Martin Houston, 29 August 1962. [AANDC-234684] George Maczynski worked there from 1966 to 1967, TRC, NRA, Beaufort-Delta Education Council Warehouse, Inuvik, NWT, Payroll, 1959 to 1966 [box 1], M. Ruyant to Department of Northern Affairs and National Resources, Payroll list of employees at the hostel for September 1966, September 1966; [GHU- 002427] Beaufort-Delta Education Council Warehouse, Inuvik, NWT, Payroll, 1967 to 1970 [box 1], Department of Northern Affairs and National Resources, Northern Administration: Paylist – Hostel, May 1967. [GHU-002435] Paul Leroux worked there from 1967 to 1979, TRC, ASAGR, Glenn Taylor, "Grollier Man Pleads Not Guilty to Sex Offences," Northern News Services, 28 November 1997, http://www.nnsl.com/frames/newspapers/1997-11/nov28_97sex.html.

255. Mandryk, "Uneasy Neighbours," 210.

256. TRC, NRA, Library and Archives Canada, RG10, volume 8798, file 371/25-13-019, part 2, R. F. Davey to William Starr, 19 July 1962; [FGA-001179] TRC, NRA, Anglican Church of Canada, General Synod Archives, ACC-MSCC-GS 75-103, series 2:15, box 24, file 3, Extract from Report on Visit of Major-General G. R. Turner to St. Paul's Anglican Indian Residential School, Cardston, Alberta, 6–8, 1958. [AAC-090593]

257. Mandryk, "Uneasy Neighbours," 210.

258. *R. v. Plint*, [1995] B.C.J. No. 3060 (B.C. S.C.); "Former Employee of Residential School Jailed for Sex Abuses," *Victoria Times–Colonist*, January 24, 2004.

259. TRC, AVS, Jean Pierre Bellemare, Statement to the Truth and Reconciliation Commission of Canada, La Tuque, Québec, 5 March 2013, Statement Number: SP104.

260. TRC, AVS, Andrew Yellowback, Statement to the Truth and Reconciliation Commission of Canada, Kamloops, British Columbia, 9 August 2009, Statement Number: 2011-5015.

261. See, for example: TRC, AVS, [Name redacted], Statement to the Truth and Reconciliation Commission of Canada, Winnipeg, Manitoba, 18 June 2010, Statement Number: 02-MB-18JU10-055; TRC, AVS, Myrna Kaminawaish, Statement to the Truth and Reconciliation Commission of Canada, Thunder Bay, Ontario, 7 January 2011, Statement Number: 01-ON-06JA11-004; TRC, AVS, Percy Tuesday, Statement to the Truth and Reconciliation Commission of Canada, Winnipeg, Manitoba, 18 June 2010, Statement Number: 02-MB-18JU10-083; TRC, AVS, Isaac Daniels, Statement to the Truth and Reconciliation Commission of Canada, Saskatoon, Saskatchewan, 22 June 2012, Statement Number: 2011-1779.

262. TRC, AVS, Marlene Kayseas, Statement to the Truth and Reconciliation Commission of Canada, Regina, Saskatchewan, 16 January 2012, Statement Number:

SP035. For gifts of candy, see: TRC, AVS, Elaine Durocher, Statement to the Truth and Reconciliation Commission of Canada, Winnipeg, Manitoba, 16 June 2010, Statement Number: 02-MB-16JU10-059; TRC, AVS, John B. Custer, Statement to the Truth and Reconciliation Commission of Canada, Winnipeg, Manitoba, 19 June 2010, Statement Number: 02-MB-19JU10-057; TRC, AVS, Louise Large, Statement to the Truth and Reconciliation Commission of Canada, St. Paul, Alberta, 7 January 2011, Statement Number: 01-AB-06JA11-012. For field trips, see: TRC, AVS, Ben Pratt, Statement to the Truth and Reconciliation Commission of Canada, Regina, Saskatchewan, 18 January 2012, Statement Number: 2011-3318.

263. See, for example: TRC, AVS, [Name redacted], Statement to the Truth and Reconciliation Commission of Canada, Winnipeg, Manitoba, 18 June 2010, Statement Number: 02-MB-18JU10-055; TRC, AVS, Leona Bird, Statement to the Truth and Reconciliation Commission of Canada, Saskatoon, Saskatchewan, 21 June 2012, Statement Number: 2011-4415; TRC, AVS, Barbara Ann Pahpasay Skead, Statement to the Truth and Reconciliation Commission of Canada, Winnipeg, Manitoba, 17 June 2010, Statement Number: 02-MB-16JU10-159.

264. TRC, AVS, Josephine Sutherland, Statement to the Truth and Reconciliation Commission of Canada, Timmins, Ontario, 8 November 2010, Statement Number: 01-ON4-6NOV10-013.

265. TRC, AVS, Marie Therese Kistabish, Statement to the Truth and Reconciliation Commission of Canada, Val d'Or, Québec, 6 February 2012, Statement Number: SP101.

266. TRC, AVS, Richard Morrison, Statement to the Truth and Reconciliation Commission of Canada, Winnipeg, Manitoba, 17 June 2010, Statement Number: 02-MB-17JU10-080.

267. For shower, see: TRC, AVS, Leonard Peter Alexcee, Statement to the Truth and Reconciliation Commission of Canada, Vancouver, British Columbia, 18 September 2013, Statement Number: 2011-3228. For lunch pail, see: TRC, AVS, Mervin Mirasty, Statement to the Truth and Reconciliation Commission of Canada, Saskatoon, Saskatchewan, 21 June 2012, Statement Number: 2011-4391.

268. TRC, AVS, Donna Antoine, Statement to the Truth and Reconciliation Commission of Canada, Enderby, British Columbia, 13 October 2011, Statement Number: 2011-3287.

269. TRC, AVS, Helen Harry, Statement to the Truth and Reconciliation Commission of Canada, Vancouver, British Columbia, 20 September 2013, Statement Number: 2011-3203.

270. TRC, AVS, Bernard Catcheway, Statement to the Truth and Reconciliation Commission of Canada, Skownan First Nation, Manitoba, 12 October 2011, Statement Number: 2011-2510; TRC, AVS, Doris Judy McKay, Statement to the Truth and Reconciliation Commission of Canada, Rolling River First Nation, Manitoba, 23 November 2011, Statement Number: 2011-2514.

271. TRC, AVS, Timothy Henderson, Statement to the Truth and Reconciliation Commission of Canada, Winnipeg, Manitoba, 28 June 2011, Statement Number: 2011-0291.

272. TRC, AVS, Nellie Ningewance, Statement to the Truth and Reconciliation Com-

mission of Canada, Sault Ste. Marie, Ontario, 1 July 2011, Statement Number: 2011-0305.

273. TRC, AVS, Flora Northwest, Statement to the Truth and Reconciliation Commission of Canada, Hobbema, Alberta, 24 July 2013, Statement Number: SP124.

274. For examples, see: TRC, AVS, Hazel Mary Anderson, Statement to the Truth and Reconciliation Commission of Canada, Winnipeg, Manitoba, 18 June 2010, Statement Number: 02-MB-18JU10-034; TRC, AVS, Peter Ross, Statement to the Truth and Reconciliation Commission of Canada, Tsiigehtchic, Northwest Territories, 8 September 2011, Statement Number: 2011-0340.

275. TRC, AVS, Eric Robinson, Statement to the Truth and Reconciliation Commission of Canada, Winnipeg, Manitoba, 16 June 2010, Statement Number: SC093.

276. TRC, AVS, Lynda Pahpasay McDonald, Statement to the Truth and Reconciliation Commission of Canada, Winnipeg, Manitoba, 16 June 2010, Statement Number: 02-MB-16JU10-130.

277. For examples, see: TRC, AVS, Larry Roger Listener, Statement to the Truth and Reconciliation Commission of Canada, Hobbema, Alberta, 25 July 2013, Statement Number: SP125; TRC, AVS, Mary Vivier, Statement to the Truth and Reconciliation Commission of Canada, Winnipeg, Manitoba, 18 June 2010, Statement Number: SC110.

278. TRC, AVS, Louisa Papatie, Statement to the Truth and Reconciliation Commission of Canada, Val d'Or, Québec, 6 February 2012, Statement Number: SP101. For an example of abuse stopping as students became older, see: Fontaine, *Broken Circle*, 18–19.

279. For examples, see: TRC, AVS, Ken A. Littledeer, Statement to the Truth and Reconciliation Commission of Canada, Thunder Bay, Ontario, 26 November 2010, Statement Number: 01-ON-24-NOV10-028; TRC, AVS, Sphenia Jones, Statement to the Truth and Reconciliation Commission of Canada, Terrace, British Columbia, 29 November 2011, Statement Number: 2011-3300.

280. TRC, AVS, Lawrence Waquan, Statement to the Truth and Reconciliation Commission of Canada, Winnipeg, Manitoba, 18 June 2010, Statement Number: SC111.

281. TRC, AVS, Hazel Mary Anderson, Statement to the Truth and Reconciliation Commission of Canada, Winnipeg, Manitoba, 18 June 2010, Statement Number: 02-MB-18JU10-034.

282. TRC, AVS, Wayne Reindeer, Statement to the Truth and Reconciliation Commission of Canada, Hobbema, Alberta, 25 July 2013, Statement Number: SP125.

283. TRC, AVS, Michael Muskego, Statement to the Truth and Reconciliation Commission of Canada, Winnipeg, Manitoba, 18 June 2010, Statement Number: 02-MB-18JU10-045.

284. TRC, AVS, Josephine Sutherland, Statement to the Truth and Reconciliation Commission of Canada, Timmins, Ontario, 8 November 2010, Statement Number: 01-ON4-6NOV10-013.

285. TRC, AVS, Norman Courchene, Statement to the Truth and Reconciliation Commission of Canada, Winnipeg, Manitoba, 16 June 2010, Statement Number: 02-MB-16JU10-065.

286. For examples, see: TRC, AVS, Ben Pratt, Statement to the Truth and Reconcilia-tion Commission of Canada, Regina, Saskatchewan, 18 January 2012, Statement Number: 2011-3318; TRC, AVS, Amelia Galligos-Thomas, Statement to the Truth and Reconciliation Commission of Canada, Victoria, British Columbia, 13 April 2012, Statement Number: 2011-3975.

287. TRC, AVS, Violet Rupp Cook, Statement to the Truth and Reconciliation Com-mission of Canada, Bloodvein First Nation, Manitoba, 25 January 2012, State-ment Number: 2011-2565.

288. For examples, see: TRC, AVS, Ivan George, Statement to the Truth and Reconcil-iation Commission of Canada, Mission, British Columbia, 18 May 2011, State-ment Number: 2011-3472; TRC, AVS, Dorothy Jane Beaulieu, Statement to the Truth and Reconciliation Commission of Canada, Fort Resolution, Northwest Territories, 28 April 2011, Statement Number: 2011-0379; TRC, AVS, Lorna Morgan, Statement to the Truth and Reconciliation Commission of Canada, Winnipeg, Manitoba, 17 June 2010, Statement Number: 02-MB-16JU10-041.

289. Ruben, "Abraham Ruben," 136.

290. For examples, see: TRC, AVS, Stella Marie Tookate, Statement to the Truth and Reconciliation Commission of Canada, Timmins, Ontario, 9 November 2010, Statement Number: 01-ON-8-10NOV10-003; TRC, AVS, Richard Hall, Statement to the Truth and Reconciliation Commission of Canada, Vancouver, British Columbia, 18 September 2013, Statement Number: 2011-1852.

291. TRC, AVS, William Garson, Statement to the Truth and Reconciliation Com-mission of Canada, Split Lake First Nation, Manitoba, 24 March 2011, Statement Number: 2011-0122.

292. TRC, AVS, Percy Thompson, Statement to the Truth and Reconciliation Com-mission of Canada, Hobbema, Alberta, 25 July 2013, Statement Number: SP125.

293. TRC, AVS, Alice Ruperthouse, Statement to the Truth and Reconciliation Commission of Canada, Val d'Or, Québec, 5 February 2012, Statement Number: SP100.

294. TRC, AVS, Albert Elias, Statement to the Truth and Reconciliation Commis-sion of Canada, Inuvik, Northwest Territories, 1 July 2011, Statement Number: SC092.

295. TRC, AVS, Denis Morrison, Statement to the Truth and Reconciliation Com-mission of Canada, Winnipeg, Manitoba, 17 June 2010, Statement Number: 02-MB-17JU10-028.

296. TRC, AVS, Bob Baxter, Statement to the Truth and Reconciliation Commis-sion of Canada, Thunder Bay, Ontario, 24 November 2010, Statement Number: 01-ON-24NOV10-012.

297. TRC, AVS, Clara Quisess, Statement to the Truth and Reconciliation Commis-sion of Canada, Winnipeg, Manitoba, 17 June 2010, Statement Number: 02-MB-17JU10-032.

298. TRC, AVS, Louisa Birote, Statement to the Truth and Reconciliation Commis-sion of Canada, La Tuque, Québec, 5 March 2013, Statement Number: SP104.

299. See, for example: TRC, AVS, Ruth Chapman, Statement to the Truth and Recon-ciliation Commission of Canada, Winnipeg, Manitoba, 16 June 2010, Statement

Number: 02-MB-16JU10-118; TRC, AVS, Gordon James Pemmican, Statement to the Truth and Reconciliation Commission of Canada, Winnipeg, Manitoba, 18 June 2010, Statement Number: 02-MB-18JU10-0069; TRC, AVS, Mary Vivier, Statement to the Truth and Reconciliation Commission of Canada, Winnipeg, Manitoba, 18 June 2010, Statement Number: 02-MB-18JU10-082; TRC, AVS, Roy Johnson, Statement to the Truth and Reconciliation Commission of Canada, Dawson City, Yukon, 24 May 2011, Statement Number: 2011-0203; TRC, AVS, Ken Lacquette, Statement to the Truth and Reconciliation Commission of Canada, Winnipeg, Manitoba, 18 June 2010, Statement Number: 02-MB-18JU10-052.

300. TRC, AVS, Agnes Moses, Statement to the Truth and Reconciliation Commission of Canada, Inuvik, Northwest Territories, 29 June 2011, Statement Number: SC090.

301. TRC, AVS, Don Willie, Statement to the Truth and Reconciliation Commission of Canada, Alert Bay, British Columbia, 3 August 2011, Statement Number: 2011-3284.

302. TRC, AVS, Christina Kimball, Statement to the Truth and Reconciliation Commission of Canada, Winnipeg, Manitoba, 17 January 2011, Statement Number: 03-001-10-020.

303. TRC, AVS, Noel Starblanket, Statement to the Truth and Reconciliation Commission of Canada, Regina, Saskatchewan, 16 January 2012, Statement Number: 2011-3314.

304. TRC, AVS, Geraldine Shingoose, Statement to the Truth and Reconciliation Commission of Canada, Winnipeg, Manitoba, 19 June 2010, Statement Number: 02-MB-19JU10-033.

305. TRC, AVS, Paul Andrew, Statement to the Truth and Reconciliation Commission of Canada, Inuvik, Northwest Territories, 30 June 2011, Statement Number: NNE202.

306. TRC, NRA, National Archives of Canada – Burnaby, FA 10-138, 07/1956, Perm. volume 13528, C. G. Brown, G. J. Buck, B. O. Filteau, "Report of the Educational Survey Commission on the Educational Facilities and Requirements of the Indians of Canada," July 1956, 10. [120.18398]

307. TRC, NRA, Library and Archives Canada – Ottawa, RG10, volume 8703, file 962/6-1, part 7, NAC – Ottawa, L. K. Poupore to H. M. Jones, 14 October 1957. [JOE-063234]

308. TRC, NRA, INAC – Departmental Library – Ottawa, "St. Michael's Indian School Wins Service Club Trophy," *Indian Record*, April 1946. [SMD-002822]

309. TRC, NRA, Library and Archives Canada, RG10, volume 8610, file 652/1-13, part 1, George Roussel to B. F. Neary, 25 March 1949. [SMD-001575-0001]

310. TRC, NRA, Library and Archives Canada, RG10, volume 8610, file 652/1-13, part 1, Geo.-L. Roussel to B. F. Neary, 25 March 1949. [SMD-001575-0001]

311. Marks, *They Call Me Chief*, 31. Sasakamoose played with the Chicago Blackhawks in the 1952–53 season. He was born on the Sandy Lake, Saskatchewan, reserve in 1933. TRC, NRA, INAC – Departmental Library – Ottawa, "Saskatchewan Midget Hockey Champions," *Indian Record*, Volume 12, Number 5, May 1949. [SMD-002829]

312. TRC, NRA, Library and Archives Canada, RG29, volume 792, file 344, Pratt, Gerry. "Little Indians Are Big Fighters," in the *Vancouver Sun Magazine Supplement*, 31 March 1951. [NPC-600625]

313. TRC, NRA, INAC – Departmental Library – Ottawa, "First Winner of the Tom Longboat Trophy," *The Indian Missionary Record*, Volume 15, Number 3, March 1952, 3. [IMR-000400]

314. Hughes, *Jackson Beardy*, 6–7.

315. MacGregor, *Chief*, 34–35.

316. Canadien, *From Lishamie*, 253–254.

317. Canadien, *From Lishamie*, 264–265.

318. For an example from the Presbyterian school at Shoal Lake, see: TRC, NRA, Library and Archives Canada, RG10, volume 6187, file 461-1, part 1, "Report of Inspector Semmens on the Cecilia Jaffrey [*sic*] Boarding School," 22 January 1917. [IRC-048048]

319. Library and Archives Canada, RG10, volume 4041, file 334503, Duncan Campbell Scott to Frank Pedley, 19 February 1912, cited in Wasylow, "History of Battleford Industrial School," 261–263. For Battleford capacity, see: Canada, *Annual Report of the Department of Indian Affairs, 1907*, 341.

320. Canada, *Annual Report of the Department of Indian Affairs, 1915*, xxvi.

321. Canada, *Annual Report of the Department of Indian Affairs, 1898*, 297; Canada, *Annual Report of the Department of Indian Affairs, 1910*, 474; TRC, NRA, Provincial Archives of Alberta, PAA 71.220 B16 668, unsigned letter to J. T. McNally, 22 February 1922. [OGP-090011]

322. Canada, *Annual Report of the Department of Indian Affairs 1906*, 191; Canada, *Annual Report of the Department of Indian Affairs, 1907*, xxxiii.

323. For St. Boniface closing, see: Canada, *Annual Report of the Department of Indian Affairs, 1905*, xxxiii; Canada, *Annual Report of the Department of Indian Affairs, 1906*, 191. For difficulty in recruiting, see: Canada, *Annual Report of the Department of Indian Affairs, 1896*, 362. For Calgary closing, see: Canada, *Annual Report of the Department of Indian Affairs, 1908*, 197. For Calgary recruiting problem, see: Canada, *Annual Report of the Department of Indian Affairs, 1904*, 375. For Regina closing, see: Canada, *Annual Report of the Department of Indian Affairs, 1910*, 364. For evidence of Indian Affairs' dissatisfaction with the management of the Regina school, see: TRC, NRA, Library and Archives Canada, RG10, volume 6332, file 661-1, part 1, W. M. Graham to Secretary, Indian Affairs, 17 November 1910. [RLS-000027] For the Elkhorn school, see: TRC, NRA, Library and Archives Canada, RG10, volume 3925, file 116823-1A, Clerk of the Privy Council to Superintendent General, Indian Affairs, 18 February 1918. [ELK-000248] For the Red Deer school, see: TRC, NRA, Library and Archives Canada, RG10, volume 6350, file 753-1, part 1, J. F. Woodsworth to James Endicott, 5 June 1919. [EDM-000242]

324. The government actually closed day schools in an effort to force parents to send their children to residential schools. Canada, *Annual Report of the Department of Indian Affairs, 1895*, xxi–xii.

325. For examples of the withholding of rations, see: TRC, NRA, Library and
Archives Canada, RG10, volume 1629, A. J. McNeill to D. Laird, 10 December
1901; [SAR-000404] TRC, NRA, Library and Archives Canada, RG10, volume
6320, file 658-1, part 1, David Laird to Secretary, Indian Affairs, 3 April 1906;
[PAR-000980-0000] TRC, NRA, Library and Archives Canada, RG10, volume
6320, file 658-1, part 1, Microfilm reel C-9802, M. Benson to Deputy Superintendent General, Indian Affairs, 21 February 1907. [120.00284]

326. TRC, NRA, Library and Archives Canada, RG10, volume 6475, file 918-1, part
1, [Illegible], Office of the General Superintendent, Oblate Catholic Indian Missions to Philip Phelan, 21 October 1941. [FPU-000133]

327. TRC, NRA, Library and Archives Canada, RG10, School Files, volume 6352, file
753-10, part 1, Microfilm reel C-8708, P. Phelan to J. F. Woodsworth, 22 January
1941. [EDM-003580]

328. TRC, NRA, Library and Archives Canada, RG10, volume 1346, Microfilm reel
C-13916, G. Donckele to W. R. Robertson, 23 July 1906. [KUP-004276]

329. TRC, NRA, English Language Summary of the Fort Resolution Chronicles,
Volume 1, 1903– 1942, 3. [GNN-000077-0001]

330. TRC, NRA, Library and Archives Canada, RG10, Perm. volume 6451, file 883-1,
part 1, Bella Coola Agency – Kitamaat Boarding School – General Administra-
tion, 1906–1932, FA 10-17, Microfilm reel C-8773; [KMT-095676-0001] TRC,
NRA, Library and Archives Canada, "Royal Canadian Mounted Police Report,
Re: Kitimat Indian Reserve, Re: Hanna Grant, Deceased, 15 June 1922," I.
Fougner to Secretary, Indian Affairs, 15 June 1922. [KMT-095674]

331. TRC, NRA, INAC – Resolution Sector – IRS Historical Files Collection – Ottawa,
773/25-1-003, 05/36–09/70, volume 1, RCAP, R. D. Ragan, "Extract from minutes
of Blood Indian Council Meeting March 15, 1948." [MRY-000302] For Charron's initials, see: TRC, NRA, National Archives of Canada, RG29, volume 974,
file 388-6-4, part 1, 02/1948–07/1949, B. F. Neary to P. A. Charron, 21 July 1948.
[120.03363]

332. TRC, NRA, Library and Archives Canada, RG10, volume 6262, file 578-1, part
4, A. Ogletree to Deputy Secretary, Department of Indian Affairs, 23 July 1926.
[ELK-000331]

333. TRC, NRA, Library and Archives Canada, RG10, volume 6371, file 764-1, part 1,
M. Christianson to W. M. Graham, 28 October 1927. [PUL-001008]

334. TRC, NRA, Library and Archives Canada, RG10, volume 6445, file 881-10, part
5, Agent's Report on Stuart Lake Agency for September, Robert Howe, 2 October 1940. [LEJ-002079]

335. For examples from British Columbia, see: TRC, NRA, Library and Archives Canada,
RG10, volume 6445, file 881-10, part 6, Report of Corporal L. F. Fielder, 14 October
1943; [LEJ- 001389] TRC, NRA, Library and Archives Canada – Ottawa, RG10, volume 6443, file 881-1, part 2, R. Howe to Indian Affairs Branch, 12 September 1946;
[LEJ-000855] TRC, NRA, Library and Archives Canada, RG10, volume 6445, file
881-10, part 7, R. Howe to Indian Affairs, 7 October 1946. [LEJ-001830] For Manitoba example, see: TRC, NRA, Library and Archives Canada, INAC – Resolution
Sector – IRS Historical Files Collection – Ottawa, file 501/25-1-076, volume 1, A.
G. Hamilton to Indian Affairs, 4 November 1943. [SBR-000408] For Saskatchewan
examples, see: TRC, NRA, Library and Archives Canada, RG10, volume 6302, file

650-10, part 3, R. A. Hoey to J. P. B. Ostrander, 11 September 1942; [BVL-000433] TRC, NRA, Library and Archives Canada, RG10, volume 9148, file 309-11 ACE, John Baptiste, Peter King, and Alex Sapp to Indian Agent, Battleford, 31 August 1945. [PAR-000897-0002] For Alberta examples, see: TRC, NRA, National Capital Regional Service Centre – LAC – Ottawa, file 1/18-24, volume 1 (locator #X-46-4), Rev. L. C. Schmidt to Harold McGill, 2 July 1943; [NCA-014258] TRC, NRA, Library and Archives Canada, RG10, volume 6374, file 764-10, part 2, PARC, H. A. R. Gagnon to Director, Indian Affairs Branch, 12 October 1945; [PUL-009517-0000] TRC, NRA, Library and Archives Canada, RG10, volume 6355, file 757-1, part 2, 1928–1948, John E. Pugh to Indian Affairs, 8 October 1947; [MOR-005548] TRC, NRA, Provincial Archives – Alberta, PAA 71.220 B94 3972, Principal Ermineskin Indian Residential School to Indian Affairs Branch, 31 March 1948; [OGP-032546] TRC, NRA, Library and Archives Canada, RG10, volume 6374, file 764-10, part 2, PARC, J. E. Pugh to Indian Affairs Branch, 7 March 1946; [PUL-009511] TRC, NRA, Library and Archives Canada – Edmonton, 103/6-1-764, volume 1, 09/44–12/54, C. A. F. Clark to Superintendent of Education, 9 November 1949; [IRC-048180] TRC, NRA, INAC – Resolution Sector – IRS Historical Files Collection – Ottawa, file 773/25-1-003, volume 1, 10/36–09/70, "Minutes of the Blood Band Council Held in The Indian Agency Office," 22 November 1949, annotated by C. A. F. Clark. [IRC-041373]

336. TRC, NRA, Library and Archives Canada, RG10, volume 6467, file 889-1, part 1, 12/1894– 11/1933, Vancouver Agency – Squamish Residential School – General Administration, FA 10-17, Microfilm reel C-8785, NAC, Ottawa, A. W. Vowell to the Secretary, Department of Indian Affairs, 5 April 1905. [SQU-000423]

337. TRC, NRA, Library and Archives Canada, RG10, volume 6270, file 582-1, part 1, "Extract from report on meeting Chief of Pine Creek Band," A. Ogletree, Indian Agent, 16 June 1917. [PCR-010082]

338. For an example from Morley, Alberta, see: TRC, NRA, Library and Archives Canada, NAC – Ottawa, 772/3-6, volume 1, dates 1940–1954, Minutes from the council meeting for the Stony Indian Agency, 15 October 1946, 3. [MOR-006118] For an example from Lestock, Saskatchewan, see: TRC, NRA, Library and Archives Canada, RG10, volume 8756, file 673/25-1-003, 25 August 1949. [MRS-046113-0001]

339. TRC, NRA, Library and Archives Canada, RG10, volume 8756, file 673/25-1-003, J. P. B. Ostrander to Neary, 24 January 1950. [MRS-046113-0005]

340. For an example from the Presbyterian school at Shoal Lake, Ontario, see: TRC, NRA, Library and Archives Canada, RG10, volume 6187, file 461-1, part 1, Chief Kesik, Chief Redsky, and three others to McKenzie, 28 March 1917. [CJC-000006-0002]

341. TRC, NRA, Library and Archives Canada, RG10, volume 6187, file 461, part 1, "Report of the Commission of Presbytery appointed to investigate conditions at 'Cecilia Jeffries [sic] Boarding School,'" 26 February 1918. [CJC-000847-0001]

342. TRC, NRA, Library and Archives Canada, RG10, volume 6187, file 461-1, part 1, "Report of the Commission of Presbytery appointed to investigate conditions at 'Cecilia Jeffries [sic] Boarding School,'" 26 February 1918. [CJC-000847-0001]

343. TRC, NRA, Library and Archives Canada, volume 6332, file 661-1, part 2, petition from parents to Crooked Lakes Agency, 25 July 1949. [IRC-041159] Although Indian Affairs official J. P. B. Ostrander opposed replacing the teacher,

he did report that she kept a strap on display in her class. He said, "If she does not use it for punishment, at least she keeps it on display as a threat of punishment, which does not promote harmony in the classroom." TRC, NRA, Library and Archives Canada, volume 6332, file 661-1, part 2, J. P. B. Ostrander to Indian Affairs Branch, Department of Mines and Resources, 12 August 1949. [RLS-000512-0000]

344. TRC, NRA, Library and Archives Canada, RG10, volume 6187, file 461-1, part 2, Mr. Paget to Mr. Ferrier, 21 August 1928. [CJC-001354]

345. TRC, NRA, Library and Archives Canada, RG10, volume 6254, file 575-10, part 1, A. G. Smith to Secretary, Indian Affairs, 29 December 1936. [BIR-002631]

346. For an example of a request for an investigation into a death, see: TRC, NRA, Library and Archives Canada, RG10, volume 6332, file 661-1, part 2, Garnet Neff to T. G. Murphy, 26 January 1935; [RLS-000366-0001] TRC, NRA, Library and Archives Canada, RG29, volume 2917, file 851-1-A673, part 1, Memorandum to Mr. McLean, 13 January 1914. [NPC-603178] For an example of a complaint regarding discipline, see: TRC, NRA, Library and Archives Canada, RG10, volume 6200, file 466-1, part 3, H. H. Craig to H. A. Snell, 29 July 1937. [MSC-000080- 0001] For an example of working on behalf of an injured student, see: TRC, NRA, Library and Archives Canada, RG10, volume 6327, file 660-1, part 3, William Hall to Indian Affairs, 30 April 1936. [PLD-000746] For an example of seeking a discharge, see: TRC, NRA, Library and Archives Canada, volume 12333, box 19, part 1, 1936–1939, NAC, J. D. Caldwell to [Severed], 16 March 1939. [KUP-004496]

347. TRC, NRA, Library and Archives Canada – Ottawa, RG85, volume 1505, file 600-1-1, part 1, N.W.T. – General Policy File – Education and Schools, 1905–1944, Extract From Act. Sgt. G. T. Makinson's Report-Resolution, N.W.T., 3 July 1937. [FRU-010059]

348. Cuthand, "Native Peoples," 382–383; Kulchyski, "Considerable Unrest," 100.

349. Goodwill and Sluman, *John Tootoosis*, 155.

350. Goodwill and Sluman, *John Tootoosis*, 156.

351. Both the 1905 fire at the Saint-Paul-des-Métis, Alberta, school and the 1930 fire at the Cross Lake, Manitoba, school were set by students. The Saint-Paul fire resulted in one death; the Cross Lake fire, in thirteen deaths. For the Saint-Paul fire, see: Stanley, "Alberta's Half-Breed Reserve," 96–98. For the Cross Lake fire, see: TRC, NRA, Library and Archives Canada, RG10, volume 6260, file 577-1, part 1, J. L. Fuller to A. McNamara, 8 March 1930; [CLD-000933- 0000] William Gordon to Assistant Deputy and Secretary, Indian Affairs, 10 March 1930. [CLD-000934]

352. Wilson, *Missionary work*, 167–170.

353. TRC, NRA, Library and Archives Canada, RG10, volume 6032, file 150-40A, part 1, "Regulations Relating to the Education of Indian Children" (Ottawa: Government Printing Bureau, 1894). [AGA-001516-0000]

354. See, for examples: Canada, *Annual Report of the Department of Indian Affairs, 1893*, 104; Canada, *Annual Report of the Department of Indian Affairs, 1902*, 423.

355. See, for example: TRC, NRA, Library and Archives Canada, RG10, volume 6258, file 576-10, part 9, "Royal Canadian Mounted Police Report, Re: Thomas

'Tommy' Linklater et al.," 23 September 1936; [BRS-000240-0006] TRC, NRA, Library and Archives Canada, RG10, volume 6258, file 576-10, part 9, "Royal Canadian Mounted Police Report Re: Thomas 'Tommy' Linklater et al.," 20 October 1936; [BRS-000240-0005] TRC, NRA, Library and Archives Canada, RG10, volume 6209, file 468-10, part 2, "Royal Canadian Mounted Police Report, Re: Abner Elliott and Leonard Beeswax, truants," 13 October 1938. [MER-001043-0001] TRC, NRA, Library and Archives Canada, RG10, volume 6209, file 468-10, part 2, "Royal Canadian Mounted Police Report, Re: Abner Elliott and Leonard Beeswax, truants," 11 January 1939. [MER-001048-0001]

356. For Duncan Sticks, see: TRC, NRA, Library and Archives Canada, RG10, volume 6436, file 878-1, part 1, Statement of Reverend Henry Boening, 3 March 1902; [IRC-047093] Statement of Joseph Fahey, 3 March 1903; [IRC-047092] TRC, NRA, Library and Archives Canada, RG10, volume 6436, file 878-1, part 1, Statement of Antonio Boitano, 1 March 1902. [IRC-047086] For William Cardinal, see: TRC, NRA, Library and Archives Canada, RG10, volume 3921, file 116818-1B, J. F. Woodsworth to Secretary, Indian Affairs, 25 November 1918. [EDM-000956] For unnamed boy from The Pas, Manitoba, school, see: TRC, NRA, Anglican Church of Canada, General Synod Archives Anglican Church of Canada GS 75-103, B17, "Minutes of meeting of Indian and Eskimo Commission, M.S.C.C., Held on Tuesday, January 11th, 1927," 11. [AAC-083001] For three unnamed boys from the Fort Alexander, Manitoba, school, see: St. Boniface Historical Society, Archives Deschâtelets, L 541 M27L 266, Brachet to père provincial, 20 October 1928. For Agnes Ben, see: "Find Body of Indian Girl, Long Missing," *Winnipeg Free Press*, 17 April 1930. For Percy Ochapowace, see: TRC, NRA, Library and Archives Canada, RG10, volume 6332, file 661-1, part 2, Royal Canadian Mounted Police Report, "Re: Percy Ochapowace – Death of, Ochapowace Indian Reserve, Saskatchewan," H. S. Casswell, 19 January 1935; [RLS-000365-0003] J. P. B. Ostrander to Secretary, Indian Affairs, 19 January 1935. [RLS-000365-0001] For Allen Patrick, Andrew Paul, Justa Maurice, and John Jack, see: TRC, NRA, Library and Archives Canada, RG10, volume 6446, file 881-23, part 1, R. H. Moore to Secretary, Indian Affairs, 6 January 1937. [LEJ-004083-0000] For Andrew Gordon, see: TRC, NRA, Library and Archives Canada, RG10, volume 9151, file 312-11 ACE, "Royal Mounted Police Report, Re Andrew Gordon (Juvenile), Deceased," 16 March 1939. [GDC-009280- 0001] For John Kioki, Michael Sutherland, and Michael Matinas, see: TRC, NRA, Library and Archives Canada, RG10, volume 6186, file 460-23, part 1, Paul Langlois to Constable Dexter, 14 June 1941. [FTA-000105-0001] For Leonard Major, Ambrose Alexander, and Alec Francis, see: TRC, NRA, Library and Archives Canada – Ottawa, file 882-2, part 8, Kamloops Agency – Kamloops Residential School – Quarterly Returns, 1947–1952, FA 10-17, volume 6447, Microfilm reel C-8770, Library and Archives Canada – Ottawa, Indian Residential School Quarterly Return for Kamloops Indian Residential School, 30 September 1947, pages 8, 9, and 10 of 20-page portable document file; [KAM-002274] TRC, ASAGR, RCMP-564517, Royal Canadian Mounted Police, E-Div NIRS task force Final Report, M. W. Pacholuk, "Final Report of the Native Indian Residential School Task Force, Project E-NIRS," Royal Canadian Mounted Police, 49. [AGCA-564517] For Albert Nepinak, see: TRC, NRA, Library and Archives Canada, RG10, volume 6272, file 582-23, part 1, Royal Canadian Mounted Police Report, 9 April 1951. [PCR-000190] For Tom and Charles Ombash, see: TRC, NRA, National Capital Regional Service Centre – LAC – Ottawa, file 494/3-3-3, volume 1, "Provincial Police Report," G. A. McMonagle, 19 Decem-

ber 1956. [PLK-001205-0001] For Beverly Joseph and Patricia Joseph, see: TRC, NRA, INAC – Resolution Sector – IRS Historical Files Collection – Ottawa, file 961/25-2, volume 15, Admissions and Discharges – Kuper Island Residence, Cowichan Agency, B.C., 01/08/1958–02/07/1966, Control No. 34-15 IRSRC – Historical Files, J. V. Boys to Indian Commissioner for B.C., 29 January 1959. [KUP-200601] For Mabel Crane Bear and Belinda Raw Eater, see: TRC, NRA, Library and Archives Canada – Edmonton, 772/25-1, volume 1, 04/60–06/70, N. Goater to A. H. Murray, 10 March 1962. [OLD-007287-0005] For Alfred Whitehawk, see: TRC, NRA, Library and Archives Canada – Edmonton, RG10, Acc. E1996- 97/415, box 36, file 25-2-662, 1964–1966, E. Turenne to K. Kerr, 6 June 1965. [SPR-006307] For Charles Wenjack, see: TRC, NRA, The Presbyterian Church in Canada Archives, Toronto, On., Acc. 1988-7004, box 17, file 4, "Inquest Hears Tragic Tale of Runaway Boy," *Kenora Miner and News*, 18 November 1966; Coroner's Statement Upon Issuing His Warrant for Holding an Inquest in the Case of Charles Wenjack, R. Glenn Davidson, 4 November 1966; Report of Post-Mortem Examination, A-258, Charles Wenjack, 23 October 1966, Dr. Peter Pan; Adams, "The Lonely Death," 30–44. [CJC-007909] For Joseph Commanda, see: TRC, NRA, INAC – Resolution Sector – IRS Historical Files Collection – Ottawa, file 451/25-2-004, volume 2, "Report on the Death of Joseph Commanda," H. B. Rodine, 6 September 1968. [TAY-001114-0001] For Philip Swain and Roderick Keesick, see: TRC, NRA, INAC, file 487/18-2, volume 1, "2 Boys Died from Exposure," *Kenora Miner and News*, 18 December 1970; [KNR-003158-0002] P. J. Hare to Indian Affairs, 7 December 1970. [KNR-003168] For Jack Elanik and Dennis Dick, see: TRC, NRA, Anglican Church of Canada, Diocese of the Arctic, General Synod Archives, file 110-09, Stringer Hall, Accession M96-7, series 2:1, Notice of missing boys, 1972; [AGS-000341] TRC, NRA, Government of Northwest Territories Archives Confidential, Hostels, 1971–1974, Archival box 8-24, Archival Acc. G1995-004, Leonard Holman to J. Coady, 14 July 1972. [SHU-000486]

357. For examples of cases where criticism was directed against school authorities for the handling of runaways, including cases that led to fatalities, see: TRC, NRA, Library and Archives Canada, RG10, volume 6436, file 878-1, part 1, Statement of Reverend Henry Boening, 3 March 1902; [IRC-047093] TRC, NRA, Library and Archives Canada, RG10, volume 6436, file 878-1, part 1, Statement of Reverend Henry Boening, Statement of Joseph Fahey, 3 March 1903; [IRC-047092] TRC, NRA, Library and Archives Canada, RG10, volume 6267, file 580-1, part 2, W. G. Tweddell to W. M. Graham, 6 May 1931; [DRS-000588] TRC, NRA, Library and Archives Canada, RG10, volume 6332, file 661-1, part 2, Royal Canadian Mounted Police Report, "Re: Percy Ochapowace – Death of, Ochapowace Indian Reserve, Saskatchewan," H. S. Casswell, 19 January 1935; [RLS-000365-0003] TRC, NRA, Library and Archives Canada, RG10, volume 6332, file 661-1, part 2, J. P. B. Ostrander to Secretary, Indian Affairs, 19 January 1935; [RLS- 000365-0001] TRC, NRA, Library and Archives Canada, volume 6446, file 881-23, part 1, R. H. Moore to Secretary, Indian Affairs, 6 January 1937; [LEJ-004083-0000] TRC, NRA, Library and Archives Canada, RG10, volume 6309, file 654-1, part 2, "Memorandum of an inquiry into the cause and circumstances of the death of Andrew Gordon," R. W. Frayling, 11 March 1939; [GDC-028479] TRC, NRA, Library and Archives Canada, RG10, volume 11553, file 312-11, "Indian Boy Frozen on Bush Trail," *Regina Leader-Post*, 16 March 1939; [GDC-009281] TRC, NRA, Library and Archives Canada, RG10, volume 9151, file 312-11 ACE, "Royal Mounted Police Report, Re

Andrew Gordon (Juvenile), Deceased," 16 March 1939; [GDC-009280- 0001] TRC, NRA, Library and Archives Canada, RG10, volume 6278, file 584-10, part 2, Police Report, G. N. McRae, 23 April 1940; [SBR-110686-0001] TRC, NRA, Library and Archives Canada, RG10, volume 6278, file 584-10, part 2, Police Report, G. L. Tisdale, 30 April 1940; [SBR-110686-0002] TRC, NRA, Library and Archives Canada, RG10, volume 6186, file 460-23, part 1, Paul Langlois to Constable Dexter, 14 June 1941; [FTA-000105-0001] TRC, NRA, Library and Archives Canada, RG10, volume 6186, file 460-23, part 1, "Statement of Charles Kioki," 22 June 1942; [FTA-000116-0013] TRC, NRA, Library and Archives Canada, RG10, volume 6320, file 657-10, part 2, Royal Canadian Mounted Police Report, J. P. Douglas, 7 October 1944; [MDD 001704] TRC, NRA, Library and Archives Canada, RG10, volume 6320, file 657-10, part 2, Royal Canadian Mounted Police Report, T. H. Playford, 10 October 1944; [MDD-002258] TRC, NRA, Library and Archives Canada, RG10, volume 6272, file 582-23, part 1, Royal Canadian Mounted Police Report, 9 April 1951; [PCR-000190] TRC, NRA, National Capital Regional Service Centre – LAC – Ottawa, file 487/18-24, volume 1, L. A. Marshall to Indian Affairs, 20 December 1954, [KNR-001380- 0003] TRC, NRA, INAC – Resolution Sector – IRS Historical Files Collection – Ottawa, file 961/25-2, volume 15, Admissions and Discharges – Kuper Island Residence, Cowichan Agency, B.C., 01/08/1958–02/07/1966, Control no. 34-15 IRSRC – Historical Files, J. V. Boys to Indian Commissioner for B.C., 29 January 1959; [KUP-200601] TRC, NRA, Library and Archives Canada – Edmonton, 772/25-1, volume 1, 04/60–06/70, N. Goater to A. H. Murray, 10 March 1962; [OLD-007287-0005] TRC, NRA, INAC, file 487/18-2, volume 1, "2 Boys Died from Exposure," *Kenora Miner and News,* 18 December 1970; [KNR-003158- 0002] TRC, NRA, INAC, file 487/18-2, volume 1, P. J. Hare to Indian Affairs, 7 December 1970. [KNR-003168]

358. For the reporting to the Ontario Provincial Police, see: TRC, NRA, National Capital Regional Service Centre – LAC – Ottawa, file 494/3-3-3, volume 1, "Provincial Police Report," G. A. McMonagle, 19 December 1956. [PLK-001205- 0001] For the reporting to Indian Affairs, see: TRC, NRA, Library and Archives Canada, RG10, volume 8275, file 494/6-1-014, part 5, R. F. Davey to G. Swartman, 13 November 1956. [PLK-000488]

359. Porter, "Remains Found Near Residential School Are 'Non-human,'" *CBC News,* 12 July 2012, http://www.cbc.ca/news/canada/thunder-bay/remains-found-near-residential-school-are-non-human-1.1249599.

360. TRC, NRA, INAC – Resolution Sector – IRS Historical Files Collection – Ottawa, file 1/25-1-5-2, volume 1, "Regulations With Respect to Teaching, Education, Inspection, and Discipline for Indian Residential Schools, Made and Established for the Superintendent General of Indian Affairs Pursuant to Paragraph (a) of Section 114 of the Indian Act," 20 January 1953. [PAR-001203-0001]

361. TRC, NRA, INAC – Resolution Sector – IRS Historical Files Collection – Ottawa, file 901/25-13, volume 4 (locator 156-2), J. B. Bergevin to H. B. Cotnam, 1 March 1971. [NCA-012545-0000]

362. For an example from Chilliwack, British Columbia, see: TRC, NRA, Library and Archives Canada, RG10, volume 6422, file 869-1, part 1, Microfilm reel C-8754, J. Hall to F. Devlin, 19 January 1900. [COQ-000345]

363. TRC, NRA, Library and Archives Canada, RG10, volume 6308, file 653-10, part 1, "Royal Canadian Mounted Police Report Re: Douglas Shingoose and Donald

Stevenson," 23 February 1935. [FHR-001050-0001]

364. See, for examples: North-West Mounted Police, *Annual Report*, 1894, 52–53; TRC, NRA, Library and Archives Canada, RG10, volume 3920, file 116818, C. E. Somerset to Indian Commissioner, 6 October 1896; [EDM-009788] TRC, NRA, Library and Archives Canada, RG10, volume 2771, file 154845, part 1, Mohawk Institute to Hayter Reed, 18 March 1896; [TAY-003510] TRC, NRA, Library and Archives Canada, RG10, volume 6278, file 584-10, part 1, "RCMP Report regarding [Name redacted]," 16 October 1933. [SBR-110565-0001]

365. Sutherland, *Children in English-Canadian Society*, 122. For examples of prosecutions, see: TRC, NRA, Library and Archives Canada, RG10, volume 6278, file 584-10, part 1, A. H. L. Mellor to Deputy Superintendent General, Indian Affairs, 19 September 1935; [SBR-110607- 0000] TRC, NRA, Library and Archives Canada, RG10, volume 6209, file 468-10, part 1, "Royal Canadian Mounted Police report, Re: [Names redacted]," 21 November 1937; [MER-000580- 0001] TRC, NRA, Library and Archives Canada, RG10, volume 6193, file 462-10, part 3, A. D. Moore to Secretary, Indian Affairs, 16 September 1940. [CRS-000507-0000]

366. For examples of the Royal Canadian Mounted Police's being used to return students to school, see: TRC, NRA, Library and Archives Canada, RG10, volume 6330, file 660-10, part 1, R. W. Greatwood to Indian Affairs, 11 April 1930; [PLD-003278-0001] TRC, NRA, Library and Archives Canada, RG10, volume 6330, file 660-10, part 2, H. E. P. Mann to Commissioner, RCMP, 6 February 1934; [PLD-003316-0001] TRC, NRA, Library and Archives Canada, RG10, volume 6193, file 462-10, part 1, page 1/1, "Royal Canadian Mounted Police Report," 11 February 1935, C. Graham; [CRS-001237-0001] TRC, NRA, Library and Archives Canada, RG10, volume 6275, file 583-10, part 1, "Royal Canadian Mounted Police Report, Re: Frank Puckina or Edwards," 15 September 1939; [PLP-000374] TRC, NRA, Library and Archives Canada, RG10, volume 6304, file 651-10, part 1, Constable G. J. Mitchell, 9 September 1931. [MRS-045402-0001]

367. TRC, NRA, Untitled document, purportedly Chronologie Dépuis Leur Foundations, École Blue Quills (Daily Journal from their Founding, Grey Nuns at Blue Quills) 1931–1936, entry for 1 May 1932. [GNA-000404]

368. TRC, NRA, Library and Archives Canada, RG10, volume 6278, file 584-10, part 1, "RCMP's Report on Truant," Constable R. D. Toews, 23 October 1936; [SBR-110630-0001] TRC, NRA, Library and Archives Canada, RG10, volume 6278, file 584-10, part 1, Constable R. D. Toews, 8 May 1937. [SBR-110645-0001]

369. TRC, NRA, Library and Archives Canada, RG10, volume 6258, file 576-10, part 9, "Royal Canadian Mounted Police Report Re: Wallace Hahawahi, Delinquent," 28 October 1936. [BRS-000240-0004]

370. TRC, NRA, Library and Archives Canada, RG10, volume 6258, file 576-10, part 9, "Royal Canadian Mounted Police Report Re: Kenneth Thompson, Runaway Boy," 28 October 1936. [BRS-000240-0001]

371. TRC, NRA, Library and Archives Canada, RG10, volume 6258, file 576-10, part 9, "Royal Canadian Mounted Police Report Re: Peter Ryder Runaway Boy," 28 October 1936. [BRS-000240-0002]

372. TRC, NRA, Library and Archives Canada, RG10, volume 6267, file 580-1, part 2, J. Waddy, 24 November 1928. [DRS-000564]

373. TRC, NRA, Library and Archives Canada, RG10, volume 6253, file 575-5, part 5, A. G. Hamilton to Indian Affairs, November 4, 1935. [BIR-000208]

374. TRC, NRA, Library and Archives Canada, RG10, volume 6057, file 265-10, part 1, J. P. Mackey to Secretary, Indian Affairs, 16 July 1937; [SRS-006077] J. P. Mackey to Secretary, Indian Affairs, 27 July 1937. [SRS-006079]

375. TRC, NRA, Library and Archives Canada, RG10, volume 6057, file 265-10, part 2, "Royal Canadian Mounted Police Report Re: Steven LaBobe," 15 October 1938. [SRS-006090-0001]

376. TRC, NRA, Library and Archives Canada, RG10, volume 6053, file 260-10, part 1, J. P. Mackey to W. J. Cameron, 21 March 1939; [SRS-007977] TRC, NRA, Library and Archives Canada, RG10, volume 6053, file 260-10, part 1, J. P. Mackey to Secretary, Indian Affairs, 14 April 1939. [SRS-007980]

377. TRC, AVS, Ken Lacquette, Statement to the Truth and Reconciliation Commission of Canada, Winnipeg, Manitoba, 18 June 2010, Statement Number: 02-MB-18JU10-052.

378. TRC, AVS, Anthony Wilson, Statement to the Truth and Reconciliation Commission of Canada, Terrace, British Columbia, 30 November 2011, Statement Number: 2011-3303.

379. TRC, AVS, Arthur Ron McKay, Statement to the Truth and Reconciliation Commission of Canada, Winnipeg, Manitoba, 18 June 2010, Statement Number: 02-MB-18JU10-044.

380. TRC, AVS, Ivan George, Statement to the Truth and Reconciliation Commission of Canada, Mission, British Columbia, 18 May 2011, Statement Number: 2011-3472.

381. TRC, AVS, Muriel Morrisseau, Statement to the Truth and Reconciliation Commission of Canada, Winnipeg, Manitoba, 18 June 2010, Statement Number: 02-MB-18JU10-057.

382. TRC, AVS, Isaac Daniels, Statement to the Truth and Reconciliation Commission of Canada, Saskatoon, Saskatchewan, 22 June 2012, Statement Number: 2011 1779.

383. TRC, AVS, Dora Necan, Statement to the Truth and Reconciliation Commission of Canada, Ignace, Ontario, 3 June 2011, Statement Number: 2011-1503.

384. TRC, AVS, Nellie Cournoyea, Statement to the Truth and Reconciliation Commission of Canada, Inuvik, Northwest Territories, 28 June 2011, Statement Number: NNE105. Cournoyea later went on to lead the negotiation of the first comprehensive land rights agreement in the Northwest Territories for her Inuvialuit people, and later became the first Aboriginal and female premier in Canada.

385. TRC, AVS, Lawrence Waquan, Statement to the Truth and Reconciliation Commission of Canada, Winnipeg, Manitoba, 18 June 2010, Statement Number: SC111.

386. TRC, AVS, Beverley Anne Machelle, Statement to the Truth and Reconciliation Commission of Canada, Whitehorse, Yukon, 27 May 2011, Statement Number: 2011-1133.

387. TRC, NRA, INAC, file 494/18-28, volume 1, G. Swartman to Indian Affairs Branch, 12 May 1955. [PLK-002025]

388. TRC, AVS, Mel H. Buffalo, Statement to the Truth and Reconciliation Commission of Canada, Hobbema, Alberta, 24 July 2013, Statement Number: SP124.

389. Canada, *Annual Report of the Department of Indian Affairs, 1907*, 189.

390. United Church of Canada Archives, Toronto, Archive accession information: Fonds, 3282: John Chantler McDougall Fonds, 1986.291C, box 1, file 8, Mrs. J. McDougall, "Founding of the McDougall Orphanage and Training School," Historical Sketch, no date.

391. Coccola, *They Call Me Father*, 89.

392. Stocken, *Among the Blackfoot*, 1–2.

393. Kelm, "Introduction" to Butcher, *Letters of Margaret Butcher*, xi, xxvi.

394. Butcher, *Letters of Margaret Butcher*, 5.

395. TRC, AVS, Lorraine Arbez, Statement to the Truth and Reconciliation Commission of Canada, Winnipeg, Manitoba, 18 June 2010, Statement Number: 02-MB-18JU10-007.

396. TRC, AVS, Noreen Fischbuch, Statement to the Truth and Reconciliation Commission of Canada, Beaver Mines, Alberta, 3 August 2011, Statement Number: 2011-1692.

397. TRC, AVS, George Takashima, Statement to the Truth and Reconciliation Commission of Canada, Lethbridge, Alberta, 3 August 2011, Statement Number: 2011-1700.

398. TRC, NRA, Library and Archives Canada, RG10, volume 3938, file 121607, Deputy Superintendent General of Indian Affairs to A. E. Forget, Assistant Commissioner of Indian Affairs, NWT, 18 January 1895. [RIS-000385-0000]

399. Library and Archives Canada, RG10, volume 2100, file 17960, part 2, A. Sutherland to Superintendent General of Indian Affairs, 31 March 1887.

400. TRC, NRA, Library and Archives Canada, RG10, volume 8843, file 709/16-2-001, part 1, C. H. Birdsall to Dr. Dorey, 2 June 1948. [EDM-000371]

401. TRC, NRA, No document location, no document file source, H. F. Dunlop to P. Phelan, 4 November 1948. [SEC-000063]

402. TRC, NRA, No document location, no document file source, A. Noonan to L. K. Poupore, 27 November 1960. [CIS-000553]

403. TRC, NRA, Library and Archives Canada, file 883-1, part 1, Bella Coola Agency – Kitamaat Boarding School – General Administration, 1906–1932, FA 10-17, Perm. volume 6451, Microfilm reel C-8773, Library and Archives Canada, L. Spotton to C. G. Young, 28 February 1930. [KMT-095721]

404. TRC, NRA, Library and Archives Canada, RG10, volume 6377, file 767-1, part 1, M. Christianson to H. W. McGill, 2 August 1933. [JON-000073]

405. Fast, "Amelia Le Soeur (Yeomans)," http://www.biographi.ca/009004-119.01-e.php?BioId=41653 (accessed 26 May 2013); Canada, *Annual Report of the Department of Indian Affairs, 1900*, 109; Canada, *Annual Report of the Department of Indian Affairs, 1901*, 80. (Charlotte Amelia's name is mistakenly given as Annie in the annual report.)

406. TRC, AVS, Theresa Reid, Statement to the Truth and Reconciliation Commission of Canada, Powell River, British Columbia, 28 September 2011, Statement Number: 2011-0263.

407. TRC, AVS, George Takashima, Statement to the Truth and Reconciliation Commission of Canada, Lethbridge, Alberta, 3 August 2011, Statement Number: 2011-1700.

408. TRC, AVS, Olive Saunders, Statement to the Truth and Reconciliation Commission of Canada, Thunder Bay, Ontario, 7 and 8 March 2011, Statement Number: 2011-0042.

409. TRC, NRA, Provincial Archives Alberta, PAA 71.220 B161 2357, E. O. Drouin to Chief Shot on Both Sides and Blood Band Council, Indian Agency, Cardston, 27 December 1966. [OGP-022362]

410. Regina principal A. J. McLeod (1900), TRC, NRA, The United Church of Canada Archives, Toronto, Acc. No. 1979.199C, box 2, file 20, Alex Skene to Mr. McKay, 1 December 1900; [RIS- 000436] Muncey, Ontario, principal W. W. Shepherd (died after a horse-drawn cart accident in 1903), TRC, NRA, Library and Archives Canada, RG10, volume 6205, file 468-1, part 1, R. G. Howes to Deputy Superintendent General, 25 May 1903; [MER-000331] Regina principal J. A. Sinclair (1905), TRC, NRA, Library and Archives Canada, RG10, volume 3927, file 116836- 1A, Frank Pedley to W. M. Graham, 16 January 1905; [RIS-000090] Mission, British Columbia, principal Charles Marchal (diphtheria, 1906), TRC, NRA, Library and Archives Canada, RG10, volume 6468, file 890-1, part 1, Microfilm reel C-8786, A. W. Vowell to Secretary, Indian Affairs, 10 October 1906; [MIS-004766] Onion Lake, Saskatchewan, Anglican school principal John Matheson (1916), TRC, NRA, Library and Archives Canada, RG10, volume 6320, file 658-1, part 1, W. Sibbald to Secretary, Indian Affairs, 28 August 1916; [PAR-003569] Qu'Appelle, Saskatchewan, principal Joseph Hugonnard (1917), RG10, volume 6327, file 660-1, part 1, M. Kalmes to Duncan C. Scott, 13 February 1917; [PLD-000005] Shoal Lake, Ontario, principal Mr. Mathews (influenza, 1918), TRC, NRA, RG10, volume 6187, file 461-1, part 1, R. S. McKenzie to Assistant Deputy and Secretary, 23 October 1918; [CJC-000870] High River, Alberta, principal George Nordmann (influenza, 1918), Library and Archives Canada, RG10, volume 3933, file 117657-1, A. Naessens to Secretary, Indian Affairs, 7 January 1919; Gordon's, Saskatchewan, principal H. W. Atwater (1925), TRC, NRA, INAC – Resolution Sector – IRS Historical Files Collection – Ottawa, file E4974-02016, volume 4, T. J. Davies to Mr. Moore, 25 November 1925; [GDC-002528] Beauval, Saskatchewan, principal Mederic Adam (typhoid, 1930), TRC, NRA, Library and Archives Canada, RG10, volume 6300, file 650-1, part 1, O. Charlebois to Duncan Scott, 28 October 1930; [BVL-000005] Grayson, Saskatchewan, principal J. Carriere (1933), TRC, NRA, Library and Archives Canada, RG10, volume 6303, file 651-1, part 1, A. F. MacKenzie to J. P. B. Ostrander, 3 July 1933; [MRS 001401] Kamsack, Saskatchewan, principal C. Brouillet (1935), TRC, NRA, Library and Archives Canada, RG10, volume 6334, file 662-1, part 2, A. F. MacKenzie to W. Murison, 14 February 1935. [SPR-000465]

411. TRC, NRA, Library and Archives Canada, RG10, volume 1346, Microfilm reel C-13916, G. Donckele to W. R. Robertson, 1 January 1907; [KUP-004280] RG10, FA 10-1, volume 1346, Microfilm reel C-13916, Cowichan Agency – Incoming Correspondence re Kuper Island Industrial School, 1891–1907, P. Claessen to W. R. Robertson, 5 June 1907. [KUP-022198] For A. J. McLeod's initials, see: Canada, *Annual Report of the Department of Indian Affairs, 1900*, 383.

412. TRC, NRA, Anglican Church of Canada Archives, Diocese of the Arctic, M96-7, box 188, "File 8, Collected Material – Bessie Quirt, Articles written by Bessie re: Shingle Point and Fort George" "RE: First Eskimo Residential School (Anglican) – Shingle Point. Story One – Fifty Years Ago – August 1929–1979"; Library and Archives Canada, RG919-10, part 1, Fort Norman Agency – Aklavik Church of England Residential School – Admissions and Discharges, 1936–1946, FA 10-17, Perm. volume 6477, Microfilm reel C-8792, H. S. Shepherd to Philip Phelan, 30 March 1939; [ASU-001138] RG29, volume 2906, file 851-1-A486, part 3, H. S. Shepherd to P. E. Moore, 14 January 1948; [NPC-603247] RG10, volume 10728, file 484/25-2-467, part 1, H. S. Shepherd to J. L. Whitey, 17 November 1952; [MFI-001074] Anglican Church of Canada, General Synod Archives, ACC-MSCC-GS 75-103, series 2.15, box 22, file 2, "Minutes of a Meeting of the Sub-Executive Committee MSCC," 8th September 1954; [AAC-090761] Anglican Church of Canada, General Synod Archives GS 75-103, series 2-15, box 22, "Report of the Superintendent, Indian School Administration, to the M.S.C.C. Board of Management, Toronto, November 16th, 1954." [GDC-007201]

413. TRC, NRA, Library and Archives Canada, RG10, volume 6430, file 876-1, part 1, West Coast Agency – Ahousaht Residential School – General Administration, 1901–1931, FA 10-17, Microfilm reel C-8759, W. R. Woods to Dr. Young, 5 November 1929. [AST-200068-0001]

414. Methodist Church of Canada, British Columbia Conference, Port Simpson District, Ministerial Sessions, 1893, 188, quoted in Bolt, *Thomas Crosby*, 63.

415. TRC, NRA, Library and Archives Canada – Ottawa, RG10, volume 8803, file 959/25-13, part 2, Henry Cook to Frank Howard, 29 March 1960. [MIK-002122]

416. TRC, NRA, O.M.I. House – Vancouver, box 39, Fort St. John–Kakawis Family Development, folder 20, Kakawis Correspondence 1942–1979, Series One Plus Finding Aid, B.C./Yukon Local Community of O.M.I. Lacombe Canada Province [formerly St. Paul's Province], Mary Gemma to M. Kearney, 3 February 1958. [CST-800117] For background on the Benedictine Sisters of Mount Angel, see: The Benedictine Sisters of Mount Angel, "About Us, A Brief History of the Benedictine Sisters of Mt. Angel," http://www.benedictine-srs.org/history.html (accessed 12 June 2014).

417. TRC, NRA, Library and Archives Canada, RG55, FA 55-22, Acc. 1980-81/069, box 118, file 1105, part 2, Rates of Pay & Conditions of Employment of Teachers, 1964–1965, R. F. Davey to Peter Fillipoff, 25 May 1965. [AEMR-150636]

418. Bruno-Jofre, *Missionary Oblate Sisters*, 4–12, 132–139; Choquette, *Canada's Religions*, 83–84, 201; McCarthy, *From the Great River*, 156; Gresko, "Gender and Mission," 9; Huel, *Proclaiming the Gospel*, 165–166, 171; Shanahan, *Jesuit Residential School*, 5; TRC, NRA, Provincial Archives – Alberta, Acc. 78.204/5, Vital Grandin to Mother Ste. Marie, 27 September 1890; [ORC-000775] No document location, no document file source, Victor Rassier to Gerald Murphy, 15 September 1930; [BVT-000239] No document location, no document file source, M. Agatha, to Gerald Murray, 26 May 1931; [BVT-000260] TRC, NRA, Library and Archives Canada, RG10, volume 6276, file 584-3, part 1, H. B. Rayner to W. M. Graham, 26 August 1931. [SBR-000879-0001]

419. TRC, CAR, United Church Archives, Presbyterian Church in Canada, Board of Foreign Missions, Records Pertaining to Missions to Aboriginal People in Mani-

toba and the North West, 79.199C, box 3, file 29, (C0990), Austin McKitrick to Dr. R. P. MacKay, 30 September 1901, quoted in Hildebrand, "Staff Perspectives," 170. [13d-c000990-d0017-001]

420. Gagan, *Sensitive Independence*, 201.

421. Canada, *Annual Report of the Department of Indian Affairs, 1906*, 2: 52–56.

422. Grant, "Two-Thirds of the Revenue," 108–109.

423. For an example, see: Canada, *Annual Report of the Department of Indian Affairs, 1893*, 172.

424. TRC, NRA, Library and Archives Canada, file 886-24, part 1, Skeena River Agency – Crosby Girls Residential School [Port Simpson] – Audit Reports 1935–1948, FA 10-17, Perm. volume 6458, Microfilm reel C-8779; Library and Archives Canada – Ottawa, "Crosby Girls' Home, United Church of Canada, Cost of Operations for Fiscal Year 1934–35." [PSM-200049-0003]

425. TRC, NRA, Library and Archives Canada, RG10, volume 8845, file 963/16-2, part 1, July 3, 1936, Re: Kamloops Residential School, Roman Catholic. [KAM-002000]

426. TRC, NRA, Anglican Diocese of Cariboo Archives Section #205, St. George Indian Residential School, Card D.C. 2C11, Lytton-St.-George's School, #88.44, "All Saints Indian Residential School Staff Manual 2nd Revision, 1967, Mr. A. W. Harding, Vice-Principal," 26–27. [AEMR-177341]

427. Canada, *Annual Report of the Department of Indian Affairs, 1896*, 366.

428. TRC, NRA, Anglican Church of Canada, General Synod Archives, ACC-MSCC-GS 75-103, series 9:08, box 131, file 5-3, "The Indian Residential School Commission of the Mission Society of the Church of England in Canada, An Outline of the Duties of Those Who Occupy Positions on the Staff at the Society's Indian Residential Schools, No. III, The Teacher." [AAC-090142]

429. TRC, NRA, Library and Archives Canada, RG10, volume 6462, file 888-1, part 1, H, EGN-007951, F. J. C. Ball to D. C. Scott, 5 May 1921. [GRG-022150-0000]

430. TRC, NRA, Library and Archives Canada, RG10, volume 6028, file 118-7-1, part 1, E. B. Glass to Dr. Sutherland, 4 September 1896. [WFL-000648-0002]

431. Hare and Barman, "Good Intentions," 168, 205, 206, 216.

432. Buck, *Doctor Rode Side-Saddle*, 114, 133.

433. Buck, *Doctor Rode Side-Saddle*, 92.

434. Brandon, Manitoba, principal T. Ferrier in 1903; Mount Elgin, Ontario, principal S. R. McVitty in 1913; and Kuper Island, British Columbia, principal W. Lemmens in 1915—all used the word "evil" in describing tendencies in Aboriginal culture. Canada, *Annual Report of the Department of Indian Affairs, 1903*, 342–343; TRC, NRA, Library and Archives Canada, RG10, volume 6205, file 468-1, part 1, Public Archives Canada, S. R. McVitty, "Helping the Indian: How it Is Done at Mount Elgin Industrial Institute," *The Christian Guardian*, 31 May 1913; [MER-0376] RG10, volume 1347, Microfilm reel C-13916, W. Lemmens to W. R. Robertson, 10 February 1915. [KUP-004240]

435. See, for example, *Algoma Missionary News* (April 1877): 14, quoted in Wilson, "Note on Shingwauk Industrial Home," 69; Butcher, *Letters of Margaret Butcher*, 26.

436. TRC, NRA, Library and Archives Canada, RG10, volume 6057, file 265-10, part 1, J. P. Mackey to Father MacNeil, 5 October 1936. [SRS-000280-0003]

437. Bush, *Western Challenge*, 27.

438. Fisher, *Contact and Conflict*, 185–188; Usher, *William Duncan*, 126.

439. TRC, NRA, Anglican Church of Canada, General Synod Archives, MSCC, GS 75-103, series 2-15, box 29, file 10, Anglican document no. 52.63, Victoria Ketcheson and Patricia Watson, 29 November 1952. [PAR-001992]

440. TRC, NRA, Document location to be determined, Hance/Aleck/Michell – Anglican Church of Canada and Anglican Church of Cariboo List of Documents, Helen Clafton to Bishop Dean, 5 March 1957. [ANG-063238]

441. Canada, *Annual Report of the Department of Indian Affairs, 1930*, 17.

442. TRC, NRA, Library and Archives Canada, RG10, volume 6200, file 466-1, part 2, "Successful Graduates." [TAY-004294-0002]

443. TRC, NRA, Library and Archives Canada, RG10, volume 2006, file 7825-1A, "Report on the Mohawk Institute and Six Nations Board School," 30 August 1895, 43. [TAY-003821-0000]

444. TRC, NRA, Library and Archives Canada, RG10, volume 6200, file 466-1, part 2, A. F. MacKenzie to H. W. Snell, 7 May 1936. [TAY-003085-0002]

445. Canada, *Annual Report of the Department of Indian Affairs, 1903*, 402.

446. TRC, NRA, United Church of Canada Archives, Acc. No. 1979.199C, box 5, file 60, J. A. Sinclair to R. P. MacKay, 26 April 1904. [RIS-000306]

447. TRC, NRA, Library and Archives Canada, RG10, volume 6255, file 576-1, part 2, J. Doyle to Secretary, Indian Affairs, 14 September 1932. [BRS-000234]

448. Canada, *Annual Report of the Department of Indian Affairs, 1960*, 56.

449. TRC, AVS, Stanley McKay, Statement to the Truth and Reconciliation Commission of Canada, Winnipeg, Manitoba, 13 July 2011, Statement Number: 2011-0269

450. Kirkness, *Creating Space*, 3–12, 29–40.

451. Kirkness, *Creating Space*, 29–30.

452. TRC, NRA, Library and Archives Canada, RG10, file 494/1-13-014, volume 1, T. B. Jones to R. F. Davey, 21 June 1963. [PLK-001867] For Spence as a residential school student, see: Canada, Special Joint Committee, 1947, 1066–1067.

453. TRC, NRA, INAC – Resolution Sector – IRS Historical Files Collection – Ottawa, file 494/25- 1-014, volume 2, "The Anglican Indian Residential School, Sioux Lookout, Ontario," 10 June 1965. [PLK-000304-0001]

454. TRC, NRA, INAC – Resolution Sector – IRS Historical Files Collection – Ottawa, file 487/25-1- 014, R. F. Davey to Giollo Kelly, 10 June 1966. [CJC-000308]

455. TRC, NRA, The Presbyterian Church in Canada Archives, Toronto, ON, Acc. 1988-7004, box 43, file 4, Giollo Kelly to Mrs. Colin Wasacase, 8 July 1966. [NCA-009161-0002]

456. For Mission, see: TRC, NRA, "Historic Transfer of Authority," *Fraser Valley Record*, 5 September 1973. [OMS-000307] For Kamloops, see: TRC, NRA, Library

and Archives Canada – Burnaby, RG10, FA 10-138, Acc. v85-86/353, file 963/1-13, Perm. volume 6 [502372], part 1, Student Residence Establishment, 1969–78, NAC – Burnaby, A. H. Friesen to A. H. Noonan, 18 April 1973. [KAM-008144] For Blue Quills, Alberta, see: TRC, NRA, INAC – Resolution Sector – IRS Historical Files Collection – Ottawa, file 779/25-2-009, volume 1 (Ctrl #55-4), "Confidential: Notes: Re Blue Quills," undated. [NCA-007302] For Prince Albert, see: TRC, NRA, INAC – Resolution Sector – IRS Historical Files Collection – Ottawa, file 601/25-13-1, J. B. Freeman to James A. Roberts, 2 April 1973. [PAR-019374] For Duck Lake, see: TRC, NRA, INAC – Resolution Sector – IRS Historical Files Collection – Ottawa, GRS Files, box 8A, file 15, D. Seesequasis to H. Kolakowski, 3 February 1982. [GDC-014654-0004] For Qu'Appelle, see: LaRose, "Wrecker's ball Claims White Calf Collegiate," http://www.ammsa.com/publications/saskatchewan-sage/wreckers-ball-claims-white-calf-collegiate-0. For Fort George, see: TRC, NRA, INAC – Resolution Sector – IRS Historical Files Collection – Ottawa, file 371/25-1-019, volume 2, Right Rev. James A. Watton to A. Gill, 7 September 1971. [FGA-000225-0001] TRC, NRA, INAC – Resolution Sector – IRS Historical Files Collection – Ottawa, NCR-E4974-1 (Encl 1), volume 3, (Ctrl #446-19), Saskatchewan Region, Student Residences: An Issue Management Discussion Paper, 8 February 1994. [NCA-016023-0002]

457. TRC, NRA, INAC – Resolution Sector – IRS Historical Files Collection – Ottawa, NCR-E4974-1 (Encl 1), volume 3, (Ctrl #446-19), Saskatchewan Region, Student Residences: An Issue Management Discussion Paper, 8 February 1994. [NCA-016023-0002]

458. TRC, NRA, Anglican Church of Canada, General Synod Archives, file 1, Visit Reports of the Superintendent 02/54–12/54, pg. 004126-004227, Accession GS 75-103, series 2:15, box 24, "Superintendent's Visit to Chooutla School, Carcross, Y.T., December 3th–6th, 1954." [DYK-201620]

459. TRC, CAR, General Synod of the Anglican Church of Canada Archives, Archive accession information: MSSC Indian School Administration, Visit Reports, 1954–62, file 2 (1955–56), "Superintendent's Visit to St. John's Residential School, Wabasca, Alberta, 26th August, 1956." [13a-c000034-d0002-022]

460. General Synod of the Anglican Church of Canada Archives, Missionary Society of the Church of England in Canada, Indian School Administration – Visit Reports, Committees, Textual Records, 1903–1968, Indian and Eskimo Residential Schools and Indian School Administration, 1921–1977, GS75-103, box 23, file 10, "Superintendent's Visit to St. Philip's School, Fort George – March 24–25," 1953. [13a-c000032-d0025-001]

461. TRC, CAR, The General Synod of the Anglican Church of Canada Archives, ACC-MSCC-GS 75-103, series 2:15, box 24, file 2, Superintendent's Visit to St. Philip's School, Fort George, QC, January 16 and 17, 1956. [13a-c000034-d0002-004]

462. TRC, AVS, Jeanne Rioux, Statement to the Truth and Reconciliation Commission of Canada, Vancouver, British Columbia, 18 September 2013, Statement Number: 2011-3207.

463. TRC, AVS, Mary Chapman, Statement to the Truth and Reconciliation Commission of Canada, Vancouver, British Columbia, 4 October 2011, Statement Number: 2011-1529.

464. Vitaline Elsie Jenner, Statement to the Truth and Reconciliation Commission

of Canada, Winnipeg, Manitoba, 16 June 2010, Statement Number: 02-MB-16JU10-131.

465. Coates, *A Global History of Indigenous Peoples*, 244–245.

466. United Nations, *United Nations Declaration on the Rights of Indigenous Peoples*; Coates, *A Global History of Indigenous Peoples*, 244–245.

467. Smith, *Apology to First Nations People*, http://www.united-church.ca/beliefs/policies/1986/a651 (accessed 23 October 2014).

468. The Missionary Oblates of Mary Immaculate, *An Apology to the First Nations of Canada by the Oblate Conference of Canada*, http://www.cccb.ca/site/images/stories/pdf/oblate_apology_english.pdf (accessed 27 October 2014)

469. For the Anglican apology, see: Hiltz, *A Step Along the Path: Apology by Archbishop Fred Hiltz*, http://www.anglican.ca/relationships/files/2011/06/Apology-English.pdf (accessed 27 October 2014). For the Presbyterian apology, see: Presbyterian Church in Canada, *The Confession of the Presbyterian Church in Canada as Adopted by the General Assembly*, http://presbyterian.ca/?wpdmdl=92& (accessed 27 October 2014); The United Church of Canada, *Apology to Former Students of United Church Indian Residential Schools, and to Their Families and Communities*, http://www.united-church.ca/beliefs/policies/1998/a623 (accessed 27 October 2014).

470. "Bernard's Lawsuit Helped Natives Nationwide," *The Daily News*, http://www.canada.com/story_print.html?id=983a8b88-a8ac-4e09-9e5c-b2c0e207ac3d.

471. Canadian Broadcasting Corporation, *The Journal*, Barbara Frum interview with Phil Fontaine, 30 October 1990, http://archives.cbc.ca/society/education/clips//11177.

472. Lleweyn, "Dealing with the Legacy," 253 at 261.

473. Assembly of First Nations, *Assembly of First Nations Report*, 11.

474. *Cloud v. Canada (Attorney General)* 2004 CanLII 45444 (ON CA).

475. Canada, House of Commons Debates (11 June 2008), 6850.

476. Canada, House of Commons Debates (11 June 2008), 6851.

477. Canada, House of Commons Debates (11 June 2008), 6852.

478. Canada, House of Commons Debates (11 June 2008), 6853.

479. Canada, House of Commons Debates (11 June 2008), 6855.

480. Canada, House of Commons Debates (11 June 2008), 6855.

481. Canada, House of Commons Debates (11 June 2008), 6855.

482. Canada, House of Commons Debates (11 June 2008), 6856.

483. Canada, House of Commons Debates (11 June 2008), 6856.

CHAPTER THREE: THE LEGACY

1. For an example of a student who started drinking while in school, see: Nabigon, *Hollow Tree*, 5.

2. TRC, NRA, INAC–Resolution Sector–IRS Historical Files Collection – Ottawa, file 6-21-1, volume 2 (Ctrl #27-6), H. M. Jones to Deputy Minister, 13 December 1956. [NCA-001989-0001]

3. For a discussion that places both child welfare and residential schools in the context of the ongoing colonization of Aboriginal people, see: McKenzie and Hudson, "Native Children."

4. TRC, AVS, Genine Paul-Dimitracopoulos, Statement to the Truth and Recon ciliation Commission of Canada, Halifax, Nova Scotia, 27 October 2011, State ment Number: 2011-2862.

5. TRC, AVS, Alma Mann Scott, Statement to the Truth and Reconciliation Com mission of Canada, Winnipeg, Manitoba, 17 June 2010, Statement Number: 02-MB16JU10-016.

6. TRC, AVS, Norma Kassi, Statement to the Truth and Reconciliation Commis sion of Canada, Inuvik, Northwest Territories, 29 June 2011, Statement Number: NNE203.

7. Royal Commission on Aboriginal Peoples, as cited in Sinha and Kozlowski, "Structure of Aboriginal Child Welfare in Canada," 4, http://ir.lib.uwo.ca/iipj/vol4/iss2/2.

8. Johnston, *Native Children*, 57.

9. Canada, Statistics Canada, *Aboriginal People in Canada*, 19.

10. TRC, NRA, The Presbyterian Church in Canada Archives, Toronto, ON, Tyler Bjornson File, 'Presbyterian Research,' "Presbyterian Indian Residential School Staff Handbook," 1. [IRC-041206]

11. Canada, *Annual Report of the Department of Indian Affairs*, 1942, 154; Canada, *Annual Report of the Department of Indian Affairs*, 1943, 168; Canada, *Annual Report of the Department of Indian Affairs*, 1944, 177; Canada, *Annual Report of the Department of Indian Affairs*, 1945, 190; Canada, *Annual Report of the Department of Indian Affairs*, 1946, 231; Canada, *Annual Report of the Department of Indian Affairs*, 1947, 236; Canada, *Annual Report of the Department of Indian Affairs*, 1948, 234; Canada, *Annual Report of the Department of Indian Affairs*, 1949, 215; Canada, *Annual Report of the Department of Indian Affairs*, 1950, 86–87; Canada, *Annual Report of the Department of Indian Affairs*, 1951, 34–35; Canada, *Annual Report of the Department of Indian Affairs*, 1952, 74–75; Can ada, *Annual Report of the Department of Indian Affairs*, 1953, 82–83; Canada, *Annual Report of the Department of Indian Affairs*, 1954, 88–89; Canada, *Annual Report of the Department of Indian Affairs*, 1955, 78–79; Canada, *Annual Report of the Department of Indian Affairs*, 1956, 76–77; Canada, *Annual Report of the Department of Indian Affairs*, 1956–57, 88–89; Canada, *Annual Report of the De partment of Indian Affairs*, 1958, 91; Canada, *Annual Report of the Department of Indian Affairs*, 1959, 94; Canada, *Annual Report of the Department of Indian Affairs*, 1960, 94; Canada, *Annual Report of the Department of Indian Affairs*, 1961, 102; Canada, *Annual Report of the Department of Indian Affairs*, 1962, 73; Canada, *Annual Report of the Department of Indian Affairs*, 1963, 62.

12. Canada, Statistics Canada, *2011 National Household Survey Aboriginal Demographics*, https://www.aadnc-aandc.gc.ca/eng/1376329205785/1376329233875.

13. Canadian Human Rights Commission, *Report on Equality Rights*, 3, 12, 32.

14. Sharpe, et al., *Effect of Increasing Aboriginal Educational Attainment*, vii.

15. Canada, Statistics Canada, *Aboriginal People Living Off-reserve*, 15.

16. Canada, Statistics Canada, *Census Inuit Table*: 89-636-x, http://www.statcan.gc.ca/pub/89-636-x/89-636-x2008001-eng.htm.

17. Wilson and Macdonald, *Income Gap*, 8.

18. Wilson and Macdonald, *Income Gap*, 4.

19. MacDonald and Wilson, *Poverty or Prosperity*, 6.

20. Wilson and Macdonald, *Income Gap*, 14.

21. Assembly of First Nations, *Breaking the Silence*, 25–26.

22. TRC, AVS, Michael Sillett, Statement to the Truth and Reconciliation Commission of Canada, Halifax, Nova Scotia, 27 October 2011, Statement Number: 2011-2870.

23. TRC, NRA, INAC – Resolution Sector – IRS Historical Files Collection – Ottawa, file 81/25-1 (Ctrl #240-13), R. Morris to Chiefs, Petahbun [Pehtabun] Area, 9 February 1979, 2–3. [NCA-001721]

24. TRC, AVS, Conrad Burns, Statement to the Truth and Reconciliation Commission of Canada, Regina, Saskatchewan, 17 January 2012, Statement Number: SP036.

25. TRC, AVS, Mary Courchene, Statement to the Truth and Reconciliation Commission of Canada, Pine Creek First Nation, Manitoba, 28 November 2011, Statement Number: 2011-2515.

26. Brass, *I Walk in Two Worlds*, 13.

27. According to UNCESO, 36 percent of Canada's Aboriginal languages are critically endangered, 18 percent are severely endangered, and 16 percent are definitely endangered. The remaining languages are all vulnerable. Moseley and Nicolas, *Atlas of the World's Languages*, 117.

28. Canada, Statistics Canada, *Aboriginal Peoples and Language*, http://www12.statcan.gc.ca/nhsenm/2011/as-sa/99-011-x/99-011-x2011003_1-eng.cfm.

29. Canada, Statistics Canada, *Aboriginal Peoples and Language*, http://www12.statcan.gc.ca/nhsenm/2011/as-sa/99-011-x/99-011-x2011003_1-eng.cfm; Canada, Statistics Canada, *Population Reporting an Aboriginal Identity*, http://www.statcan.gc.ca/tables-tableaux/sum-som/l01/cst01/demo38a-eng.htm; Canada, Statistics Canada, *Aboriginal Languages in Canada*, http://www.statcan.gc.ca/pub/11-008-x/2007001/9628-eng.htm.

30. Library and Archives Canada, RG10, volume 3957, file 140754-1, P. H. Bryce to F. Pedley, 5 November 1909.

31. For long-term differences in the Aboriginal and non-Aboriginal tuberculosis death rates in Canada, see: Wherritt, *Miracle of the Empty Beds*, 251–253.

32. TRC, AVS, Katherine Copenace, Statement to the Truth and Reconciliation

Commission of Canada, Winnipeg, Manitoba, 16 June 2010, Statement Number: 02-MB-16JU10-129.

33. Taylor, "Grollier Meeting Emotional," 23 January 1998, http://www.nnsl.com/frames/newspapers/1998-01/jan23_98grol.html.

34. Canada, *Annual Report of the Department of Indian Affairs*, 1905, 278.

35. Smylie, "Review of Aboriginal Infant Mortality Rates," 147.

36. Canada, Statistics Canada, *Mortality Rates among Children and Teenagers*, http://www.statcan.gc.ca/pub/82-003-x/2012003/article/11695-eng.htm.

37. Canada, Statistics Canada, *Select Health Indicators of First Nations People*, http://www.statcan.gc.ca/daily-quotidien/130129/dq130129b-eng.htm.

38. First Nations Centre, *First Nations Regional Longitudinal Health Survey*, 114.

39. Kirmayer et al., *Suicide Among Aboriginal People*, xv, 22.

40. Canada, Indian Residential Schools Adjudication Secretariat, Adjudication Secretariat Statistics, http://iap-pei.ca/information/stats-eng.php (accessed 20 February 2015). By the end of 2014, it had awarded $2.69 billion in compensation for sexual and serious physical abuse under the Independent Assessment Process established by the Indian Residential Schools Settlement Agreement.

41. TRC, AVS, Daniel Andre, Statement to the Truth and Reconciliation Commission of Canada, Whitehorse, Yukon, 23 May 2011, Statement Number: 2011-0202.

42. Canada, Statistics Canada, *Adult Correctional Services in Canada, 1995–1996*, http://www.statcan.gc.ca/pub/85-002-x/85-002-x1997004-eng.pdf; Canada, Statistics Canada, *Adult Correctional Services in Canada, 2011* 2012, http://www.statcan.gc.ca/pub/85-002-x/2014001/article/11918-eng.htm#a5.

43. Canada, Statistics Canada, *Adult Correctional Services in Canada, 2011–2012*, http://www.statcan.gc.ca/pub/85-002-x/2014001/article/11918-eng.htm#a5.

44. Canada, Statistics Canada, *Youth Correctional Services in Canada, 2011–2012*, http://www.statcan.gc.ca/pub/85-002-x/2014001/article/11917-eng.htm#a5; Canada, Department of Justice, Youth Justice Research, *One-Day Snapshot*, 3. These figures do not include Saskatchewan, which has a high rate of Aboriginal youth incarceration.

45. Canada, Public Health Agency of Canada, *Fetal Alcohol Spectrum Disorder* (FASD), http://www.phac-aspc.gc.ca/hp-ps/dca-dea/prog-ini/fasd-etcaf/index-eng.php; Ospina and Dennett, *Review on the Prevalence of Fetal Alcohol Spectrum Disorders*, iii.

46. Canada, Public Safety Canada, Fetal Alcohol Spectrum Disorder, 5, http://www.publicsafety.gc.ca/cnt/rsrcs/pblctns/ftl-lchl-spctrm/ftl-lchl-spctrm-eng.pdf.

47. Canada, Correctional Service of Canada, *Fetal Alcohol Spectrum Disorder* (FASD), iv, http://www. publicsafety.gc.ca/lbrr/archives/cn21451-eng.pdf.

48. A study done for the Aboriginal Healing Foundation drew links among the intergenerational trauma of residential schools, alcohol addictions, and the prevalence of FASD in Aboriginal communities. Tait, *Fetal Alcohol Syndrome*.

49. Canada, Statistics Canada, *Violent Victimization of Aboriginal People*, http://wgc.ca/pub/85-002-x/2011001/article/11415-eng.pdf.

50. Canada, Statistics Canada, *Violent Victimization of Aboriginal Women*, http://
    www.statcan.gc.ca/pub/85-002-x/2011001/article/11439-eng.pdf.

51. Royal Canadian Mounted Police, *Missing and Murdered Aboriginal Women*, 3,
    http://www.rcmp-grc.gc.ca/pubs/mmaw-faapd-eng.pdf.

CHAPTER FOUR: RECONCILIATION

1. TRC, AVS, Alma Mann Scott, Statement to the Truth and Reconciliation Commission of Canada, Winnipeg, Manitoba, 17 June 2010, Statement Number:
   02-MB-16JU10-016.

2. Media coverage on the call for an inquiry on missing and murdered Aboriginal
   women has been extensive. See, for example: "Women's Memorial March in
   Vancouver Attracts Hundreds," *CBC News*, 14 February 2015, http://www.cbc.
   ca/news/canada/british-columbia/womens-memorial-march-in-vancouver-
   attracts-hundreds-1.2957930; "Murdered and Missing Aboriginal Women
   Deserve Inquiry, Rights Group Says," *CBC News*, 12 January 2015, http://www.
   cbc.ca/news/politics/murdered-and-missing-aboriginal-women-deserve-inqui-
   ry-rights-group-says-1.2897707; Ken S. Coates, "Aboriginal Women Deserve
   Much More than an Inquiry," *National Post*, 16 February 2015, http://news.
   nationalpost.com/2015/02/16/ken-s-coates-aboriginal-women-deservemuch-
   more-than-an-inquiry/. On economic development issues, see, for example:
   Jeff Lewis, "TransCanada CEO Says Canada Needs to Resolve Conflicts over
   Pipelines," *Globe and Mail*, 4 February 2015, http://www.theglobeandmail.com/
   report-on-business/economy/transcanadaceo-says-canada-needs-to-resolve-
   conflicts-over-pipelines/article22798276/; Daniel Schwartz and Mark Gollom,
   "NB Fracking Protests and the Fight for Aboriginal Rights," *CBC News Canada*,
   19 October 2013, http://www.cbc.ca/news/canada/n-b-fracking-protests-and-
   the-fight-for-aboriginal-rights-1.2126515; Michael MacDonald, "Shale Gas
   Conflict in New Brunswick Underscores Historical Grievances, Rights of First
   Nations," *Toronto Star*, 25 December 2013, http://www.thestar.com/news/
   canada/2013/12/25/shale_gas_conflict_in_new_brunswick_underscores_his-
   toric_grievances_rights_of_first_nations.html.

3. On the role of the courts in Aboriginal rights and reconciliation, see: Joseph
   Brean, "'Reconciliation' with First Nations, Not the Charter of Rights &
   Freedoms, Will Define the Supreme Court in Coming years, Chief Justice
   Says," *National Post*, 13 March 2014, http://news.nationalpost.com/2014/03/13/
   reconciliation-with-first-nations-not-the-charter-of-rights-freedoms-will-
   define-the-supreme-court-in-coming-years-chief-justice-says/. On Aboriginal
   rights cases, see, for example: "6 Landmark Rulings on Native Rights," *CBC
   News*, 8 January 2013, http://www.cbc.ca/news/canada/6-landmark-rulings-on-
   native-rights-1.1316961. On day schools litigation, see, for example: "Residential
   School Day Scholars Launch Class-action Lawsuit," *CBC News*, 16 August 2012,
   http://www.cbc.ca/news/canada/british-columbia/residential-school-day-schol-
   ars-launchclass-action-lawsuit-1.1146607; Dene Moore, "Federal Appeal Court
   Gives OK on Hearing First Nations' Day-school Suit," *Canadian Press*, 4 March
   2014, http://www.ctvnews.ca/canada/federal192appeal-court-gives-ok-on-
   hearing-first-nations-day-school-suit-1.1713809. On Sixties Scoop legislation,
   see, for example: "Sixties Scoop Case Moves Forward as Class-action Lawsuit,"
   CBC News, 3 December 2014, http://www.cbc.ca/news/canada/thunder-bay/

sixties-scoop-case-moves-forward-as-class-action-lawsuit-1.2859332; Diana Mehta, "'Sixties Scoop' Class-action Lawsuit to Proceed," *Canadian Press*, 4 December 2014, http://www.ctvnews.ca/canada/60s-scoop-class-action-lawsuit-to-proceed-1.2132317.

4. Miller, *Lethal Legacy*, vi.

5. TRC, AVS, Mary Deleary, Statement to the Truth and Reconciliation Commission of Canada, Winnipeg, Manitoba, 26 June 2014, Statement Number: SE049.

6. TRC, AVS, Archie Little. Statement to the Truth and Reconciliation Commission of Canada, Victoria, British Columbia, 13 April 2012, Statement Number: SP135.

7. McKay, "Expanding the Dialogue," 107. McKay was the first Aboriginal moderator of the United Church of Canada (1992 to 1994).

8. TRC, AVS, Jessica Bolduc, Statement to the Truth and Reconciliation Commission of Canada, Edmonton, Alberta, 30 March 2014, Statement Number: ABNF401.

9. Truth and Reconciliation Commission of Canada, *Educating Our Youth*, video, 19 September 2013, http://www.trc.ca/websites/trcinstitution/index.php?p=3 (accessed 10 February 2014).

10. TRC, AVS, Patsy George, Statement to the Truth and Reconciliation Commission of Canada, Vancouver, British Columbia, 21 September 2013, Statement Number: BCNE404.

11. TRC, AVS, Dave Courchene, Statement to the Truth and Reconciliation Commission of Canada, Winnipeg, Manitoba, 25 June 2014, Statement Number: SE048.

12. The mandate of the Truth and Reconciliation Commission of Canada is listed under Schedule N of the Indian Residential Schools Settlement Agreement, http://www.residentialschoolsettlement.ca/settlement.html (accessed 5 March 2015). In accordance with the TRC's mandate, the Commission was required to recognize "the significance of Aboriginal oral and legal traditions in its activities," Schedule N, 4(d); and "witness, support, promote and facilitate truth and reconciliation events at both the national and community levels," Schedule N, 1(c). The term *witness* "refers to the Aboriginal principle of 'witnessing,'" Indian Residential Schools Settlement Agreement, Schedule N, 1(c), n1. Aboriginal oral history, legal traditions, and the principle of witnessing have deep historical roots and contemporary relevance for reconciliation. Indigenous law was used to resolve family and community conflict, to establish Treaties among various Indigenous nations, and to negotiate nation-to-nation treaties with the Crown. For a comprehensive history of Aboriginal–Crown Treaty making from contact to the present, see: Miller, *Compact, Contract, Covenant*. The term *witness* is in reference to the Aboriginal principle of witnessing, which varies among First Nations, Métis, and Inuit peoples. Generally speaking, witnesses are called to be the keepers of history when an event of historic significance occurs. Through witnessing, the event or work that is undertaken is validated and provided legitimacy. The work could not take place without honoured and respected guests to witness it. Witnesses are asked to store and care for the history they witness and to share it with their own people when they return home. For Aboriginal peoples, the act of witnessing these events comes with a great responsibility to

remember all the details and be able to recount them accurately as the foundation of oral histories. See: Thomas, "Honouring the Oral Traditions," 243–244.

13. TRC, AVS, Jim Dumont, Statement to the Truth and Reconciliation Commis-
     sion of Canada, Winnipeg, Manitoba, 26 June 2014, Statement Number: SE049.

14. TRC, AVS, Wilfred Whitehawk, Statement to the Truth and Reconciliation
     Commission of Canada, Key First Nation, Saskatchewan, 21 January 2012, State-
     ment Number: SP039.

15. TRC, AVS, Vitaline Elsie Jenner, Statement to the Truth and Reconciliation
     Commission of Canada, Winnipeg, Manitoba, 16 June 2010, Statement Number:
     02-MB-16JU10-131.

16. TRC, AVS, Daniel Elliot, Statement to the Truth and Reconciliation Commis-
     sion of Canada, Victoria, British Columbia, 13 April 2012, Statement Number:
     SP135.

17. TRC, AVS, Clement Chartier, Statement to the Truth and Reconciliation Com-
     mission of Canada, Saskatoon, Saskatchewan, 22 June 2013, Statement Number:
     SNE202.

18. TRC, AVS, Steven Point, Statement to the Truth and Reconciliation Commis-
     sion of Canada, Vancouver, British Columbia, 20 September 2013, Statement
     Number: BCNE304.

19. TRC, AVS, Merle Nisley, Statement to the Truth and Reconciliation Commis-
     sion of Canada, Thunder Bay, Ontario, 14 December 2011, Statement Number:
     2011-4199.

20. TRC, AVS, Tom Cavanaugh, Statement to the Truth and Reconciliation Com-
     mission of Canada, Victoria, British Columbia, 14 April 2012, Statement Num-
     ber: SP137.

21. TRC, AVS, Ina Seitcher, Statement to the Truth and Reconciliation Commission
     of Canada, Victoria, British Columbia, 14 April 2012, Statement Number: SP136.

22. TRC, AVS, Evelyn Brockwood, Statement to the Truth and Reconciliation Com-
     mission of Canada, Winnipeg, Manitoba, 18 June 2010, Statement Number:
     SC110.

23. Indian Residential Schools Settlement Agreement, Schedule N, Principles, 1,
     http://www.residentialschoolsettlement.ca/settlement.html (accessed 5 March
     2015).

24. Johnston, "Aboriginal Traditions," 141–159.

25. TRC, AVS, Barney Williams, Statement to the Truth and Reconciliation Com-
     mission of Canada, Winnipeg, Manitoba, 26 June 2014, Statement Number:
     SE049.

26. TRC, AVS, Stephen Augustine, Statement to the Truth and Reconciliation Com-
     mission of Canada, Winnipeg, Manitoba, 25 June 2014, Statement Number:
     SE048.

27. TRC, AVS, Reg Crowshoe, Statement to the Truth and Reconciliation Commis-
     sion of Canada, Winnipeg, Manitoba, 26 June 2014, Statement Number: SE049.

28. TRC, AVS, Kirby Littletent, Statement to the Truth and Reconciliation Com-
     mission of Canada, Regina, Saskatchewan, 16 January 2012, Statement Number:
     SP035.

29. TRC, AVS, Simone (last name not provided), Statement to the Truth and Reconciliation Commission of Canada, Inuvik, Northwest Territories, 1 July 2011, Statement Number: SC092.

30. TRC, AVS, Patrick Etherington, Statement to the Truth and Reconciliation Commission of Canada, Winnipeg, Manitoba, 17 June 2010, Statement Number: SC108.

31. TRC, AVS, Maxine Lacorne, Statement to the Truth and Reconciliation Commission of Canada, Inuvik, Northwest Territories, 29 June 2011, Statement Number: SC090.

32. TRC, AVS, Barney Williams, Statement to the Truth and Reconciliation Commission of Canada, Vancouver, British Columbia, 21 September 2013, Statement Number: BCNE404.

33. TRC, AVS, Honourable Chuck Strahl, Statement to the Truth and Reconciliation Commission of Canada, Winnipeg, Manitoba, 16 June 2010, Statement Number: SC093.

34. TRC, AVS, Archbishop Fred Hiltz, Statement to the Truth and Reconciliation Commission of Canada, Inuvik, Northwest Territories, 1 July 2011, Statement Number: NNE402.

35. TRC, AVS, Anonymous, Statement to the Truth and Reconciliation Commission of Canada, Regina, Saskatchewan, 17 January 2012, Statement Number: SP036.

BIBLIOGRAPHY

PRIMARY SOURCES

1. TRUTH AND RECONCILIATION
COMMISSION DATABASES

The endnotes of this report often commence with the abbreviation TRC, followed by one of the following abbreviations: ASAGR, AVS, CAR, IRSSA, NRA, RBS, and LAC. The documents so cited are located in the Truth and Reconciliation Commission of Canada's database. At the end of each of these endnotes, in square brackets, is the document identification number for each of these documents. The following is a brief description of each database.

Active and Semi-Active Government Records (ASAGR) Database: The Active and Semi-Active Government Records database contains active and semi-active records collected from federal governmental departments that potentially intersected with the administration and management of the residential school system. Documents that were relevant to the history and/or legacy of the system were disclosed to the Truth and Reconciliation Commission of Canada (TRC) in keeping with the federal government's obligations in relation to the Indian Residential Schools Settlement Agreement (IRSSA). Some of the other federal government departments included, but were not limited to, the Department of Justice, Health Canada, the Royal Canadian Mounted Police, and National Defence. Aboriginal Affairs and Northern Development Canada undertook the responsibility of centrally collecting and producing the records from these other federal departments to the TRC.

Audio/Video Statement (AVS) Database: The Audio/Video Statement database contains video and audio statements provided to the TRC at community hearings and regional and national events held by the TRC, as well as at other special events attended by the TRC.

Church Archival Records (CAR) Database: The Church Archival Records database contains records collected from the different church/religious entities that were involved in administration and management of residential schools. The church/religious entities primarily included, but were not limited to, entities associated with the Roman Catholic Church, the Anglican Church of Canada, the Presbyterian Church in Canada, and the United Church of Canada. The records were collected as part of the TRC's mandate, as set out in the Indian Residential Schools Settlement Agreement, to "identify sources and create as complete an historical record as possible of the IRS system and legacy."

Indian Residential Schools School Authority (IRSSA) Database: The Indian Residential Schools School Authority database is comprised of individual records related to each residential school, as set out by the IRSSA.

National Research and Analysis (NRA) Database: The National Research and Analysis database contains records collected by the National Research and Analysis Directorate, Aboriginal Affairs and Northern Development Canada, formerly Indian

Residential Schools Resolution Canada (IRSRC). The records in the database were originally collected for the purpose of research into a variety of allegations, such as abuse in residential schools, and primarily resulted from court processes such as civil and criminal litigation, and later the Indian Residential Schools Settlement Agreement (IRSSA), as well as from out-of-court processes such as Alternative Dispute Resolution. A majority of the records were collected from Aboriginal Affairs and Northern Development Canada. The collection also contains records from other federal departments and religious entities. In the case of some records in the database that were provided by outside entities, the information in the database is incomplete. In those instances, the endnote in the report reads, "No document location, no document file source."

Red, Black and School Series (RBS) Database: The Red, Black and School Series database contains records provided by Library and Archives Canada to the TRC. These three sub-series contain records that were originally part of the "Headquarters Central Registry System," or records management system, for departments that preceded the current federal department of Aboriginal Affairs and Northern Development Canada. The archival records are currently related to the Department of Indian Affairs and Northern Development fonds and are held as part of Library and Archives Canada's collection.

Library and Archives Canada Archival Records Container (LACAR) and Document Databases: The LACAR Records Container and Document databases contain records collected from Library and Archives Canada (LAC). The archival records of federal governmental departments that potentially intersected with the administration and management of Indian Residential Schools were held as part of Library and Archives Canada's collection. Documents that were relevant to the history and/or legacy of the Indian Residential School system were initially collected by the Truth and Reconciliation Commission, in conjunction with Aboriginal Affairs and Northern Development Canada, as part of their mandate, as set out in the Indian Residential School Settlement Agreement. The collection of records was later continued by Aboriginal Affairs and Northern Development Canada, based on the federal government's obligation to disclose documents in relation to the Indian Residential Schools Settlement Agreement.

2. INDIAN AFFAIRS ANNUAL REPORTS, 1864–1997

Within this report, *Annual Report of the Department of Indian Affairs* denotes the published annual reports created by the Government of Canada, and relating to Indian Affairs over the period from 1864 to 1997.

The Department of Indian Affairs and Northern Development was created in 1966. In 2011, it was renamed Aboriginal Affairs and Northern Development. Before 1966, different departments were responsible for the portfolios of Indian Affairs and Northern Affairs.

The departments responsible for Indian Affairs were (in chronological order):

• The Department of the Secretary of State of Canada (to 1869)

• The Department of the Secretary of State for the Provinces (1869–1873)

• The Department of the Interior (1873–1880)

- The Department of Indian Affairs (1880–1936)
- The Department of Mines and Resources (1936–1950)
- The Department of Citizenship and Immigration (1950–1965)
- The Department of Northern Affairs and National Resources (1966)
- The Department of Indian Affairs and Northern Development (1966 to the present)

The exact titles of Indian Affairs annual reports changed over time, and were named for the department.

3. LIBRARY AND ARCHIVES CANADA

RG10 (Indian Affairs Records Group): The records of RG10 at Library and Archives Canada are currently part of the R216, Department of Indian Affairs and Northern Development fonds. For clarity and brevity, in footnotes throughout this report, records belonging to the RG10 Records Group have been identified simply with their RG10 information. Where a copy of an RG10 document held in a TRC database was used, the TRC database holding that copy is clearly identified, along with the RG10 information connected with the original document.

4. OTHER ARCHIVES

Provincial Archives of British Columbia

5. GOVERNMENT PUBLICATIONS

Audette, L. A. *Report on The Commission, under Part II of the Inquiries Act, to investi-gate and report the circumstances in connection with the alleged flogging of Indian pupils recently at Shubenacadie, in The Province of Nova Scotia, 17 September 1934.*

Brennan, Shannon. "Violent victimization of Aboriginal women in the Canadian provinces, 2009." *Juristat*, 17 May 2011. Catalogue no. 85-002-x. Ottawa: Statistics Canada, 2011. http://www.statcan.gc.ca/pub/85-002-x/2011001/article/11439-eng.pdf.

Bryce, P. H. *Report on the Indian Schools of Manitoba and the North-West Territories.* Ottawa: Government Printing Bureau, 1907.

Canada. Canadian Human Rights Commission. *Report on Equality Rights of Aborigi-nal People.* Ottawa: Government of Canada, 2013.

Canada. Department of Justice. *A One-Day Snapshot of Aboriginal Youth in Custody Across Canada: Phase II.* Ottawa: Department of Justice, February 2004. http://www.justice.gc.ca/eng/rp-pr/cj-jp/yj-jj/yj2-jj2/yj2.pdf.

Canada. Indian Residential Schools Adjudication Secretariat. "Adjudication Secre-

tariat Statistics, from September 19, 2007 to January 31, 2015." http://iap-pei.ca/
information/stats-eng.php (accessed 20 February 2015).

Canada. Parliament. House of Commons. *Debates*, 5th Parliament, 1st Session, 9 May
1883. Ottawa: Queen's Printer, 1883.

Canada. Parliament. Special Joint Committee of the Senate and House of Commons
Appointed to Examine and Consider *The Indian Act*. *Minutes of Proceedings and
Evidence*. Ottawa, 1946–1949. (Cited as Canada, S.J.C.).

Canada. Prime Minster Stephen Harper. "Statement of Apology – to former students
of Indian Residential Schools." 11 June 2008. http://www.aadnc-aandc.gc.ca/eng
/1100100015644/1100100015649.

Canada. Public Health Agency of Canada. "Fetal Alcohol Spectrum Disorder (FASD)."
http://www.phac-aspc.gc.ca/hp-ps/dca-dea/prog-ini/fasd-etcaf/index-eng.php
(accessed 18 April 2015).

Canada. Public Safety Canada, Aboriginal Corrections Policy Unit. *Fetal Alcohol Spectrum Disorder and the Criminal Justice System*. 2010. http://www.publicsafety.
gc.ca/cnt/rsrcs/pblctns/ftl-lchlspctrm/ftl-lchl-spctrm-eng.pdf.

Canada. Royal Canadian Mounted Police. *Missing and Murdered Aboriginal Women: A
National Operational Overview*. Catalogue no. PS64-115/2014E-PDF. 2014. http://
www.rcmp-grc.gc.ca/pubs/mmaw-faapd-eng.pdf (accessed 31 December 2014).

Canada. Royal Commission on Aboriginal Peoples. *Report of the Royal Commission
on Aboriginal Peoples*. Ottawa: Supply and Services Canada, 1996.

Canada. *Statement of the Government of Canada on Indian Policy*. Presented to the
first session of the 28th Parliament by the Honourable Jean Chrétien, Minister
of Indian Affairs and Northern Development. Ottawa: Queen's Printer, 1969.

Canada. Statistics Canada. "2006 Inuit Census Tables." Catalogue no. 89-636-x. 2013.
http://www.statcan.gc.ca/pub/89-636-x/89-636-x2008001-eng.htm.

Canada. Statistics Canada. "Aboriginal People in Canada: First Nations People, Metis
and Inuit: National Household Survey 2011." Catalogue no. 99-011-X2011001.
2013. http://www12.statcan.gc.ca/nhs-enm/2011/as-sa/99-011-x/99-011-
x2011001-eng.cfm.

Canada. Statistics Canada. "Aboriginal Peoples and Language. National Household
Survey (NHS), 2011." Catalogue no. 99-011-X2011003. 2013. http://www12.
statcan.gc.ca/nhs-enm/2011/assa/99-011-x/99-011-x2011003_1-eng.cfm.

Canada. Statistics Canada. "Fact Sheet – 2011 National Household Survey Aboriginal
Demographics, Educational Attainment and Labour Market Outcomes." 2013.
https://www.aadnc-aandc.gc.ca/eng/1376329205785/1376329233875.

Canada. Statistics Canada. "Mortality rates among children and teenagers living in Inuit
Nunangat, 1994 to 2008." *Health Reports*, 18 July 2012. Catalogue no. 82-003-X.
2012. http://www.statcan.gc.ca/pub/82-003-x/2012003/article/11695-eng.htm.

Canada. Statistics Canada. "Select health indicators of First Nations people living off
reserve, Métis and Inuit, 2007 to 2010." *The Daily*, 29 January 2013. http://www.
statcan.gc.ca/daily-quotidien/130129/dq130129b-eng.htm.

Canada. Statistics Canada. *Educational Portrait of Canada, 2006 Census*. Catalogue no.
97-560-X. 2008.

Canada. Truth and Reconciliation Commission of Canada. *Educating our Youth* (video). 19 September 2013. http://www.trc.ca/websites/trcinstitution/index. php?p=3 (accessed 10 February 2014).

Canada. Truth and Reconciliation Commission of Canada. *Indian Residential Schools Settlement Agreement.* Schedule N. http://www.residentialschoolsettlement.ca/ settlement.html (accessed 5 March 2015).

Canada. Truth and Reconciliation Commission of Canada. *Truth and Reconciliation Commission: Interim Report.* Winnipeg: Truth and Reconciliation Commission of Canada, 2012.

Davin, Nicholas Flood. *Report on Industrial Schools for Indians and Half-Breeds.* Report produced for the Minister of the Interior. Ottawa: 1879.

Fraser, R. D. "Section B: Vital Statistics and Health." In *Historical Statistics of Canada,* edited by F. H. Leachy. Second edition. Ottawa: Statistics Canada, 1983. http:// www.statcan.gc.ca/pub/11-516-x/sectionb/4147437-eng.htm.

Indian and Métis Conference, Committee of the Community Welfare Planning Council. *Survey of Canadian History Textbooks.* Winnipeg: Submission to the Curriculum Revision Committee, Manitoba Department of Education, 1964.

MacPherson, Patricia H., Albert E. Chudley, and Brian A. Grant. *Fetal Alcohol Spectrum Disorder (FASD) in a Correctional Population: Prevalence, Screening, and Characteristics.* Ottawa: Correctional Service of Canada, 2011. http://www. publicsafety.gc.ca/lbrr/archives/cn21451-eng.pdf.

Munch, Christopher. "Youth correctional statistics in Canada, 2010/2011." *Juristat,* 11 October 2012. Catalogue no. 85-002-X. Ottawa: Statistics Canada, 2012. https:// www.publicsafety.gc.ca/lbrr/archives/jrst11716-eng.pdf.

Perreault, Samuel. "Admissions to adult correctional services in Canada, 2011/2012." *Juristat,* 27 March 2014. Catalogue no. 85-002-X. Ottawa: Statistics Canada, 2014. http://www.statcan.gc.ca/pub/85-002-x/2014001/article/11918-eng.htm#a5.

Perreault, Samuel. "Violent victimization of Aboriginal people in the Canadian provinces, 2009." *Juristat,* 11 March 2011. Catalogue no. 85-002-X. Ottawa: Statistics Canada, 2011. http://wgc.ca/pub/85-002-x/2011001/article/11415-eng.pdf.

Quebec. *Rapport de la Commission royale d'enquête sur l'enseignement dans la province de Québec.* Quebec: Government of Quebec, 1966. http://classiques.uqac.ca/ contemporains/quebec_commission_parent/rapport_parent_4/rapport_par-ent_vol_4.pdf (accessed 7 August 2012).

Reed, Micheline, and Peter Morrison. "Adult Correctional Services in Canada 1995–96." *Juristat,* March 1997. Catalogue no. 85-002-XPE. Ottawa: Statistics Canada, 1997. http://www.statcan.gc.ca/pub/85-002-x/85 002 x1997004-eng.pdf.

Rosenthal, Jeffrey S. "Statistical Analysis of Deaths at Residential Schools: Conducted on behalf of the Truth and Reconciliation Commission of Canada." January 2015.

Ryerson, Egerton. "Report on Industrial Schools, 26 May 1847." In *Statistics Respecting Indian Schools.* Ottawa: Government Printing Bureau, 1898.

Ryerson, Egerton. *Report on a System for Public Elementary Instruction for Upper Canada.* Printed by order of the Legislative Assembly of Upper Canada. Montreal: Lovell & Gibson, 1847.

United States. Board of Indian Commissioners. *Eighteenth Annual Report of the Board of Indian Commissioners, 1886*. Washington: Government Printing Office, 1887.

Zietsma, Danielle. "Aboriginal People Living Off-reserve and the Labour Market: Estimates from the Labour Force Survey, 2008–2009." Catalogue no. 710588-X, no. 2. Ottawa: Statistics Canada, 2010. http://www.statcan.gc.ca/pub/71-588-x/71-588-x2010001-eng.pdf.

6. LEGISLATION

An Act for the gradual enfranchisement of Indians, Statutes of Canada 1869, chapter 42. (Reproduced in Venne, *Indian Acts*, 11.)

An Act further to amend "The Indian Act, 1880," Statutes of Canada 1884, chapter 27, section 3. (Reproduced in Venne, *Indian Acts*, 93.)

An Act respecting Indians [Indian Act], Statutes of Canada 1951, chapter 29, sections 113–122, 169–172.

An Act to amend and consolidate the laws respecting Indians, Statutes of Canada 1880, chapter 28, section 72. (Reproduced in Venne, *Indian Acts*, 75.)

Great Britain. *Rupert's Land and North-Western Territory Order* (Order of Her Majesty in Council Admitting Rupert's Land and the North-Western Territory into the Union), 23 June 1870. Schedule A, *Rupert's Land Act* 1868, 31–32 Vict., chapter 105 (U.K.). http://www.justice.gc.ca/eng/rppr/csj-sjc/constitution/lawreg-loireg/p1t32.html.

The Public Schools Act, Revised Statutes of Manitoba 1954, chapter 215, pages 923–1,114.

7. LEGAL CASES

Cloud v. Canada (Attorney General), [2004] O.J. No 4924, 247 D.L.R. (4th) 667.

Fontaine v. Canada (Attorney General), 2011 ONSC 4938 (CanLII), 7. [Reasons for Decision of Winkler CJO, Court File No 00-CV-192059CP].

R. v. Comeau, [1998] N.W.T.J. No. 34 (NTSC).

R. v. Plint, [1995] B.C.J. No. 3060 (BCSC).

8. OTHER SOURCES

United Nations General Assembly. *United Nations Declaration on the Rights of Indigenous Peoples*. Adopted by the General Assembly, 2 October 2007.

SECONDARY SOURCES

1. BOOKS AND PUBLISHED REPORTS

Ahenakew, Edward. *Voices of the Plains Cree*. Edited by Ruth M. Buck. Toronto: Mc-Clelland and Stewart, 1973.

Amagoalik, John. *Changing the Face of Canada: The Life Story of John Amagoalik*. Edited by Louis McComber. Life Stories of Northern Leaders 2. Iqaluit: Nunavut Arctic College, 2007.

Armitage, David. *The Ideological Origins of the British Empire*. Cambridge: Cambridge University Press, 2000.

Assembly of First Nations. *Assembly of First Nations Report on Canada's Dispute Resolution Plan to Compensate for Abuses in Indian Residential Schools*. Ottawa: Assembly of First Nations, 2004.

Assembly of First Nations. *Breaking the Silence: An Interpretive Study of Residential School Impact and Healing as Illustrated by the Stories of First Nation Individuals*. Ottawa: Assembly of First Nations, 1994.

Auger, Donald J. *Indian Residential Schools in Ontario*. Ontario: Nishnawbe Aski Nation, 2005.

Axtell, James. *The Invasion Within: The Contest of Cultures in Colonial North America*. New York: Oxford University Press, 1985.

Baker, Simon. *Khot-La-Cha: The Autobiography of Chief Simon Baker*. Compiled and edited by Verna J. Kirkness. Vancouver: Douglas and McIntyre, 1994.

Banner, Stuart. *How the Indians Lost Their Land: Law and Power on the Frontier*. Cambridge, Massachusetts: The Belknap Press of Harvard University Press, 2005.

Barron, Laurie F. *Walking in Indian Moccasins: The Native Policies of Tommy Douglas and the CCF*. Vancouver: University of British Columbia Press, 1997.

Bartels, Dennis A., and Alice L. Bartels. *When the North Was Red*. Montreal and Kingston: McGill-Queen's University Press, 1995.

Bayly, C. A. *The Birth of the Modern World: 1780–1914*. Oxford: Blackwell Publishing, 2004.

Bloch, Alexia. *Red Ties and Residential Schools: Indigenous Siberians in a Post-Soviet State*. Philadelphia: University of Pennsylvania Press, 2004.

Blue Quills First Nations College. *Pimohteskanaw, 1971–2001: Blue Quills First Nations College*. St. Paul, Alberta: Blue Quills First Nations College, 2002.

Bolt, Clarence. *Thomas Crosby and the Tsimshian: Small Shoes for Feet Too Large*. Vancouver: University of British Columbia Press, 1992.

Brass, Eleanor. *I Walk in Two Worlds*. Calgary: Glenbow Museum, 1987.

Bruno-Jofre, Rosa. *The Missionary Oblate Sisters: Vision and Mission*. Montreal and Kingston: McGill-Queen's University Press, 2005.

Bryce, P. H. *The Story of a National Crime: Being an Appeal for Justice to the Indians of Canada; the Wards of the Nation, Our Allies in the Revolutionary War, Our Brothers-in-Arms in the Great War*. Ottawa: James Hope and Sons, 1922.

Buck, Ruth Matheson. *The Doctor Rode Side-Saddle*. Toronto: McClelland and Stewart, 1974.

Bush, Peter. *Western Challenge: The Presbyterian Church in Canada's Mission on the Prairies and North, 1885–1925*. Winnipeg: Watson and Dwyer Publishing, 2000.

Butcher, Margaret. *The Letters of Margaret Butcher: Missionary-Imperialism on the North Pacific Coast*. Edited by Mary-Ellen Kelm. Calgary: University of Calgary Press, 2006.

Canadian Welfare Council. *Indian Residential Schools: A Research Study of the Child Care Programs of Nine Residential Schools in Saskatchewan*. Prepared for the Department of Indian Affairs and Northern Development. Ottawa: Canadian Welfare Council, 1967.

Canadien, Albert. *From Lishamie*. Penticton: Theytus Books, Limited, 2010.

Carter, Sarah. *Lost Harvests: Prairie Indian Reserve Farmers and Government Policy*. Montreal and Kingston: McGill-Queen's University Press, 1990.

Chartrand, Larry N., Tricia E. Logan, and Judy D. Daniels. *Métis History and Experience and Residential Schools in Canada*. Ottawa: Aboriginal Healing Foundation, 2006.

Choquette, Robert. *Canada's Religions: An Historical Introduction*. Ottawa: University of Ottawa Press, 2004.

Choquette, Robert. *The Oblate Assault on Canada's Northwest*. Ottawa: University of Ottawa Press, 1995.

Coates, Kenneth. *A Global History of Indigenous Peoples: Struggle and Survival*. Basingstoke, England: Palgrave Macmillan, 2004.

Coccola, Nicolas. *They Call Me Father: Memoirs of Father Nicolas Coccola*. Edited by Margaret Whitehead. Vancouver: University of British Columbia Press, 1988.

Cole, Douglas, and Ira Chaikin. *An Iron Hand Upon the People: The Law Against the Potlatch on the Northwest Coast*. Vancouver: Douglas & McIntyre, 1990.

Cronin, Kay. *Cross in the Wilderness*. Vancouver: Mitchell Press, 1960.

Daschuk, James. *Clearing the Plains: Disease, Politics of Starvation, and the Loss of Aboriginal Life*. Regina: University of Regina Press, 2013.

Diffie, Bailey W., and George D. Winius. *Foundations of the Portuguese Empire, 1415–1580*. Minneapolis: University of Minnesota Press, 1978.

Dion, Joseph F. *My Tribe the Crees*. Edited and with an introduction by Hugh Dempsey. Second edition. Calgary: Glenbow Museum, 1996.

Duchaussois, J. R. *The Grey Nuns in the Far North (1867–1917)*. Toronto: McClelland and Stewart, 1919.

Elliott, John H. *Empires of the Atlantic World: Britain and Spain in America, 1492–1830*. New Haven, Connecticut: Yale University Press, 2007.

Erasmus, Peter. *Buffalo Days and Nights*. Calgary: Fifth House Publishers, 1999. First published 1976 by Glenbow-Alberta Institute.

Fear-Segal, Jacqueline. *White Man's Club: Schools, Race, and the Struggle of Indian Acculturation*. Lincoln: University of Nebraska, 2007.

First Nations Centre. *First Nations Regional Longitudinal Health Survey (RHS) 2002/03*. Ottawa: First Nations Centre, 2005.

Fisher, Robin. *Contact and Conflict: Indian-European Relations in British Columbia, 1774–1890*. Second edition. Vancouver: University of British Columbia Press, 1992.

Fontaine, Theodore. *Broken Circle: The Dark Legacy of Indian Residential Schools*. Vancouver: Heritage House, 2010.

Frichner, Tonya Gonnella. "Preliminary Study of the Impact on Indigenous Peoples of the International Legal Construct Known as the Doctrine of Discovery." New York: United Nations, Permanent Forum on Indigenous Issues, 2010.

Gagan, Rosemary R. *A Sensitive Independence: Canadian Methodist Women Missionaries in Canada and the Orient, 1881–1925*. Montreal and Kingston: McGill-Queen's University Press, 1992.

Getty, A. L., and Antoine S. Lussier. *As Long as the Sun Shines and Water Flows: A Reader in Canadian Native Studies*. Vancouver: University of British Columbia Press, 1983.

Goodwill, Jean, and Norma Sluman. *John Tootoosis*. Winnipeg: Pemmican Publications, 1984.

Graham, Elizabeth. *The Mush Hole: Life at Two Indian Residential Schools*. Waterloo: Heffle Publishing, 1997.

Hamilton, W. D. *The Federal Indian Day Schools of the Maritimes*. Fredericton, New Brunswick: Micmac-Maliseet Institute, University of New Brunswick, 1986.

Head, Edmund Walker, Froome Talfourd, Thomas Worthington, and Richard T. Pennefather. *Report of the Special Commissioners appointed on the 8th of September 1856, to Investigate Indian Affairs in Canada*. Toronto: Stewart Derbishire and George Desbarats, 1858.

Hobsbawm, E. J. *On Empire: America, War and Global Supremacy*. New York: Pantheon Books, 2008.

Howe, Stephen. *Empire: A Very Short Introduction*. Oxford: Oxford University Press, 2002.

Huel, Raymond J. A. *Proclaiming the Gospel to the Indians and Métis*. Edmonton: University of Alberta Press, 1996.

Hughes, Kenneth James, and Jackson Beardy. *Jackson Beardy, Life and Art*. Winnipeg: Canadian Dimension Publishers, 1979.

Hyam, Ronald. *Britain's Imperial Century, 1815–1914: A Study of Empire and Expansion*. Third edition. Basingstoke, England: Palgrave Macmillan, 2002.

Indian Chiefs of Alberta. *Citizens Plus*. 1970. Reprinted in *Aboriginal Policy Studies* 1, no. 2 (2011): 188–281.

Jaenen, Cornelius. *Friend and Foe: Aspects of French-Amerindian Cultural Contact in the Sixteenth and Seventeenth Centuries*. Toronto: McClelland and Stewart, 1976.

Johnston, Patrick. *Native Children and the Child Welfare System*. Toronto: Canadian Council on Social Development in association with J. Lorimer, 1983.

Johnston, Sheila M. F. *Buckskin & Broadcloth: A Celebration of E. Pauline Johnson Tekahionwake, 1861–1913*. Toronto: Natural Heritage/Natural History, 1997.

Kirkness, Verna J. *Creating Space: My Life and Work in Indigenous Education*. Winnipeg: University of Manitoba Press, 2013.

Kirmayer, Laurence, Gregory Brass, Tara Holton, Ken Paul, Cori Simpson, Caroline Tait. *Suicide Among Aboriginal People in Canada*. Ottawa: Aboriginal Healing Foundation, 2007.

LaViolette, Forrest. *The Struggle for Survival: Indian Cultures and the Protestant Ethic in British Columbia*. Toronto: University of Toronto Press, 1961.

Lux, Maureen K. *Medicine that Walks: Disease, Medicine, and Canadian Plains Native People, 1880–1940*. Toronto: University of Toronto Press, 2001.

Macdonald, David, and Daniel Wilson. *Poverty or Prosperity: Indigenous Children in Canada*. Ottawa: Canadian Centre for Policy Alternatives, 2013.

MacGregor, Roy. *Chief: The Fearless Vision of Billy Diamond*. Toronto: Viking, 1989.

Magnuson, Roger. *Education in New France*. Montreal, Kingston: McGill-Queen's University Press, 1992.

Marks, Don. *They Call Me Chief: Warriors on Ice*. Winnipeg: J. Gordon Shillingford, 2008.

McCarthy, Martha. *From the Great River to the Ends of the Earth: Oblate Missions to the Dene, 1847–1921*. Edmonton: University of Alberta Press; Western Canadian Publishers, 1995.

McGregor, Heather E. *Inuit Education and Schools in the Eastern Arctic*. Vancouver: University of British Columbia Press, 2010.

McMillan, Alan D., and Eldon Yellowhorn. *First Peoples in Canada*. Vancouver and Toronto: Douglas & McIntyre, 2004.

McNally, Vincent J. *The Lord's Distant Vineyard: A History of the Oblates and the Catholic Community in British Columbia*. Edmonton: University of Alberta Press, 2000.

Miller, J. R. *Compact, Contract, Covenant: Aboriginal Treaty Making in Canada*. Toronto: University of Toronto Press, 2009.

Miller, J. R. *Lethal Legacy: Current Native Controversies in Canada*. Toronto: McClelland and Stewart, 2004.

Miller, J. R. *Skyscrapers Hide the Heavens: A History of Indian-White Relations in Canada*. Second edition. Toronto: University of Toronto Press, 2000.

Milloy, John S. *A National Crime: The Canadian Government and the Residential School System, 1879–1986*. Winnipeg: University of Manitoba Press, 1999.

Moine, Louise. *My Life in a Residential School*. Saskatchewan: Provincial Chapter Imperial Order of Daughters of the Empire, Saskatchewan, in Cooperation with the Provincial Library of Saskatchewan, 1975.

Montour, Enos. *Brown Tom's Schooldays*. Edited by Elizabeth Graham. Waterloo, Ontario: The Author, 1985.

Moorhouse, Geoffrey. *The Missionaries*. Philadelphia and New York: J. B. Lippincott Company, 1973.

Moran, Bridget. *Stoney Creek Woman: The Story of Mary John*. Vancouver: Arsenal Pulp Press, 1997.

Morley, Alan. *Roar of the Breakers: A Biography of Peter Kelly*. Toronto: Ryerson Press, 1967.

Morris, Alexander. *The treaties of Canada with the Indians of Manitoba and the North-West Territories, Including the Negotiations on which they were Based, and Other Information Relating thereto.* Saskatoon: Fifth House Publishers, 1991. First published, Toronto: Belfords, Clarke and Company, 1880.

Moseley, Christopher, editor. *Atlas of the World's Languages in Danger.* 3rd edition. Paris: UNESCO Publishing, 2010.

Nabigon, Herb. *The Hollow Tree: Fighting Addiction with Traditional Native Healing.* Montreal: McGill-Queen's University Press, 2006.

National Indian Brotherhood. *Indian Control of Indian Education: Policy Paper Presented to the Minister of Indian Affairs and Northern Development.* Ottawa: National Indian Brotherhood, 1972.

Newman, Morton. *Indians of the Saddle Lake Reserve.* Edmonton: Human Resources and Development Council, 1967.

Ospina, Maria, and Liz Dennett. *Systematic Review on the Prevalence of Fetal Alcohol Spectrum Disorders.* Edmonton: Institute of Health Economics, 2013.

Pagden, Anthony. *Peoples and Empires: A Short History of European Migration and Conquest from Greece to the Present.* New York: Modern Library, 2001.

Pagden, Anthony. *Spanish Imperialism and the Political Imagination: Studies in European and Spanish-American Social and Political Theory, 1513–1830.* New Haven, Connecticut: Yale University Press, 1990.

Pagden, Anthony. *The Lords of All the World: Ideologies of Empire in Spain, Britain and France c. 1500–c. 1800.* New Haven, Connecticut: Yale University Press, 1995.

Parker, R. A. *Uprooted: The Shipment of Poor Children to Canada, 1867–1917.* Bristol, UK: Policy Press, 2010.

Peake, Frank A. *The Bishop Who Ate His Boots: A Biography of Isaac O. Stringer.* Toronto: Anglican Church of Canada, 1966.

Pettipas, Katherine. *Severing the Ties that Bind: Government Repression of Indigenous Ceremonies on the Prairies.* Winnipeg: University of Manitoba Press, 1994.

Primrose, A. P. (5th Earl of Rosebery). *Australian speechlets, 1883–84.*

Quassa, Paul. *We Need to Know Who We Are: The Life Story of Paul Quassa.* Edited by Louis McComber. Translated by Letia Qiatsuk. Volume 3, Life Stories of Northern Leaders. Iqaluit: Nunavut Arctic College, 2008.

Quiring, David M. *CCF Colonialism in Northern Saskatchewan: Battling Parish Priests, Bootleggers, and Fur Sharks.* Vancouver: University of British Columbia Press, 2004.

Ray, Arthur J. *An Illustrated History of Canada's Native People: I have lived here since the world began.* Toronto: Key Porter, 2010.

Rompkey, William. *The Story of Labrador.* Montreal and Kingston: McGill-Queen's University Press, 2003.

Seed, Patricia. *Ceremonies of Possession in Europe's Conquest of the New World, 1492–1640.* Cambridge, Massachusetts: Cambridge University Press, 1995.

Shanahan, David F. *The Jesuit Residential School at Spanish: "More than Mere Talent."* Toronto: Canadian Institute of Jesuit Studies, 2004.

Sharpe, Andrew, Jean-François Arsenault, Simon Lapointe, and Fraser Cowan. *The Effect of Increasing Aboriginal Educational Attainment on the Labour Force, Output and the Fiscal Imbalance.* Ottawa: Centre for the Study of Living Standards, 2009.

Snow, John. *These Mountains Are Our Sacred Places: The Story of the Stoney Indians.* Toronto: Samuel Stevens, 1977.

Sprague, D. N. *Canada's Treaties with Aboriginal People.* Winnipeg: University of Manitoba, Faculty of Law, Canadian Legal History Project, 1991.

Standing Bear, Luther. *My People the Sioux.* Boston: Houghton Mifflin Company, 1928.

Stocken, H. W. Gibbon. *Among the Blackfoot and Sarcee.* Introduction by Georgeen Barrass. Calgary: Glenbow Museum, 1976.

Sutherland, Neil. *Children in English-Canadian Society: Framing the Twentieth-Century Consensus.* Waterloo: Wilfrid Laurier University Press, 2000.

Tait, Caroline L. *Fetal Alcohol Syndrome among Aboriginal People in Canada: Review and Analysis of the Intergenerational Links to Residential Schools.* Ottawa: Aboriginal Healing Foundation, 2003.

Thiong'o, Ngugi wa. *Dreams in a Time of War: A Childhood Memoir.* London: Vintage Books, 2011.

Trudel, Marcel. *The Beginnings of New France: 1524–1663.* Toronto: McClelland and Stewart, 1973.

Usher, Jean. *William Duncan of Metlakatla: A Victorian Missionary in British Columbia.* Publications in History 9. Ottawa: National Museums of Canada, 1974.

Vanderburgh, Rosamond M. *The Canadian Indian in Ontario's School Texts: A Study of Social Studies Textbooks, Grade 1 through 8.* Port Credit, Ontario: University Women's Club of Port Credit, Study Group on the Canadian Indian Eskimo, 1968.

Venne, Sharon H., editor. *Indian Acts and Amendments 1868–1975, An Indexed Collection.* Saskatoon: University of Saskatchewan, Native Law Centre, 1981.

Waldram, James, D. Ann Herring, and T. Kue Young. *Aboriginal Health in Canada: Historical, Cultural, and Epidemiological Perspectives.* Second edition. Toronto: University of Toronto Press, 2006.

Weaver, Sally M. *Making Canadian Indian Policy: The Hidden Agenda, 1968–70.* Toronto: University of Toronto Press, 1981.

Wherrett, George Jasper. *The Miracle of the Empty Beds: A History of Tuberculosis in Canada.* Toronto: University of Toronto Press, 1977.

Williams, Robert A. *The American Indian in Western Legal Thought: The Discourses of Conquest.* Oxford: Oxford University Press, 1990.

Wilson, Daniel, and David Macdonald. *The Income Gap between Aboriginal Peoples and the Rest of Canada.* Ottawa: Canadian Centre for Policy Alternatives, 2010.

Wilson, E. F. *Missionary Work among the Ojebway Indians.* London, 1886.

Wood, Ellen Meiksins. *Empire of Capital.* New York: Verso Books, 2003.

Wood, Ellen Meiksins. *The Origin of Capitalism: A Longer View.* London: Verso Books, 2002.

2. BOOK CHAPTERS AND ARTICLES

Adams, Ian. "The Indians: An Abandoned and Dispossessed People." *Weekend Magazine* 15, no. 31 (31 July 1965).

Adams, Ian. "The Lonely Death of Charlie Wenjack." *Maclean's* (February 1967): 30–44.

Banner, Stuart. "Why Terra Nullius? Anthropology and Property Law in Early Australia." *Law and History Review* 23, no. 1 (Spring 2005): 95–132.

Barron, F. Laurie. "The Indian Pass System in the Canadian West, 1882–1935." *Prairie Forum* 13, no. 1 (Spring 1988): 25–42.

Blondin-Andrew, Ethel. "New Ways of Looking for Leadership." In *Leading in an Upside-Down World: New Canadian Perspectives on Leadership*, edited by J. Patrick Boyer, 59–70. Toronto: Dundurn Press, 2003.

Brown, Judith. "Economic Organization and the Position of Women among the Iroquois." *Ethnohistory* 17 (1970): 151–167.

Carney, Robert. "The Grey Nuns and the Children of Holy Angels: Fort Chipewyan, 1874–1924." In *Proceedings of the Fort Chipewyan and Fort Vermilion Bicentennial Conference*, edited by P. A. McCormack and R. Geoffrey Ironside. Edmonton: Boreal Institute for Northern Studies, University of Alberta, 1990.

Chartrand, Larry N. "Métis Residential School Participation: A Literature Review." In *Métis History and Experience and Residential Schools in Canada*, by Larry N. Chartrand, Tricia E. Logan, and Judy D. Daniels, 5–55. Ottawa: Aboriginal Healing Foundation, 2006.

Côté, M. M. "St. Albert, Cradle of the Catholic Church in Alberta." *Canadian Catholic Historical Association Report* 32 (1965): 29–35.

Cuthand, Stan. "The Native Peoples of the Prairie Provinces in the 1920s and 1930s." In *Sweet Promises: A Reader on Indian-White Relations in Canada*, edited by J. R. Miller, 381–392. Toronto: University of Toronto Press, 1991.

Driver, Felix. "Discipline Without Frontiers? Representations of the Mettray Reformatory Colony in Britain, 1840–1880." *Journal of Historical Sociology* 3 (September 1990): 272–93.

Elias, Lillian. "Lillian Elias." In *We Were So Far Away: The Inuit Experience of Residential Schools*, 47–62. Ottawa: Legacy of Hope, 2010.

Erickson, Lesley. "'Bury Our Sorrows in the Sacred Heart': Gender and the Métis Response to Colonialism the Case of Sara and Louis Riel, 1848–83." In *Unsettled Pasts: Reconceiving the West through Women's History*, edited by Sarah Carter, Lesley Erickson, Patricia Roome, and Char Smith, 17–46. Calgary: University of Calgary Press, 2005.

Fingard, Judith. "The New England Company and the New Brunswick Indians, 1786–1826: A Comment on Colonial Perversion of British Benevolence." *Acadiensis* 1, no. 2 (Spring 1972): 29–42.

Fiske, Jo-Anne. "Fishing Is Women's Business: Changing Economic Roles of Carrier Women and Men." In *Native Peoples, Native Lands: Canadian Indians, Inuit, and Metis*, edited by Bruce Cox, 186–198. Ottawa: Carleton University Press, 1987.

Friesen, Jean. "Magnificent Gifts: The Treaties of Canada with the Indians of the Northwest 1869- 1876." In *The Spirit of the Alberta Indian Treaties*, edited by Richard T. Price, 203-13. Edmonton: University of Alberta Press, 1999.

Grant, John W. "Two-Thirds of the Revenue: Presbyterian Women and Native Indian Missions." In *Changing Roles of Women within the Christian Church in Canada*, edited by E. G. Muir and M. F. Whiteley, 99-116. Toronto: University of Toronto Press, 1995.

Hare, Jan, and Barman, Jean. "Good Intentions Gone Awry: From Protection to Confinement in Emma Crosby's Home for Aboriginal Girls." In *With Good Intentions: EuroCanadian and Aboriginal Relations in Colonial Canada*, edited by D. Nock and C. Haig-Brown, 179-198. Vancouver: University of British Columbia Press, 2006.

Hepburn, D. W. "Northern Education: Facade for Failure." *Variables: The Journal of the Sociology Club* (University of Alberta) 2, no. 1 (February 1963): 16-21.

Jaenen, Cornelius J. "Education for Francization: The Case of New France in the Seventeenth Century." In *Indian Education in Canada*. Vol. 1, *The Legacy*, edited by Jean Barman, Yvonne Hebert, and Don McCaskill. Vancouver: University of British Columbia Press, 1986.

Johns, Robert. "A History of St Peter's Mission and of Education in Hay River, NWT Prior to 1950." *Musk Ox*, no. 13 (1973): 22-32.

Johnston, Darlene. "Aboriginal Traditions of Tolerance and Reparation: Introducing Canadian Colonialism." In *Le Devoir de Memoire et les Politiques du Pardon*, edited by Micheline Labelle, Rachad Antoinius, and Georges Leroux, 141-159. Quebec: Presses de l'Universite de Quebec, 2005.

Kelm, Mary-Ellen. "Introduction." In *The Letters of Margaret Butcher: Missionary-Imperialism on the North Pacific Coast*, by Margaret Butcher, xi-xxxi. Edited by Mary-Ellen Kelm. Calgary: University of Calgary Press, 2006.

Klein, Laura. "Mother as Clanswoman: Rank and Gender in Tlingit Society." In *Women and Power in Native North America*, edited by Laura Klein and Lillian Ackerman, 28-45. Norman: University of Oklahoma Press, 1995

Krech, Shepard III. "Nutritional Evaluation of a Mission Residential School Diet: The Accuracy of Informant Recall." *Human Organization* 37 (1978): 186—190.

Kulchyski, Peter. "'A Considerable Unrest': F. O. Loft and the League of Indians." *Native Studies Review* 4, nos. 1 and 2 (1988): 95-117.

Lleweyn, Jennifer. "Dealing with the Legacy of Native Residential School Abuse in Canada: Litigation, ADR and Restorative Justice." *University of Toronto Law Journal* 52 (2002): 253-300.

Mandryk, Murray. "Uneasy Neighbours: White-Aboriginal relations and agricultural decline." In *Writing Off the Rural West: Globalization, Governments and the Transformation of Rural Communities*, edited by Roger Epp and Dave Whitson, 205-221. Edmonton: University of Alberta Press with the Parkland Institute, 2001.

McKay, Stan. "Expanding the Dialogue on Truth and Reconciliation—In a Good Way." In *From Truth to Reconciliation: Transforming the Legacy of Residential Schools*, edited by Marlene Brant Castellano, Linda Archibald, and Mike DeGagne, 103-115. Ottawa: Aboriginal Healing Foundation, 2008.

McKenzie, Brad, and Pete Hudson. "Native Children, Child Welfare, and the Coloni-zation of Native People." In *The Challenge of Child Welfare*, edited by Ken Levitt and Brian Wharf, 125–141. Vancouver: University of British Columbia Press, 1985.

Perry, Adele. "Metropolitan Knowledge, Colonial Practice, and Indigenous Woman-hood." In *Contact Zones: Aboriginal and Settler Women in Canada's Colonial Past*, edited by Myra Rutherdale and Katie Pickles. Vancouver: University of British Columbia Press, 2005.

Renaud, André. "Indian Education Today." *Anthropologica* (1958): 1–49.

Ruben, Abraham. "Abraham Ruben." In *We Were So Far Away: The Inuit Experience of Residential Schools*, edited by Heather L. Igloliorte. Ottawa: Legacy of Hope Foundation, 2010.

Sadowski, Edward G. "Preliminary report on the investigation into missing school files for the Shingwauk Indian Residential School." Algoma University College, Shingwauk Project Archives, November 2006.

Sinha, V., and A. Kozlowski. "The Structure of Aboriginal Child Welfare in Canada." *International Indigenous Policy Journal* 4, no. 2 (2013): article 2. http://ir.lib.uwo. ca/iipj/vol4/iss2/2.

Sluman, Norma. "The Text Book Indian." *Toronto Education Quarterly* 5, no. 3 (1967).

Smylie, J. "A Review of Aboriginal Infant Mortality Rates in Canada: Striking and Persistent Aboriginal/Non-Aboriginal Inequities." *Canadian Journal of Public Health* 101, no. 2 (2010): 143–148.

Stanley, George F. G. "Alberta's Half-Breed Reserve: Saint-Paul-des-Métis, 1896–1909." In *The Other Natives: The Metis*, vol. 2, edited by A. S. Lussier and D. B. Sealey, 75–107. Winnipeg: Manitoba Metis Federation Press, 1978.

Stevenson, Winona. "The Red River Indian Mission School and John West's 'Little Charges' 1820–1833." *Native Studies Review* 4, nos. 1 and 2 (1988): 129–65.

Stonechild, Blair. "The Indian View of the 1885 Uprising." In *Sweet Promises: A Reader on Indian-White Relations in Canada*, edited by J. R. Miller, 259–76. Toronto: University of Toronto Press, 1991.

Taylor, J. Garth. "Northern Algonquians on the Frontiers of 'New Ontario,' 1890–1945." In *Aboriginal Ontario: Historical Perspectives on the First Nations*, edited by Edward S. Rogers and Donald B. Smith. Toronto: Dundurn Press, 1994.

Taylor, John Leonard. "Canada's Northwest Indian Policy in the 1870s: Traditional Premises and Necessary Innovations." In *The Spirit of the Alberta Indian Treaties*, edited by Richard T. Price, 3–7. Edmonton: University of Alberta Press, 1999.

Thomas, Robina Anne (Qwul'sih'yah'maht). "Honouring the Oral Traditions of My Ancestors through Storytelling." In *Research as Resistance: Critical, Indigenous, and Anti-Oppressive Approaches*, edited by Leslie Brown and Susan Strega, 237–54. Toronto: Canadian Scholars Press/Women's Press, 2005.

Tobias, John L. "Protection, Civilization, Assimilation: An Outline History of Canada's Indian Policy." In *Sweet Promises: A Reader on Indian-White Relations in Canada*, edited by J. R. Miller, 212–40. Toronto: University of Toronto Press, 1991.

Upton, L. F. S. "The Origins of Canadian Indian Policy." *Journal of Canadian Studies* 8, no. 4 (November 1973): 51–60.

Van Camp, Rosa. "Bishop Paul Piché." *Arctic Profiles* 42, no. 2 (1989): 168–170.

Wolfe, Patrick. "Settler Colonialism and the Elimination of the Native." *Journal of Genocide Research* 8, no. 4 (2006): 387–409.

3. THESES AND DISSERTATIONS

Brandak, George Michael. "A Study of Missionary Activity in the Diocese of Athabasca, 1884–1903." MA thesis, Waterloo Lutheran University, 1972.

Callahan, Ann B. "On Our Way to Healing: Stories from the Oldest Living Generation of the File Hills Indian Residential School." MA thesis, University of Manitoba, 2002.

Carney, Robert. "Relations in Education Between the Federal and Territorial Governments and the Roman Catholic Church in the Mackenzie District, Northwest Territories, 1867–1961." PhD dissertation, University of Alberta, 1971.

Foran, Timothy Paul. "'Les Gens de cette place': Oblates and the Evolving Concept of Métis at Île-à-la-Crosse, 1845–1898." PhD dissertation, University of Ottawa, 2011.

Gresko, Jacqueline Kennedy. "Gender and Mission: The Founding Generations of the Sisters of Saint Ann and the Oblates of Mary Immaculate in British Columbia 1858–1914." PhD dissertation, University of British Columbia, 1999.

Gull, Norman Andrew. "The 'Indian Policy' of the Anglican Church of Canada from 1945 to the 1970s." MA thesis, Trent University, 1992.

Kennedy, Jacqueline. "Qu'Appelle Industrial School. White 'Rites' for the Indians of the Old North-West." MA thesis, Carleton University, 1970.

Persson, Diane Iona. "Blue Quills: A Case Study of Indian Residential Schooling." PhD dissertation, University of Alberta, 1980.

Pettit, Jennifer Lorretta. "'To Christianize and Civilize': Native Industrial Schools in Canada." PhD dissertation, University of Calgary, 1997.

Wasylow, Walter Julian. "History of Battleford Industrial School for Indians." Masters of Education thesis, University of Saskatchewan, 1972.